ERASMUS:

HIS LIFE, WORKS, AND INFLUENCE

Erasmus
Charcoal drawing by Albrecht Dürer, 1520
The Louvre, Paris

Cornelis Augustijn

ERASMUS

His Life, Works, and Influence

translated by
J.C. Grayson

UNIVERSITY OF TORONTO PRESS

Toronto Buffalo London

Originally published as
Erasmus von Rotterdam: Leben – Werk – Wirkung
© C.H. Beck'sche Verlagsbuchhandlung
(Oscar Beck) München 1986
English translation
© University of Toronto Press 1991
Toronto Buffalo London
Printed in Canada

The English translation from the Dutch original
was supported by a grant from the Prins Bernhard Fonds.

ISBN 0-8020-5864-7

Printed on acid-free paper

Canadian Cataloguing in Publication Data

Augustijn, C., 1928–
Erasmus

Translation of: Erasmus, vernieuwer van kerk en
theologie.
ISBN 0-8020-5864-7

1. Erasmus, Desiderius, d. 1536. I. Title.

B785.E64A915 1991   199'.492   C91-095059-8

Contents

꙰

Illustrations

᪥

Erasmus

frontispiece

Foreword

If I begin by stating that my aim in this book is to introduce the reader to the present state of research on Erasmus, this is only half the truth. Of course, that is my aim, and I hope that some readers will be helped in their own study by this introduction and stimulated to produce work of their own in the field of the history of humanism and the Reformation. The period is fascinating, if only because of the great changes that society underwent at that time. In many respects, it was then that the foundations of modern western civilization were laid. But I have more in mind than this. I have a certain image of Erasmus, an image formed by reading many studies on him written from very different viewpoints, but shaped even more by patient reading of Erasmus' own works and those of many of his contemporaries. I want to take the reader with me and show him what I see in Erasmus and the exciting age in which he lived. As I do so, I hope to find a way which avoids both colourlessness and idiosyncrasy.

I have given references primarily, therefore, to the writings of Erasmus himself and only occasionally to secondary sources. For the most part I have used the English translation of *The Collected Works of Erasmus*; in a few instances I have supplied my own. At the beginning of the notes to each chapter I give a limited choice of important studies on the matters dealt with in that chapter. My only criterion in choosing them has been that very varied points of view, certainly including those which differ from mine, ought to be represented, provided that they are argued in a responsible way. That does not mean that much that I do not mention has no value in my eyes. Some restriction is inevitable given the present extent of the literature. The bibliography gives references for those who wish to go more deeply into Erasmus research.

ERASMUS:

HIS LIFE, WORKS, AND INFLUENCE

ONE

Introduction

❧

'Erasmus stands apart.'[1] This judgment can be found in the second part of the *Epistolae obscurorum virorum* (*Letters of Obscure Men*), in which the humanist avant-garde of 1517 gave free rein to their bitter satire against the established order in society, church, and scholarship. Erasmus, they were convinced, eluded all classification; he was a man apart. Almost twenty years later Luther called him an eel, and added: 'No one can grasp him but Christ alone.'[2] There is something hard to fathom in Erasmus, and every biography must take this into account. The elusiveness is not the fault of lack of sources, for Erasmus wrote a great deal. Immediately after his death his most faithful friends prepared an edition of his collected works compiled according to his own instructions and partly including editions revised by himself. This edition appeared between 1538 and 1540 in nine thick volumes. Between 1703 and 1706 a new edition was published at Leiden, which is still the standard one for most of his works.

Modern Erasmus scholarship began with the publication of his letters by P.S. Allen and his wife from 1906, and with Huizinga's biography of 1924. Allen's edition was a masterpiece, the indispensable foundation for all further reliable work. Huizinga even said, in dedicating his own biography to the Allens, that he was offering them a bunch of flowers picked in their own garden. And rightly so. It is significant that he laid all the stress on the young Erasmus. A solid basis was still lacking for the later years, for Allen had not got beyond 1521. But though the flowers were from the Allens' garden, the bouquet came from Huizinga. His book has deservedly become a classic. With a grand unity of conception, he portrayed Erasmus as a man, a genius, and a real personality. For all his admiration, he was by no means uncritical of Erasmus, whose pettiness sometimes irritated him as much as his greatness fascinated him. Huizinga was also very sensitive to the elusiveness of Erasmus. He described him as 'a master of reserve,' by which he meant not simply reticence prompted only by caution or fear but a quality intrinsic to his character.

Huizinga's book has determined the image of Erasmus in the Netherlands, but not elsewhere. Although translations had appeared in both English and German before the second world war, they exercised little influence. English-speaking readers had the biography by Preserved Smith, published shortly before that of Huizinga. Smith's book is well-written, reliable, and scholarly, but it does not display much breadth of vision. In Germany, Huizinga's book had no influence. The German verdict on Erasmus had long been fixed, and underwent no further alteration. In reality, one must speak of two pictures, which agree on one point: the image of Erasmus was determined by that of Luther, to whom he formed, as it were, the antitype. Sometimes Luther was seen primarily as the 'German Hercules' of the prints of a Basel artist (perhaps Holbein), as the solitary man of strength who took up the struggle against the tyranny of Rome in Germany. Luther was then the adversary of all abuses in the church, the only one who dared to make a stand against them. And Erasmus? He saw the faults at least as clearly, and even before Luther raised his voice against them, mocked the abuses, and scoffed at the church. But he was no man of action: he was fearful and cowardly, there was no martyr's blood in his veins, and he knowingly denied the truth that he recognized. Luther was the hero of the faith, Erasmus the betrayer. Others saw Luther much more as the man who attacked the doctrine of the church of his day. He discovered that man is justified by faith alone, and attacked the church because it obscured this truth and gave man a greater share in the winning of salvation. For those who held this view, Erasmus was the man of 'sermon on the mount' Christianity, for whom practical life lived by a strict moral code was paramount, and who understood nothing of Luther's deepest intentions. In this interpretation, the contradiction between them was expressed most profoundly in their works on the bondage and the freedom of the will. In them Erasmus was unmasked: he lacked true religious fervour.

Yet another picture of Erasmus was that developed in France during the thirties by Augustin Renaudet. On the basis above all of Erasmus' letters from the 1520s Renaudet depicted his relationship to the reformers and to the defenders of the old church. An impressive portrait emerges, rather reminiscent of Huizinga's in its emphasis on Erasmus' individuality. Unlike Huizinga, however, Renaudet deals more with the older Erasmus, and outlines how he came to choose his own position, independent both of Rome and of Wittenberg. Renaudet speaks of the 'modernism' of Erasmus, a rather ambiguous term which he develops in such a way that something of the Enlightenment of the eighteenth century or of the Catholic modernism of the second half of the nineteenth century is already discernible in Erasmus.

After the war, it was a long time before Erasmus again drew the attention of the scholarly world. The flood of studies published since the sixties has revealed a new Erasmus, a theologian first and foremost, and one whom we have to take seriously. Both Protestant and Catholic authors, among whom North Americans are increasingly prominent, subscribe to this view. For a long time Erasmus was underrated as a theologian, but now he is placed in the medieval tradition, and is shown to be acquainted with discussions on the doctrines of sin and grace and interested in theological subtleties. This wave of interest has given the impetus to the new edition of his collected works, which has been making steady progress since 1969, and to the publication of his letters and writings in French, German, and English translations.

What then is the point of a new biography, when the image of Erasmus has become so diffuse? I have four objectives. In the first place I intend to bring together the results of recent scholarship in the various languages. This might seem to go without saying, but the reality is that research is still pursued independently in French-, English-, and German-speaking countries. In particular, French and German research are almost completely separate from each other. In this book I hope to achieve a synthesis of modern research.

In the second place I attempt not to measure Erasmus by the standards of others but to offer him the chance to be himself. He has been unfortunate in having constantly been judged by the measure of Luther. It was natural that he should fall short of it. Erasmus was already in his early fifties when Luther first came to public attention, a sober fact that is often overlooked. It had taken a long time for him to find himself and know precisely what he wanted. By 1518 or 1519, however, when the world first heard of Luther, Erasmus had already produced his most important works and had a clearly defined goal in mind, a goal that must be judged on its own merits. Allowing Erasmus to speak for himself establishes even more clearly his independence with regard to the Enlightenment. We cannot give Erasmus credit for the Enlightenment because his thought contained the seeds of ideas that were to flower in the eighteenth century. Comparison with a later period of intellectual history has some point, just as comparison with Luther has a point, but only after Erasmus himself has been heard and has been placed in his own time.

A third important concern of this book is the position of Erasmus in the years between 1500 and 1520. In this period, in which his life's work was prepared and a great deal of it achieved, Erasmus was anything but a solitary figure. He belonged to the world of the humanists, and during those years became one of the key figures in it. It was a little world, an intellectual élite, isolated from the rest of society. Some of its members were to be found in the universities, some in the courts of princes and of the magnates of the church; some belonged to the urban establishment; some, on the other hand, lived solitary lives; all were wholly and absolutely devoted to the ideal of *bonae litterae*, the culture of classical antiquity, which had once again sprung into life and was to renew society. Resistance to this ideal from established scholars, above all the theologians and dialecticians, only strengthened the *esprit de corps* of the humanists. Our picture of Erasmus becomes clearer if we can see him in this context and identify the particular group to which he belonged, that of the biblical humanists.

With that I come to the last point which is characteristic of this biography. Rather than the biographical details, I want to stress what is peculiar to Erasmus, his essential contribution to the culture of his time: the integration of the humanist method into theology and the transformation this brought about. Of course Erasmus was not alone in this achievement; as has been said, he had his own place in a group of kindred spirits. That place was unique. In that lies the truth of the old verdict: Erasmus stands apart, he is unique.

TWO

Europe in 1500

The life of Erasmus reflects the world of the last thirty years of the fifteenth century and the first thirty years of the sixteenth. His letters and writings show us the Netherlands, Paris, Oxford and Cambridge, northern Italy, Rome, the cities of the Rhineland and especially Basel. Through him we meet the princes of his age and see something of the life of the cities, especially of the prosperous bourgeoisie. Because the church and religion played a large role in his life, popes, bishops, and monasteries also call for our attention. The cultural life of the time stands in the foreground. From his youth Erasmus was intensely concerned with the three great intellectual forces of his time: the *devotio moderna*, scholastic theology, and humanism. It is not necessary to go into great detail about all three; they will appear in their proper places in his life as a matter of course. In this chapter a few broad brush strokes are sufficient to sketch the main outlines of his environment.

The northern Netherlands, where Erasmus passed the first twenty-five years of his life, was a remote but not a backward region, relatively highly urbanized. In the province of Holland, where this development had gone furthest, about half of the population lived in towns and cities by 1500. Though the province was one of the first urbanized regions of Europe, its population was known as rustic and rather crude, if trustworthy, humane, and amenable. These are the qualities Erasmus himself names in his explanation of the Latin proverb *Auris batava*, that is, a Dutch, unrefined taste.[1] His explanation turns into a eulogy of Holland as a land of plenty, of friendliness, conviviality, and domestic life. It is also a land of intellectual mediocrity. In Erasmus' opinion, this was perhaps because of its luxurious life, perhaps also because of the values it upheld: righteous living was more esteemed than intellectual distinction.

Between 1500 and 1521 Erasmus spent most of his time, when in the Netherlands, in the southern provinces, the modern Belgium and Luxembourg. Their population was about the same as that of the north, at a rough estimate about 800,000 to 900,000. Life was more vigorous there than in the north; it was the home of most of the nobility, on whom had fallen an important political role in the second half of the fifteenth century. Brussels was its administrative centre, Mechelen the judicial capital, Antwerp with its 50,000 inhabitants a true metropolis and the market-place of commerce and industry, Louvain the only university town. From the eighties and nineties on the Netherlands was gradually absorbed into the Hapsburg empire. Although it was only after Erasmus' death that the last province, Gelderland, fell into the hands of Charles v, Erasmus himself had already been ordained a priest in 1492 by the bishop of Utrecht, David of Burgundy, who was a natural son of Philip the Good, great-grandfather of Charles v.

Similar developments occurred in the rest of western Europe. In Spain, France, and England the unitary state was either taking shape at this time or had already been formed. In these states national self-consciousness was already deeply rooted, partly as a result of the long wars of England against France and of Spain against the Moors. Unity meant centralization, and everywhere the recognized centre was the prince with his officials. For the last twenty years of Erasmus' life, Europe was dominated by three great rulers: Francis i of France from 1515, Henry viii of England from 1509, and Charles v, king of Spain, lord of the Austrian Hapsburg hereditary lands and ruler of the Netherlands 1515–16, and elected Holy Roman Emperor in 1519.

The Holy Roman Empire of the German nation consisted of a great many cities and territories, only held together to some degree from the twenties by the *Reichsregiment*. Ninety per cent of the Empire was still agrarian, the cities were small, and in social, financial, and political affairs the church still exerted greater power here than elsewhere in Europe. The upper Rhine valley, which was to play a great part in Erasmus' life from 1514, was prosperous and culturally at the forefront of German life. The archbishop's court at Mainz and the episcopal seats in Constance, Basel, Strasbourg, Speyer, Worms, and Würzburg were centres of culture. Basel, Freiburg, Tübingen, Heidelberg, and Mainz had universities, while there were schools and circles of humanists in Sélestat, Strasbourg, Pforzheim, and in most of the university cities. Not least important were the flourishing printing presses.

The cities occupied an important position in the structure of society despite their small populations. Erasmus' birthplace, Rotterdam, may have had 7,000 inhabitants, and his beloved Basel about 10,000. Antwerp and Paris were great cities. The cities formed separate administrative units with one or more mayors, a single council, or a great and small council. Although this administrative structure permitted some popular influence on the government of the cities, one should be careful not to speak of democracy. A contemporary, hearing that term, thought of anarchy, and spoke instead of aristocracy – which was much closer to the reality. In practice, urban oligarchies, small groups held together by family ties and financial interests, held power. True, changes were taking place. In many cities the guilds, the leaders of which represented a less well-off stratum of society, demanded a share in the administration. The city also held an important position in economic life. Although there was no absolute distinction between town and country, trade and industry were centred in cities, so that capital formation was also concentrated in them. Thanks to their position of economic power, the cities formed a certain counterbalance to the power of the princes, although over the long term they were to be the losers.

Nor were the cities to be neglected in the sphere of culture. Cultural life was still largely concentrated at the courts of princes and nobles, but the cities were growing in importance. This development had begun with the rise of the universities as typically urban institutions. Schools had followed, and with the growth of prosperity there was more scope for artists. An important phenomenon was the printing presses, which had won a place for themselves in the second half of the fifteenth century. The cultural life of the city was often concentrated not on a single point, but grouped around various institutions: the university, the school, the bishop and chapter, the printers, the artists. A few examples from towns that played a role in Erasmus' life may illustrate this. Antwerp had no university; its vigorous cultural life centred on its artists and printing presses. Louvain was completely dominated by its university. Basel had a university, but after 1500 the circle around the printers Johann Amerbach and later Johann Froben formed the true seed-bed for a literary and scholarly output that won fame far beyond the city itself.

The greatest power in the world of those days was the church, and that in three respects: as an administrative structure, as an economic factor, and as a religious-intellectual force. Rome and the papacy were the centre of the administrative organization, and in Italy a formidable political and military power as well. When Erasmus arrived in northern Italy in 1506, Pope Julius II was about to make his entry as a victorious general into Bologna. The papacy had reached its lamentable nadir. There is little to be said in favour of Julius' successor, Leo x (1513–21), as a spiritual leader of western Christendom. Erasmus enthusiastically praised Leo – unlike Julius II, for whom he never had a good word – as the pope of peace and the patron of *bonae litterae*, the true culture attained by the study of classical antiquity. As for Adrian VI (1522–3) and Clement VII (1523–34), Erasmus judged them by their attitude in the conflict with Luther and his followers and by the patronage that they offered to him personally. What was true of the popes was true of the bishops too; spiritual leadership was the last quality that mattered. For the most part, bishops' sees were occupied by the sons of noble families, and the unification of ecclesiastical office and secular power had disastrous results. A typical example is the bishop whose service Erasmus entered, Hendrik van Bergen, bishop of Cambrai in the southern Netherlands. He belonged to a noble family that had risen in the service of the Burgundians. Having himself been designated from the outset for a career in the church, he did not shrink from using force to maintain his rights – or what he supposed to be his rights. As chancellor of the Order of the Golden Fleece he held the highest spiritual dignity of the Burgundian court, and as such was active in Hapsburg politics and often entrusted with diplomatic missions. The life of an ecclesiastical potentate like Hendrik had nothing at all in common with that of the faithful.

The economic and financial power of the church had much to do with this. It owned extensive lands, in some districts half of all land holdings. For three centuries, ever increasing revenues of all kinds had been added to them. The administrative system of the church was kept in being by money: every appointment had to be paid for, every ecclesiastical action cost money. The accumulation of church prebends in one hand made the system even more objectionable. The clergy's hunger for cash was enormous and manifest at all levels. Everyone came into contact with it whenever a child was baptized, a marriage solemnized, an indulgence acquired, a will drawn up. In spite of all plans and efforts at reform, before the Council of Trent the church saw no opportunity to improve matters. Anyone who has browsed through the pages of Erasmus' *Colloquies* will recall the grotesque stories he tells, and almost forget that a great part of Erasmus' own income throughout his life was directly or indirectly drawn from this source, the gifts of high prelates, for example.

The commercialization of ecclesiastical functions does not mean that the lower clergy could wallow in luxury. Of course there were good prebends to be had at the lower level, but they often fell into the hands of the already wealthy higher clergy. To advance from the lower ranks to the higher was exceptional. The church paid no attention to theological training. Most candidates were ordained priests after a very summary education, or none at all; the examination was confined to a superficial investigation and re-quired minimal knowledge. The prospects of the ordinands were poor. Around the beginning of the sixteenth century, only one-third of the 5,000 secular clergy in the diocese of Utrecht were employed in the cure of souls. The others served as chantry priests, whose only task was to read a number of masses. Then there were the regular clergy. In late medieval society the religious orders were powerful and numerous. In the diocese of Utrecht at the start of the century, there were about 13,000 monks and nuns. These 18,000 clergy, secular and regular, or roughly three per cent of the total population, lived, even if not at a very high level, at the expense of a society scarcely able to bear such a burden. In cities, above all in episcopal seats, this percentage could rise to ten. Nor were the prospects for regular clergy encouraging. In the 1480s, when Erasmus entered or was placed in the monastery, he could look forward to a life of submission and humility, the possibility of rising to prior, perhaps at the price of flattery or dishonesty a bursary for study, and, given great good luck, a position in the chancery of a high dignitary of the church.

Something of the religious power of the church has already been described in the above. The skyline of the city was determined by its church spires, its streetscape by its churches, cloisters, chapels, secular clergy, monks, and nuns. This is illustrative of the reality of religious life. Popular piety had flourished greatly, processions and pilgrimages were popular, the veneration of Mary and the saints was at the centre of attention. The fraternities with their stress on certain cults and fixed religious goals were popular. The penitential preachers, often Franciscans, found eager audiences, especially in Lent. Every guild had its own chapel in church, its own priest, and its own special feast days. In the greater churches masses for the dead were read daily at all altars. Certain saints won popularity, in the fifteenth century above all the fourteen auxiliary saints who each lent their aid in particular cases, St Erasmus, for example, in the case of intestinal illnesses. Religious life was characterized by excess and the multiplication of ceremonies. All this is typical of the intensity of piety. Hell and heaven were realities, human existence was played out between the creation and the last judgment, between the beginning and the end of the world. The beginning of history could be dated, paradise had its place on the map, heaven as the home of God and the blessed was as real as hell-fire.

Because of all this, the church exercised a burdensome authority. It alone could impart salvation to the faithful through the sacraments. This was a service to mankind, and people expected a great deal from the ecclesiastical community and its servants. But it also gave the church a position of unprecedented power, for it laid a claim to the life and the conscience of every man. Abuse was to be expected and was practised without compunction, most notoriously in the practice of issuing indulgences. This went far beyond the bounds of the official doctrine of the church and had degenerated into a scandalous device for raising money by persistently appealing to love for deceased family members who might be suffering in purgatory. Yet in spite of signs of decay, the church and religion were not in decay. Though the call for a reformation in head and members had been voiced for over a century, the church itself was attacked only sporadically.

In 1500 the *devotio moderna* and the piety characteristic of it still dominated the religious climate of much of the Netherlands and the Rhineland. The movement owed its origin to the deacon Geert Groote (1340–84) from Deventer. Many are familiar with the *Imitation of Christ*, in which Thomas a Kempis (c 1380–1471) gave classic expression to the movement's ideal of piety. The most distinctive trait of its spirituality was inwardness, the path from the multifarious forms of expression of communal service of God to the silence of one's own soul. Emotional life reached its fulfilment in a new way, not in the depths of an intense mysticism but in withdrawal from life in the world to the serenity of a hidden communing with God. The *devotio moderna* was exemplified by Geert Groote's intentions at the time of his conversion never to strive for a prebend, never to serve an ecclesiastical dignitary for the sake of money, and never to chase after a degree in theology, because he did not wish to win profit, rich benefices, or fame. Was this a criticism of the practices of the church? Implicitly it was. Yet their own lives were of most concern to the followers of the *devotio moderna*; explicit criticism of the church hardly ever arose. They respected all the laws of the church, even though they held themselves in the last resort to be bound only by the gospel. Nor did they see any clash between the two ideals of obedience, because the external world of the church and the internal world of one's own life with God remained separate. In Erasmus' day, the *devotio moderna* had long lost its original freshness. It had run into the sands of a rather pedestrian, unworldly, legalistic way of life and spirituality, neither of them capable of offering inspiration. Erasmus' own experience of it was entirely negative: a petty and small-minded cloistered existence, typified by arbitrary rules, slavish obedience to trivial regulations, little undisturbed sleep, bad food. The posture – the glance, according to the rules, had always to be fixed on the ground – reflected the attitude to life.

No discussion of the intellectual climate of a given period can leave the universities out of account. For the period around 1500 this means first and foremost theology. It cannot be called a golden age, even if historians are no longer quite so ready to dismiss it as an age of theological decadence. The great theological conflicts of the later Middle Ages had been fought out and offered little impetus for renewal. Even in Paris, where Erasmus studied, things were no better than in other places, in spite of the fame of the university. As everywhere else, theology at Paris was developing along two main lines, biblical exegesis and systematic theology. The study of the Bible was not undergoing any new developments. Biblical scholars were still following the pattern marked out by the great exegetical works of the Middle Ages. But even within this framework, activity in Paris was slight. It is characteristic that editions of the text of the Bible or the great medieval commentaries on it in the second half of the fifteenth century were either published late or not at all in Paris. The same is true of editions of the Fathers of the church. Systematic theology was also stagnant, still dominated by scholasticism, in Paris as elsewhere. It had a respectable tradition, and had proceeded for centuries by the well-tried method of *quaestio* and *summa*. The *quaestio*, 'question' or 'query,' proceeded from a theological question that was illuminated, as in a conversation, in dispute, by pros and cons from all sides and led to a conclusion, while the counter-arguments were then answered from the solution reached. In the *summa*, the *quaestiones* were systematically arranged. The intention was not to produce a fully worked out structure, but to develop an open system that could be elaborated and corrected. In this field too the creative force had dried up by the end of the fifteenth century at the University of Paris. The form had outgrown the content, the method was retained but not renewed, and the only question of substance that still excited the Paris theologians concerned the immaculate conception of Mary: was the mother of Jesus free of the original sin with which all mankind is stained, from the first moment of her conception?

It would be unfair to judge scholastic theology by the symptoms of degeneracy that it displayed or by the biting satire of Erasmus. Once a strictly philological approach to texts began to gain ground, scholasticism soon came under sharp critical fire. The real goal of scholastic method was not, in the last analysis, to arrive at the correct, *ad verbum* interpretation of a pronouncement, but to learn the truth. It was therefore permissible to bend the text for the sake of the truth, the correct insight. In this way, it was thought, justice was done to the intention of the author, since he likewise had no other goal but to serve the truth. What held good for the treatment of texts in general in the application of scholastic method also applied to the text of the Bible. If a philological approach to the text of the Bible and the Fathers of the church was to emerge, it could only set to work outside the existing context of the method hitherto followed. The renewal had to come from outside.

So we come to a last component of the intellectual life of this period, the humanist movement, which had achieved a recognized place in society in 1500. It was characterized by its orientation towards classical antiquity, both Latin and Greek. Of course, knowledge of the Latin authors had never been wholly lost in the Middle Ages, but in the fourteenth century the humanists began to rediscover important Latin texts that had been little read in the previous centuries. They were copied and, from the middle of the fifteenth century, issued in print, sometimes with learned commentaries. Greek authors had suffered much more, for the knowledge of Greek was rare. For this reason the humanists' services to Greek literature were even greater. From the middle of the fourteenth century, countless Greek manuscripts were brought to the West, knowledge of the language was revived, and editions of Greek texts were printed. We can scarcely imagine today the emotions this aroused, the excitement a scholar felt when he heard that the lost books of Livy's history of Rome might have surfaced again in manuscript. Willibald Pirckheimer of Nürnberg, a contemporary of Erasmus, even called in a medium in an attempt to discover where they might be found. Knowledge also trickled down to a wider audience as translations into the vernacular languages became fashionable. In the hundred years between 1450 and 1550, apart from editions of the early Christian authors, more than four hundred editions of translations from Latin and Greek into German are known – evidence of a large and continuing demand.

Where did this interest in the classics come from? One answer is that Latin was used by the humanists themselves. Poems, speeches, legal pleas, historical works, letters – all appeared in Latin. The study of the classical authors provided the indispensable basis, for it alone could form a good style, but there was more to it than this. The *bonae litterae* or *politiores litterae* gave access to learning, erudition, and wisdom. These terms are really untranslatable. They do not mean *belles-lettres* or the study of literature, but rather 'good' or 'polite' or 'polished' letters – found above all in the classical authors but also in the great examples of the modern age, especially the Italian humanists – to which one had to apply oneself in order to become a true, full person. The ultimate goal was an attitude to life, wisdom rather than learning. We see it in Erasmus, who held that moral philosophy, cosmography, and the history of classical antiquity furnished more wisdom in one year than Odysseus gained in twenty years of dangerous and disastrous wanderings.[2] Without the classics, all other sciences were deaf and blind,[3] without them life meant nothing. The ancients lived in the golden age – and how deep we have sunk now! In all of this there is a strongly Stoic concept of life: fortunate is the well-balanced man who needs no one else, is independent of fortune, and who knows how to develop his own capacities.

In this world the book had a unique value. The correspondence of the humanists is to a great extent concerned with books, with new editions, and how to come by them. The printed book, often published in *de luxe* editions, very early became a status symbol. But perhaps more important than the masterpieces of typography were the ephemera, little pamphlets reflecting the great events of the day or polemical writings in which rival doctrines clashed. It is well known that Erasmus knew how to exploit the possibilities of printing. Many of his letters can be compared to a leading article in a newspaper, intended to influence public opinion. But in this respect too, he was one among many. It is noteworthy that all the great reformers saw a link between the book and the Reformation: only the printed book made the transfer of knowledge and the exercise of influence possible on a large scale.

At first the humanists, some of them laymen, some clerics, were mainly in the service of princes, bishops, or cities, where their first duty was to compose official documents, to prepare and possibly give speeches, and to make pleas in court. In addition, they were active from the beginning in the universities, as teachers of rhetoric.

Around 1500, humanists were also employed in all kinds of schools, maintained by cities and the church, as educators. Some of them were authors of the new textbooks that taught grammar as simply as possible and inculcated a good style. Like every other new group they set themselves up against the existing order, against the old method of teaching, and above all against scholasticism. Its barbarous Latin drew their particular fire, and the scholastic method, worn out as it was by its antiquated, foolish, and futile questions, fared equally badly at their hands. Yet the humanists by no means lived in a world of their own, separate from the representatives of the old disciplines. Johann Eck, for example, later the dogged adversary of Luther, had in happier days been a soundly trained theologian, who worked by the old methods, but was also in contact with all the German humanists and certainly aware of new developments. At first he was reasonably moderate in his attacks on Luther; for Luther, like himself, belonged to the new intelligentsia.

Thus old and new intermingled in every field.

THREE

Youth and Student Years

Hard facts about Erasmus' life are lacking until his ordination as a priest in 1492. Everything remains vague and uncertain, and the brief account of his early life that follows can only be given subject to that reservation. In part, this is because source material is scant. For the first twenty-five years of Erasmus' life we have at our disposal only thirty letters, the same number of poems, some scattered statements by Erasmus himself of a later date, and one work from his hand. A brief sketch of his life until 1524 published in the seventeenth century, which purports to be autobiographical, was a later forgery. This state of affairs is not unusual, but it is less usual to find that the details supplied by Erasmus cannot be reconciled with each other in any way. Even the year of his birth is uncertain; it was probably 1469, but 1466 and 1467 are not impossible and can be supported from his own statements. Erasmus' father was a priest, Gerard or Gerrit, and it was from his relationship with a woman from Gouda that Erasmus' elder brother Pieter and a few years later he himself were born. Children of priests were numerous. In the diocese of Utrecht, a century later, about a quarter of the priests lived more or less officially with a woman. Yet it was this circumstance that induced Erasmus to throw a smoke-screen around his youth. He felt his origin to be a stain. His baptismal name, Erasmus, was taken from one of the fourteen auxiliary saints who were popular in the fifteenth century; he added 'Roterodamus' from his birthplace, Rotterdam; 'Desiderius,' which appeared later, was a literary decoration.

We know little of Erasmus' youth. He went to school in Gouda, and some years later attended the school of the chapter of St Lebuinus in Deventer, where the *devotio moderna* had some influence. Here the well-known humanist Alexander Hegius was his teacher for a short time, and here he met the famous Rodolfus Agricola. He studied the normal subjects of the Latin school of the day, in which Latin and rhetoric took up much of the time. He was also taught some dialectic, but he never acquired a taste for it. Probably his guardians placed him and his brother at a school in 's-Hertogenbosch after the death of their father, and in 1487 the two boys were sent to monasteries, Erasmus to Steyn near Gouda which belonged to the order of the Augustinian canons. By his own account he was a slow learner and had in general been badly taught. The latter is a stock lament of the humanists; the former may well be true, for Erasmus was no child prodigy, and the first thirty years of his life show no sign of any special talent.

We are able to get some sort of grasp of Erasmus from his years in the cloister. Was he put there against his will? That is the version he gave later, putting the blame on his guardians, who, he claimed, acted out of greed for money. More probably, the truth is that the young man of about twenty had few other possibilities open to him and as little reluctance as enthusiasm. More confidence can be placed in the complaints he later made about the way of life forced upon him, which must have become burdensome for a young man who was not physically strong and rather unworldly, his mind bent on higher things. The many charges that he later brought against monastic life in general and its representatives in particular derive from his own experiences. The monastery was strict, it strove to practise humility, obedience, and continual self-control as the highest virtues, and was wholly directed towards contemplation and worship. But when Erasmus later portrays himself as the only man of refinement among boors, there is some exaggeration involved. Letters have been preserved from his monastic days, to friends in and out of the cloister, which show that some kindred spirits had found each other. The letters will have been intended in the first place as literary exercises, but at the same time they reveal deep friendships. 'Considering that my affection for you is and always has been so deep, dearest Servatius, that I value you more than my very eyes and life, and in a word, myself, what is it that makes you so hard-hearted that you not only refuse to love him who loves you so well but do not even regard him with esteem?'[1] This is how one of Erasmus' letters begins, and he continues in the same strain, making several elegant citations from classical authors. There are others like this one. Huizinga points out that sentimental friendships were part of good style in the fifteenth century. Erasmus, who later became so reserved, had to unlearn the habit of laying himself open to people and making himself vulnerable.

The classical authors – in this letter Terence and Virgil – are not mere decoration. The circle had been touched by the ideal of *bonae litterae*, the cultivation of classical literature. They were in the grip of antiquity, especially of the Latin language. Erasmus and his friends wrote poems and felt themselves to be poets, with a feeling for language and a sensitivity to the music of words. But words bring content, a new world of beauty in stark constrast to the flat, dreary present. There was a fashionable yearning for beauty, but that is not all. Even then, Erasmus must have acquired a reasonable knowledge of Latin authors. In one letter he names fifteen almost nonchalantly,[2] and the quality of his own letters shows that he had read them. He had also read a number of Italian humanists, among them Francesco Filelfo, Agostino Dati, Poggio Bracciolini, and especially Lorenzo Valla; of the Fathers he knew St Augustine and above all St Jerome, who was to remain his guiding star throughout his life.

In rustic Holland Erasmus and his circle of friends may have formed an exception, but in Europe as a whole there were many monks who played with language and fell under the spell of a distant world, but at length reconciled themselves to their lot. From the first work by Erasmus that we have, it is clear that he was given to more serious reflection. It is his *De contemptu mundi (On Disdaining the World)*, which he wrote towards the end of the 1480s.[3] The theme, encouragement to adopt the monastic life, was already hackneyed, and at first sight his treatment of it is traditional. What are we to think of such chapter headings as 'It is dangerous to remain in the world,' 'Spurn wealth!' 'Positions of honour are meaningless and uncertain'?[4] In this case a first impression is misleading. As we read, we discover that the work is a eulogy of monastic life, but from very definite motives. It is concerned essentially with the excellence of the solitary life, as it had been praised in classical antiquity. Erasmus does not associate monastic life with general Christian ideals, but rather with the general human ideal, as it had been realized by the aristocrats of the spirit. One has the impression that Erasmus cannot be content to be a monk and to have humanist interests, but must strive to combine the two ways of life. We find the same striving in his poems, in which one can detect a turn to religious motifs. But he does not succeed in reaching a synthesis in this work. He attempts to give meaning to a way of life that he evidently already felt to be meaningless.

In 1493 Erasmus seized the chance which was offered to him. He became secretary to the bishop of Cambrai, Hendrik van Bergen, who needed a good Latinist. In spite of an order in 1514 from the prior of Steyn, Servatius Rogerus, the same man to whom he had written his letters of friendship twenty-five years earlier, Erasmus never returned. Around 1507 he laid aside the habit of his order because, he says, in Italy his clothing was taken for that of those who visited the victims of the plague, so that he had to endure disagreeable treatment.

But back to 1493. The post at the bishop's court did not suit him, nothing came of the bishop's intended journey to Rome, and Erasmus found himself travelling around the southern Netherlands in his master's entourage. He had reason enough to complain of the unhappy fate that denied him the opportunity to study. We know virtually nothing, however, about his life in this period. He himself mentions briefly, and without comment, the events in a convent near Valenciennes, where the nuns were possessed by evil spirits. We catch a glimpse of his zeal for study in the report of a monk from the monastery of Groenendael near Brussels that Erasmus, while staying there, found works by Augustine and studied them so eagerly that he even took them with him to his cell at night. The monks laughed at him for neglecting all the other books in order to immerse himself in this Father of the church – and that in the very place where the great mystic Ruusbroec had lived for many years.[5] Erasmus had no interest in making a career in the service of a prince of the church, for his goal was to study. He was eager to go to Paris, the centre of learning.

In the last months of his stay in the Netherlands, or perhaps during his early days in Paris, where he lived from 1495, Erasmus wrote a dialogue defending the rights of the study of *bonae litterae*.[6] The title *Antibarbari* (*The Antibarbarians*), under which the work was published in 1520, speaks for itself. It is noteworthy that even this early Erasmus chose the dialogue form, which he was later to handle in such masterly fashion in the *Colloquies*. At this stage, however, he was still rather clumsy in his use of it, as the Paris humanist Robert Gaguin rightly remarked.[7] The setting of the dialogue in the Brabant countryside, where several friends gather to enjoy a quiet conversation over a good meal, is no less typical. Such a scene recurs several times in Erasmus' later works. He had in fact worked on the book in the country, perhaps on the bishop's estate at Halsteren near Bergen-op-Zoom.

In the meantime Erasmus' thought had not stood still. The problems posed in the *Antibarbari* were different from those of *De contemptu mundi*. Monastic life no longer played any role, for now the question was a larger one, whether classical civilization and learning could be linked to the Christian faith. Erasmus starts by asking how it was possible for true culture to have lost so much of its vigour. One of the partners in the conversation points to the Christian religion as an important cause, citing several reasons. From the earliest days there had been Christians who thought it scandalous to be familiar with pagan literature. This attitude, in his opinion, stemmed from a misguided zeal for the faith or a natural aversion to literature or even simple idleness. Some hated what they did not know; for others it was a matter of piety: they contented themselves with the virtue of *simplicitas*, simplicity or naivety. Finally, he says, religion and culture are not by their nature easy partners: 'Unlettered religion has something of flabby stupidity, which is violently distasteful to those who know letters.'[8] Erasmus himself rejected such a distinction between piety and culture. He was convinced that God had not failed to manifest himself outside of Judaism, even in the centuries before the coming of Christ. The entire culture of classical antiquity contained God's preparation for the highest good, which Christ was to bring. And does not the highest civilization always approach the highest good?[9] Yet Erasmus did not achieve a true synthesis. He pointed to several positive examples, in particular the attitudes of Jerome and Augustine. He lashed at the pride of the more recent theologians who only spoke well of themselves and their cronies, who in their own eyes knew everything, anti-academics as they were, the opposite of the Academics of ancient times, the philosophers who preferred to suspend judgment.[10] But he was unable to suggest how a union could be achieved in his own time. He did not go beyond defending the right of *bonae litterae* against the scholastic theologians, who considered this study futile and dangerous. The polemic tone prevailed, and Erasmus offered no positive solution.

Even so, the *Antibarbari* was of no little importance. It marks a stage in Erasmus' development. Here for the first time he revealed what was to become the central theme of his whole work: how can one, with a good conscience, be both a man of culture and a Christian?

Apart from some interruptions for journeys to the Netherlands, Erasmus remained in Paris from 1495 to 1499. For a time he found accommodation at the Collège de Montaigu, where Jan Standonck of Mechelen wielded the sceptre. Standonck was a harsh master. The pupils at the hostel for poor students were given wretched food and lodging and even humiliated or beaten. Erasmus saw it with his own eyes and himself suffered from the poor treatment. Thirty years later he still recalled it with a shudder.[11] He was none too strong, could not cope with a hard regime, and had a modern feeling for hygiene. Within a year he left and took lodgings in a large student residence. The years that followed were no easier. His bursary from the bishop was inadequate, and he was always short of money. At the age of thirty he still had to humiliate himself by begging for his allowance or serving as tutor to the wealthy sons of noble or well-off bourgeois families. Erasmus' complaints in this respect should be taken seriously, but of course they do not tell the whole truth. He also describes the colourful procession, held after it had rained for three months and the Seine had overflowed its banks – and behold, the sky cleared![12] He enjoyed a battle between his landlady and the maid, whom he had advised to pull off the landlady's headpiece and then to go for her hair![13] He found a friend in the genial humanist Fausto Andrelini, with whom he exchanged notes during a dull lecture, and whom he remembered twenty-five years later as a skirt-chaser and hater of theologians.[14] Can it be pure chance that it was to Andrelini of all men that he wrote of the custom he found in England, where the girls greeted you on arrival and departure with kisses on all sides?[15] At any rate there were those in Brabant who had tales to tell of an Erasmus who ran into debt, was a lazy man about town, and had an eye for female beauty.[16]

The Paris years represented a settling of accounts with the past rather than a new beginning. Through Standonck and Jan Mombaer, a kindred spirit of Standonck who had come to Paris to carry out reforms in certain monastic houses in the neighbourhood, Erasmus again came into contact with the *devotio moderna*. He had already become acquainted with it to some extent during his school years and came to know it more deeply in the monastery of Steyn, which was under the influence of the movement. The question of the influence of the *devotio moderna* on Erasmus has been hotly disputed. Paul Mestwerdt, probably incorrectly, rated it highly. There can hardly be any question of essential contacts during Erasmus' school years, and his years in the monastery were not the happiest days of his life. Standonck and Mombaer certainly did not have a positive influence on his judgment. He wrote several short informal letters to Mombaer during his Paris years, and was familiar with Mombaer's *Rosetum*. The title *Rose-garden* was in Erasmus' opinion presumptuous: inside it you found nothing but thistles and darnel.[17] No wonder! The best known part of the work, the *Chiropsalterium*, taught a method of arousing pious thoughts using the thumb, which felt the inside of the other fingers: each part of each finger stood for a different reflection. This kind of thing was certainly not in harmony with Erasmus' ideals. His verdict on Standonck is known to us, and his statement that in Montaigu 'even the walls have a theological character'[18] makes it amply clear that Erasmus did not distinguish the teaching methods of this hated institution from the theology taught there. This hard and legalistic form of the *devotio moderna*, typical of its days of decline, was not attractive, and we hear no more of it from Erasmus.

He had gone to Paris to study theology and was intent on winning the title of doctor.[19] For unknown reasons he never reached this goal. It is still unclear which lectures he attended, but we know that he was introduced to scholastic theology in its Scotist form, which went back to Duns Scotus. What impression it made on

Erasmus we learn from two letters, one from the middle of his Paris period, one from the time in England, where he had discovered that another theology was also possible. A single glance at the second letter is enough: the lectures were hair-splitting, sophistical quibbling, which made men into quarrelsome pseudo-scholars, one dispute followed another, all quarrels about nothing, and 'we sometimes debate questions of a sort intolerable to truly religious men.' It is just a glimpse, and it is true that Erasmus claims to be attacking only the degenerate theologians and not the true masters.[20] We shall return later to the question whether Erasmus learned anything from scholasticism, in spite of his aversion to it, but the letter from Paris makes clear the deeper reason behind his rejection of it. Erasmus relates the tale of Epimenides, familiar from antiquity. He lay sleeping in a cave for no less than forty-seven years before he awoke at last. He was fortunate, says Erasmus, for most of the theologians of our day never wake up at all. Once Epimenides awoke, everything seemed changed, so that he began to doubt himself. 'He went to his city and there found everything new: he could not recognize the walls, the streets, the coinage, the very people; dress, behaviour, speech, all were altered. Such is the mutability of human affairs.' He walked about, recognized only by a pair of boon companions who had been his friends.[21] This Epimenides was for Erasmus the image of the scholastic theologians of his own day. They had fallen asleep, stuck to the old ways, and went about the modern world like men in a daze.

In the same letter Erasmus gives us a self-portrait: 'If only you could see your Erasmus sitting agape among those glorified Scotists, while "Gryllard" lectures from a lofty throne. If you could but observe his furrowed brow, his uncomprehending look and worried expression, you would say it was another man ... I am trying with might and main to say nothing in good Latin, or elegantly, or wittily.'[22] These are the words of the spokesman of a new generation and a new attitude to life.

Did Erasmus have any positive experiences in Paris? He had, in the circles of the Paris humanists, among whom Robert Gaguin, the general of the Trinitarian order, was the acknowledged master. He became acquainted with Gaguin, who gave him his first chance to publish something. At the end of Gaguin's *De origine ... Francorum* a couple of pages were left blank in the 1495 printing, and Erasmus was one of those who speedily supplied a contribution, in his case a eulogy of Gaguin. He published a few other small pieces, but the Paris circle was not yet very interested in him. There were more important men, who had achieved more. So Erasmus passed his student years and made use of the opportunities the Paris milieu offered. The result was one or two small publications; for the most part he spent his time reading, memorizing, excerpting from, and interpreting Latin authors. That he had to take such pains for the sake of his young pupils was not, in the long run, merely a waste of time. Erasmus felt nothing but reluctance for this work, for he was no schoolmaster and was never to become one. But his lessons led to textbooks of Latin for beginners, which were later to become incredibly popular. In his reading he was struck by the many proverbs and sayings, and began to collect them. That too was the preliminary stage of a work which later became famous, the collection of proverbs to which he gave the name of *Adages*.

One should not forget that there were many more in the same position: men of around thirty, clerics with little zeal for the church or theology, reasonably well schooled in Latin literature and full of admiration for the beauty of that language, but without money, and forced to scrape together an income from a casual patron or a couple of pupils, all of them cherishing the idea of going to Rome, the centre of the world.

FOUR

Erasmus in the
World of the Humanists

๛

In 1499 Erasmus was a young, unknown man of letters. In 1514 he described himself as old, grey-haired, and in poor health.[1] He was then probably forty-five years old, and the path to success was open to him. Although the fifteen years in between were of primary importance, we are not particularly well informed about them. The correspondence comprises about 200 letters, of which 150 are by Erasmus. This is not a great number, and they are very unevenly distributed. From the years from 1502 to 1508 we have 45 letters, while not a single letter from Erasmus has survived from the years 1509 and 1510. In addition, many of the letters – and this is true of later years also – were published by Erasmus, or by his friends, whom he authorized to make any alterations they thought necessary. We must bear in mind that they may have been revised. Besides the letters, there is a number of publications that give us an insight into Erasmus' interests and his intellectual world, as do scattered statements by third parties towards the end of this period, when he had become well known. This state of affairs is not bad, but it compels us to be very cautious in pointing to developments in Erasmus' thinking. Apparent differences may be due to the chances of survival or the revision of the material.

In 1499 Erasmus had been intent on going to Rome. He went to England instead, in particular to London and Oxford. In the ensuing years he travelled a great deal: 1499–1500 England, 1500–1 Paris and Orléans, 1501–4 the Netherlands, 1504–5 Paris, 1506–9 Italy, 1509–14 England. Such a summary makes clear, in the first place, that Erasmus became alienated from his original environment. After

1504 he never lived in the Netherlands again, and in the previous years he had preferred the southern provinces to the north. In 1501 he had spent one and a half months in Holland; but it was to his great dissatisfaction: he had wasted his time. He repeats it: 'Wasted, I say, for nothing is so much lost [as is lost time].'[2] He was repelled by the immoderate eating, the lack of refinement, and the contempt of study.[3] Second, we see that Erasmus lived in the centres of the humanist movement: Italy, both the north and Rome, was a self-evident requirement, England the country he preferred. The Rhineland with its important humanist traditions was still missing. The years of special importance were those Erasmus passed in England and the period in Italy.

His first visit to England brought Erasmus the recognition he ardently desired. He had gone there as tutor of William Blount, Lord Mountjoy. The twenty-year-old lord, later a tutor of Prince Henry, proved to have connections in the highest circles. Erasmus made the acquaintance of Thomas More, later chancellor of Henry viii, and More took him to the palace where the princes and princesses lived. There he met the future king, at that time eight years old, but already a true king in his appearance, as Erasmus recalled years later.[4] His association with the high nobility is typical of this first visit, which lasted about six months. In a letter to Robert Fisher, who was then in Italy, 'where the very walls are more scholarly and articulate than human beings are with us,' and in spite of these words, he sings the praises of England: there is civilization and culture, there are men like John Colet, William Grocyn, Thomas Linacre, Thomas More – 'It is marvellous to see what an extensive and rich crop of ancient learning is springing up here.' Erasmus was so taken with England that Italy seemed to him no more than a tourist attraction. He even found the climate in England agreeable and healthy – and that was in early December![5] Between the lines we can read his joy that he had at last been 'discovered.'

He also came to know John Colet. Of course, Colet was above all a Maecenas who provided money and accommodation and had important connections. But there was more. Erasmus was deeply impressed by the lectures on the Epistles of Paul that Colet gave at Oxford in 1499. When he saw Colet again in 1510, then a preacher at St Paul's and head of the school he had refounded there, Erasmus once more fell under his spell. It is indisputable that Erasmus owed much of his intellectual development to Colet, but more difficult to determine just where this influence lay. For many years now there has been a tendency to grant Colet a decisive role. He is supposed to have been the man under whose influence Erasmus was transformed from a littérateur into a student of the Bible, so that it was through him that Erasmus' first visit to England became a turning point in his life. This view has become popular since Frederic Seebohm's persuasive book, which refers, significantly, to the 'fellow-work' of Colet, Erasmus, and More in its subtitle, appeared in 1867. Robert Stupperich disputes it,[6] and, although I do not share his reasoning, I think his opinion is justified. It was not Colet who led Erasmus to the philological study of the Bible that was to be of central importance in his life. Their methods differed too widely for that. Colet knew no Greek and gave his lectures on the basis of the Vulgate. The modern reader of the lectures must make a great effort to feel any of their attractiveness, which must have lain in Colet's personality rather than in his work. The biographical sketch that Erasmus wrote shortly after Colet's death also reveals this: it is concerned with Colet the man.[7]

Erasmus' return to Paris in 1500 was a great disappointment. Travelling was not easy in an age when the news of the death of Pope Julius II took ten days post-haste to cover the distance from Rome to Nürnberg. Erasmus often described the difficulties of travelling, mostly in a lightly ironic tone, but this time the difficulties were dramatic. While his whole stay in England had been a great experience, the customs at Dover took from him the money he had with him, twenty pounds, a sum he had never seen at one time before in his life and on which he could have lived for months. No wonder the journey from the French coast to Paris lingered in his memory as a nightmare: threatened by two Frenchmen who had provided him and a travelling companion with horses and escort, but who revealed themselves *en route* as robbers, he only reached Paris safely because he had no more money to be robbed of.[8] Erasmus continued to hold the loss of his money against England, yet he remained an anglophile. As we have seen, he had his reasons to be so.

Erasmus' stay in Italy from 1506 to 1509 also deserves mention.

He did not go there as a young student with everything to learn, but as a professional scholar with published work to his credit who wished to meet his colleagues and perfect his knowledge. Soon after his arrival he received a doctorate in theology from Turin.[9] He became familiar with Bologna, Venice, Padua, and Rome. Only a few letters from this period have been preserved, and Erasmus offers no more than scraps of reminiscences later. He mentions a bullfight – which did not please him[10] – and tells us of a pitch-dark tunnel through a mountain in the neighbourhood of Naples[11] and a visit to the grotto of the Sibyl of Cumae in the same district.[12] We hear of the humanist Girolamo Aleandro, later a bitter opponent, a better Greek scholar than Erasmus but his inferior in mastery of Latin.[13] Erasmus followed Aleandro's lectures and shared a room with him in the house of the father-in-law of the famous Venetian printer, Aldo Manuzio.[14] Later he recalled to his trusted younger friend Beatus Rhenanus the days in Venice, when he worked in the printing house like a man possessed, had manuscripts of Greek authors fetched to him there, and learned all the tricks of his trade from the most renowned humanists of the day.[15] We are given the impression, probably not inaccurate, that Italy for Erasmus meant books and manuscripts.

He visited Rome in 1509 as a well-known author and used his time well, making the acquaintance of such important men as the cardinals Domenico Grimani,[16] Raffaele Riario, and Egidio Antonini (Giles) of Viterbo, as well as Giovanni de' Medici, the future Pope Leo x. His stay was unforgettable in every respect: the climate, the landscape, the libraries, and the scholars – so many celebrities.[17] But he did not lose his critical sense. Twenty years later he recalled with a shudder the famous orator who had preached a Good Friday sermon in the presence of Pope Julius ii and many cardinals and bishops. The man spent most of his time eulogizing the pope as the almighty Jupiter, who imposed his will by a nod in France, in Germany, yes, in all the countries of the world. But Christ was no more to this preacher than one of the heroes of the ancient world, who had sacrificed their lives for Rome.[18]

Crossing the Alps was also a memorable experience. Not that we hear anything of the mountains. On his way to Italy Erasmus composed De senectute (On Old Age),[19] in which he stands back from himself and describes himself and the way in which he had lived since his youth: studying, reading, always reading. On the return journey he drafted the *Praise of Folly*, in which he distances himself from everything that passes for important in the world.

Erasmus' second stay in England, from 1509 to 1514, was no less important than the first. Immediately after the death of Henry VII, William Blount encouraged him to seize his good fortune and come to England. His letter is excited. Everything is to be different now that Henry VIII has acceded to the throne – 'Heaven smiles, earth rejoices; all is milk and honey and nectar' – and he predicts that now there will be an end of Erasmus' miseries. Humanistic style? Certainly, but also characteristic of his great expectations, and to show that he was in earnest Blount sent ten pounds for the journey, half from himself and half in the name of the archbishop of Canterbury.[20] Erasmus reacted eagerly to the invitation, but once in England his high hopes were at first disappointed. Yet he gradually won fame, much more than ten years before. As early as 1511, when he was in Paris to arrange the printing of the *Praise of Folly*, a letter from England asked, 'What of Erasmus? When will he come back? He is quite the sun of our age. If only he might come back!'[21] This sounds a bit extravagant, but it was a friend who wrote. But in 1512 Erasmus described himself as 'now almost entirely transformed into an Englishman, so extremely kind have many persons been to me, including especially the archbishop of Canterbury, my incomparable Maecenas'; and then comes a eulogy on William Warham.[22] This letter reveals the second reason for his love of England. He was honoured, but he also found the patrons he needed in order to acquire an independent position. This was not something he could achieve overnight. Not until his mid-forties, at the end of his stay in England, did Erasmus break free of his dependence on others.

What was Erasmus' life like in these fifteen years? The mere struggle to exist took much of his energy. The bitter taste of poverty meets us in his letters. In 1504 he composed a panegyric in praise of Philip the Fair, the father of Charles V, and remarked to Colet that he had never written with greater reluctance. 'For I saw that this kind of thing could not be handled without some flattery.'[23] He continued to beg from his old patrons in the Netherlands. Over the years his English benefactors became more important, but he detested even more the necessity of asking them. 'O this begging! I know you laugh at it. But I hate myself,' he erupted to Colet in 1511.[24] But the end was not yet in sight. In the same year he thanked Colet for a promise but revealed himself as understandably hurt by Colet's remark 'if you beg humbly.'[25] Why this way of life? Erasmus answered this question in a letter to an old friend, who was to ask for money for him from Anna van Borssele: 'Please explain to her how much greater is the glory she can acquire from me, by my literary works, than from the other theologians in her patronage. They merely deliver humdrum sermons; I am writing immortal works. Their uneducated nonsense finds an audience in perhaps a couple of churches; my books will be read all over the world, in the Latin west and in the Greek east and by every nation. Say that there is everywhere a huge supply of such uneducated divines as these, while such a one as I am is scarcely to be found in many generations.'[26] Was he serious? He immediately adds that his friend must be willing not to insist on the strict truth from a friend. Nevertheless, he was serious, and that in 1500, when he could still only point to the future.

Erasmus could not live by gifts alone. A great deal of his income in these years came from pupils whom he was obliged to teach or supervise. It was as a tutor that he had gone to England in 1499 and to Italy in 1506. In 1511 he gave lectures at Cambridge for a short time.[27] But on this point there is a gap between Erasmus' theory and practice. He had a high opinion of Colet as a teacher of the young, and helped him with a textbook, poems, and a sermon.[28] He ardently defended the teaching profession against theologians: no work was so meritorious in the eyes of God as teaching, no cloistered life could be compared with it, however much they despised it.[29] Yet he himself found little pleasure in it.[30] The true Erasmus of these years is depicted for us by Stephen Gardiner, later bishop of Winchester and a persecutor of Protestants under Queen Mary. In 1511 he was a boy of perhaps fifteen years old, in Paris with Erasmus, and fifteen years later he recalled how Erasmus had praised him for the salads he had made. Even afterwards he boasted, when Erasmus' name was mentioned, that he had once been his cook! But above all he remembered the books, all those books, Greek and Latin, that Erasmus was buying at that time.[31]

This is the core of Erasmus' work in those years: as a humanist he studied the classics and produced editions of their works with scholarly commentaries. It began with the *Adagiorum collectanea* of 1500, immediately after he had returned from England to Paris, a collection of 818 Latin proverbs, sayings, and metaphors, a gold mine for those who wished to write correct and polished Latin. It was the first real book that he published. All kinds of smaller works followed, of which I name only a few: an edition of Cicero's *De officiis*, of the *Disticha Catonis* and the *Mimi* of Publilius Syrus, and Latin translations of Greek authors, including Euripides, Plutarch, and Lucian. Sometimes Erasmus played down this achievement, and apologized for the fact that he, a theologian, should have spent 'a few short hours' on such work.[32] This was, of course, mere bragging. Later too, Erasmus was to assert, in a stereotyped fashion, even of important books, that he had only devoted a few days to them. But were the labour long or short, he would never become rich from it. A letter from the Paris printer Josse Bade to Erasmus gives a lively picture of the difficulties faced by authors. As if in one breath Bade writes that he has received Erasmus' manuscripts, that Erasmus has unfortunately not mentioned his price, that he cannot pay properly because his competitors will immediately reprint them, and that therefore he makes an offer which Erasmus will find absurdly low, but he must console himself with the thought that heaven will reward him, that he is making himself serviceable, and that he is helping poor Bade with all his children.[33]

Erasmus published works of other kinds as well, in 1503 the *Enchiridion* and in 1511 the *Praise of Folly*. Like the *Adages* they will be discussed later in another connection. The *Adages* and the *Praise of Folly* were popular at once, but the *Enchiridion* remained unnoticed until fifteen years later, when it suddenly caused a sensation.

Did any special trait mark Erasmus out among the humanists? There was nothing out of the ordinary about him, but in these years he began to develop his own special interests. Certain elements recur again and again. To begin with, there was the study of Greek. As early as 1500 he was immersed in it.[34] He was scraping together the money to buy Plato and to be able to afford Greek books and a Greek teacher. He had great plans –wanted to publish this and that, and above all to acquire a respectable knowledge of Greek.[35] He also intended to buy all the works of Jerome.[36] He had studied Jerome eagerly in the monastery, but now he planned to produce an edition with commentary. We regularly find both the main themes of his studies in his letters. Erasmus made good progress with Greek and by 1502 could express himself reasonably well in it, even extempore.[37] His work on Jerome was time-consuming, but we continually hear of his activities in this connection.

Why these two in particular, Greek and Jerome? Greek was indispensable, if only for the *Adages*, and Jerome was an old love. In both cases, however, there was more to it than that. With no other Father of the church did Erasmus feel such affinity as with Jerome, with no one did he identify himself so closely. For him Jerome was the *vir trilinguis*, the man of three tongues, Latin, Greek, and Hebrew; he was the translator and expositor of the Bible, a work he had only been able to accomplish through his phenomenal knowledge of languages. Jerome too it was, as no other western Father of the church, who knew the classics and made his knowledge bear fruit for theology. The bond that Erasmus sought between true learning and culture on the one hand and piety and theology on the other he found realized in Jerome. Something similar was true of Greek. When Erasmus announced his intention to devote himself to Greek with all his power, he had a well-defined goal before his eyes. As with the study of Jerome, it was to contribute 'to my reputation, indeed my salvation.' He wanted to devote himself wholly to *arcanae litterae*, or *sacrae litterae*, literally the 'hidden, sacred letters.' He had long been burning with desire to deal with the Bible.[38] In one way or another, Erasmus wanted to put the study of Greek and of Jerome at the service of the study of the Bible.

But was it quite clear to him how this was to be done? Exegesis was foremost. As early as 1499, Colet had asked Erasmus to interpret some books of the Bible. He had refused – perhaps because he did not feel properly qualified.[39] When he had not long been occupied with Greek, he ventured to write a commentary on the Epistles of Paul, but soon gave it up, for he saw that it was impossible without a knowledge of Greek.[40] In 1501 he gave an example to demonstrate the importance of Greek. In two psalms the translation of the Vulgate can only arouse the greatest misunderstandings, whereas the Greek makes the psalmist's meaning clear at once.[41] One point is remarkable: Erasmus must have known that the Greek text of the Psalms was itself a translation, and he never learned Hebrew.[42] Yet this is an important moment in his development. He came to see that one could not practise theology without one basic prerequisite, the knowledge of the languages: 'I can see what utter madness it is even to put a finger on that part of theology which is specially concerned with the mysteries of the faith unless one is furnished with the equipment of Greek as well'; without this knowledge one could not even discover the literal meaning of the Scriptures.[43] In 1504 he wrote that for three years he had been 'wholly absorbed by Greek' and that he had formed the firm resolve to devote the rest of his life to the study of Holy Scripture.[44] At that time he had already discovered, in an abbey near Louvain, the manuscript of Lorenzo Valla's *Adnotationes*, the notes on the New Testament in which the famous humanist compared the Latin translation of a number of passages with some Greek manuscripts. In 1505 Erasmus published this work with an important foreword in which he disarmed the objections of those who said that only the theologian and not the philologist could criticize the Vulgate. 'Indeed this whole business of translating the Holy Scriptures is manifestly a grammarian's function. Nor indeed is it absurd if in certain spheres Jethro has greater competence than Moses.' The comparison is revealing. Although grammar may belong to profane scholarship, it can still be of service to theology, and its help is sometimes very necessary. And to the argument that theology stands so high that it is not bound by the laws of grammar Erasmus retorts that it would be 'a novel distinction' for theologians, if they were 'to have the exclusive privilege of expressing themselves barbarously.'[45] Erasmus had found his *métier*: applying his philological skills to the study of the New Testament. All in all, Erasmus had gone beyond the point he had reached in writing the *Antibarbari*. Then he had been concerned with the integration of classical culture and Christianity; now he began to set his course towards the realization of that ideal.

What kind of man was Erasmus, who in these years gradually found his life's work? In answering this question, I am not primarily concerned with his qualities of character. Huizinga drew Erasmus' portrait; his need for purity, his sensitivity and oversensitivity, his need for friendship and amiability, his egocentrism, his suspicion, his boundless sense of freedom, the contradiction between his distaste for lies and the minor falsehoods that he sometimes needed. We see before us the not very tall, rather slight but well-proportioned figure, fair in complexion, with blond hair and blue eyes. But if we ask which, of all the characteristics that made up the man Erasmus, was the most essential, my answer is: his toughness, his undaunted tenacity, in spite of all obstacles, in holding to the goal he wanted to attain. He did not let himself be held back by poverty. His far from robust health and his numerous illnesses could not keep him from the work he had chosen. Of course the deepest essence of Erasmus escapes us, but we come close to it if we imagine him in the printing house of Aldo Manuzio in Venice, steadfastly occupied for eight months in turning the collection of eight hundred proverbs that he had published in 1500 into the bulky *Adagiorum chiliades*, with its more than 3,200 entries. Surrounded by manuscripts of Greek authors put at his disposal by the printer, he collected and explained the adages. He continued to work even when the compositors had already begun printing. So too in 1515 he sat in the printing house of Froben in Basel, imperturbably busy. Scenes like these are typical of his way of life and his restrained passion.

Erasmus had reason to be satisfied when he left England in the summer of 1514 with Basel as his first goal. During the journey, he wrote a letter to the prior of the monastery of Steyn, listing his high patrons in England: bishops, who all wished to attach him to themselves, Henry VIII, who had written him a letter in his own hand, the queen, who wished to engage him as tutor; he reported on the allowance and the gifts from Warham and other bishops, the universities, both of which desired to attract him, and last but not least, John Colet, 'a man who has married profound scholarship to exceptional devoutness.'[46] Even if reality is sometimes confused with expectation here, much remains. In the same letter he proudly lists the cardinals in Rome who have welcomed him as a brother.[47]

Yet his reason for writing this letter was sad enough. Scarcely had Erasmus crossed the channel when a letter reached him from the prior, bluntly summoning him back to the monastery and the monastic duties he had given up more than twenty years before. In

Erasmus' reply we find traces of the bitter memories of former times, the fasting, the early rising for the choral services, after which he could not sleep again, his aversion to empty ceremonies, his longing for freedom. The core of the letter is a well-argued and resolute refusal. The monastic life is not suitable for him, his vocation lies elsewhere. Erasmus shows courage in clearly recognizing his own incapacity. He states that his bodily weakness and the kidney stones from which he suffers make a return to the monastery impossible. The monastic diet, the gossip, the whole way of life – all this repels him. He can only say this because throughout the letter runs the thread of the monastic life as a 'way of life,' one possibility alongside others, preferable for some but in itself no better or worse than another way of life. This is diametrically opposed to the customary view of the monastic life as the path to perfection, which as such had greater value and was rightly called *religio*, service to God *par excellence*. In the *Enchiridion* Erasmus had already spoken of the monastic existence as a 'way of life.'[48] What he had said in general terms there he now applied to himself. It is also evidence of his courage that he says under these circumstances that the so-called 'religions,' that is, the various monastic rules, have been detrimental to Christian piety: 'How much more consonant with Christ's teaching it would be to regard the entire Christian world as a single household, a single monastery as it were, and to think of all men as one's fellow-canons and brethren, to regard the sacrament of baptism as the supreme "religion," and to consider not where one lives, but how one lives.'[49] Erasmus defends his way of life. He lists his works, and expatiates on his achievements and plans with special reference to Jerome, the New Testament, and the Epistles of Paul: 'For I have made up my mind to give up my life to sacred literature. These then are the concerns upon which I am bestowing my leisure and my busy hours alike. I have, so eminent men are saying, a talent for them which others do not possess; while I shall never have any talent for living your kind of life.'[50] This was plain speaking and the best self-portrait that Erasmus could give. If anywhere, it is here that we see that Erasmus had found himself and his path, and was not to be kept from it. Nothing is known of any answer, but in 1517 he received papal permission to live in the world.

The journey to Basel became a triumphal progress. Erasmus was splendidly received in Mainz, Strasbourg, and Sélestat by such humanists as Jakob Wimpfeling, Jakob Sturm, Beatus Rhenanus, and Ulrich von Hutten. In England Erasmus had won recognition, in Germany he was acclaimed and hailed as a German. For Hutten, Johannes Reuchlin and Erasmus were the 'two pearls of Germany, for it was through them that this nation ceased to be barbarous.'[51] Erasmus received such praise eagerly. On his return from Basel to England six months later, the situation was no different. The knight Eitelwolf vom Stein was forced by kidney stones to miss the 'Socratic symposium' at which Reuchlin, Hermannus Buschius, and others received Erasmus in Frankfurt. He complained bitterly of his ill fortune the next day when he found that Erasmus had already left, so that he would not be able to see him. Never had he regretted his illness more than at this moment, when he had missed 'the greatest man of Germany.'[52] Erasmus could be content.

FIVE

The *Enchiridion*

꿏

'His writings will best show his likeness' – so a saying which often occurs as a motto to portraits of Erasmus. In this chapter we discuss the *Enchiridion militis christiani*,[1] which may be translated as the 'handbook of the Christian soldier,' but also as the 'hand-sword' or 'dagger.' Erasmus wrote it in 1501 at the request of the wife of a soldier, the master of arms at the court of Burgundy, to win him away from his all too rough life. The present was not a great success, for the man made as much use of the book as Erasmus did of the sword he received in return.[2] On the encouragement of the Franciscan Jean Vitrier, for whom he had great admiration, Erasmus elaborated the book, and in 1503 it appeared as part of a collection of works. This history of its origin makes the nature of the work fairly clear. As the dedication tells us, Erasmus wished to 'set down ... a kind of summary guide to living, so that, equipped with it, you might attain to a state of mind worthy of Christ.'[3] He gives a manual of the practice of Christian life, written 'not in order to show off my cleverness or my style.'[4]

The *Enchiridion* does not have a clear logical arrangement. Its point of departure is life as a struggle against the demons and the world. In this struggle God gives us two weapons, prayer and knowledge, which we acquire through the intense study of Holy Scripture. Study of *litterae humanae* can serve as a preparation for this, but no more than that. Man cannot, however, carry on this heavy combat if he does not know himself, and the most important part of self-knowledge is the realization that man in his soul belongs to the divine, but in his body to the animal world. Once this foundation has been laid, Erasmus adds to it twenty-two rules by which man must abide in order to obtain true happiness. Most of them he treats briefly, but in the fifth rule, the ascent from the visible to the invisible, he goes into great detail, as he does in the sixth, which portrays Christ as the ideal of piety. The final section deals with the means of resisting a number of particular sins.

Although the origin of the book, as we have described it, is not a literary fiction, the printed edition was of course intended for a wider public. At first that was not attained. Six years later a second edition appeared, again in a collection, and from 1515 to 1517 there were six printings, all as a separate work. In 1518 Erasmus had the *Enchiridion* published for the first time by Froben of Basel, with its content unchanged, but with a new foreword in which he unmistakably took Luther under his protection against his enemies. After that, the book became immensely popular: from 1519 to 1523 twenty-nine editions appeared. The number then fell off, although in the Netherlands and in England the book was frequently reprinted. In 1525 Erasmus proudly remarked that it 'was flying to all points of the compass' and had already been translated into four modern languages.[5] In fact, there were five, to which three more were to be added before the end of the century. In the Netherlands there were at least fifteen editions in the vernacular by 1600, and there were thirteen in England.

These are sober figures, but they confront us with the question of the reason for this late-flowering but long-lasting popularity of a book that Heiko A. Oberman has called 'the dullest book in the history of piety.' Such a verdict can only refer to its outer form. Oberman however makes it clear that his verdict concerns not only the form but also the content. In his view, the work tends towards the ideal of turning the whole world into a monastery. In the latest history of dogma to appear, G.A. Benrath follows the established tradition of discussing it as a work of spiritualization and moralism: for Erasmus everything hinged on the continuing moral struggle against vice and sins. Only E.-W. Kohls passes a more positive judgment. He sees in the *Enchiridion* a theology in which God's coming to man and man's return to God – two lines which intersect in Christ – are given equal emphasis. The difficulty is that to reach this conclusion Kohls systematically asks too much of his sources, so that it is questionable whether the theology he sees is Erasmus'.[6]

Of course, we have the right to pronounce an opinion on a work written almost five centuries ago. But such an overwhelmingly negative assessment of a work that was so popular in its own day might well point instead to our failure to appreciate the situation at that time. In the sixteenth century, people of very different outlooks apparently saw a great deal in the book. It says something that it was precisely in the years of Luther's rise to prominence, when many were seized by a desire to serve God in a new way, that Erasmus' book had such success. The printings were concentrated in the Rhineland – Basel, Strasbourg, Mainz, Cologne – a region where the influence of the Reformation was strongly but not exclusively determined by Luther. In good Catholic circles too the *Enchiridion* was a success, and such men as Hieronymus Emser and the bishop of Basel were enthusiastic.[7] In England translations were made by followers of the new doctrine, while the translations into German came mainly from the Swiss, and in the Netherlands from very different sides. It is noteworthy that the regions exclusively influenced by Luther contributed no translations, and also that the *Enchiridion* lost its appeal once the confessional fronts had become fixed. Finally the book was put on the *Index,* and the verdict of Ignatius Loyola speaks volumes: he felt the Spirit of God cool in him and the ardour of his devotion stifled when he read it.

What appealed to its readers, what did they find in the *Enchiridion*? I cite two witnesses. The first is Eustachius van Zichem, a Dominican and professor at Louvain, who in 1531 issued a polemical pamphlet against the fifth rule of the *Enchiridion*. He had three criticisms. In the first place it is not acceptable to consider the visible, external service of God as inferior to inner piety. The consequence of this, according to his second objection, is that Erasmus often approaches Luther's rejection of good works in being saved. Finally he defends the value of monastic vows against Erasmus' attacks. The second charge is especially interesting. Behind it lies the idea that anyone who, like Erasmus, thinks ceremonies of less value must trust entirely to inward disposition and thus to faith.

My second witness is Paul de Rovere, chaplain of St Peter's at Louvain, who was put on trial for heresy and condemned in 1543.

One of the most serious charges against De Rovere was that he had repeatedly denigrated the ecclesiastical doctrine of purgatory in conversations with colleagues and others who had questioned whether there was such a thing as purgatory, had himself even absolutely denied it, and had also rejected masses for the dead. In the penetrating hearings at which he was questioned, De Rovere answered on this point 'that he had once read in the *Enchiridion* of Erasmus ... from his words where he says that there are in reality two ways, a way of salvation and a way of judgment, and that, whether you will or no, there is no other way and that he was as if struck by lightning when he read this.'[8] The language of the official court record is rather tortuous, but the meaning is clear. In the relevant passage of the *Enchiridion* there is no word of purgatory.[9] For De Rovere it was sufficient that the doctrine of the two ways appeared. From it he inferred that purgatory belonged to a third way, in which man himself did not decide, but let the church do his work for him.

The accusation of Eustachius van Zichem and the amazement of Paul de Rovere can help us to read the *Enchiridion* with the eyes of contemporaries. They did not complain of dullness, but were struck by the depreciation, if not the repudiation, of a great deal of the external structure of religion – ceremonial, ecclesiastical rules and usages, the special place of clerics and monks – in favour of the internal substance, on which all the emphasis was now placed. They reacted very differently: what De Rovere saw as a release from useless things and a breakthrough to the essence was for Eustachius the loss of the core of religion. But they both identified the same central point in the *Enchiridion*, the fifth rule, the encouragement to 'progress always from visible things ... to invisible.'[10] And they were right. The distinction was a most essential one for Erasmus. There are two worlds: the spiritual, where God dwells with the angels, and the visible, that of the heavenly spheres and everything contained in them. The visible world is transitory, temporary. In comparison with the invisible it is merely a shadow, a feeble reflection of the spiritual world. The ideal of the true Christian is to rise from the visible world to the invisible. Erasmus was deeply imbued with the truth of Jesus' words: 'The flesh is of no profit, it is the spirit that gives life'[11] and 'But the hour is coming and now is at hand when true worshippers will worship the Father in spirit and in truth.'¹² 'I would have had scruples,' said Erasmus of the first biblical text, 'to say: "It is of no profit"; it would have been sufficient to say: "It is of some profit, but the spirit is much more profitable." But Truth itself said: "It is of no profit." Indeed it is of so little profit that according to Paul it is fatal unless it is referred to the spirit ... The body cannot subsist without the spirit, but the spirit has no need of the body.'¹³

Erasmus can describe the opposition in many different ways: visible against invisible, flesh or body against spirit, but also the letter against the spirit, the temporary against the eternal, darkness against light. Everywhere in the Bible he finds this opposition, not only in the teaching of Jesus but also, and very strongly, in Paul. Did not Paul summon men to seek the things that were above and not those upon the earth? How he opposed the flesh to the spirit, how he called the wisdom of the flesh death and enmity to God, while the wisdom of the spirit was life and peace!¹⁴ Erasmus was profoundly convinced that he had found the core of the Bible's message here. He was aware that the idea was also to be found in classical antiquity,¹⁵ but that certainly did not make it less important: of course the ancients whom he so admired had tasted some of this truth.

When Erasmus speaks of the invisible and spiritual world he is referring first of all to heaven, but not to heaven alone. Through Christ something of heaven had been brought down to earth. If God is spirit, we too must also be spiritual beings. We express this in love, joy, peace, patience, long-suffering, goodness, kindness, gentleness, faithfulness, modesty, in short by being the image of Christ on this earth.¹⁶ Summarizing, Erasmus says: 'But why should we refer to one passage or another? Paul's whole purpose is simply this: that the flesh be despised as it is a source of contention, and that he establish us in the spirit, the source of charity and liberty.'¹⁷ There is thus no absolute separation between the world of the spirit and that of the flesh. Man has a share in both and is a pilgrim in the visible world. Not only does his path lead to the invisible world, but even in the midst of the tiresome multiplicity of visible things, the path in many ways already belongs to the heavenly world.

Such a train of thought can easily lead to a complete rejection of earthly things, but Erasmus shrinks from this last step. He is not, so he says, attacking externals as such, and certainly not those that have been approved by the church. On the contrary, ecclesiastical ceremonies can be signs of piety and help us on the way to it. For the children in Christ, those who are weak in the faith, they are even necessary – or almost necessary.[18] All these customs – fasting, regular church-going, frequent attendance at mass, the saying of many psalms – are in themselves indifferent, neither good nor bad. They can be just as much flesh as spirit. In itself this thought is revolutionary enough. But it becomes more serious as Erasmus continually shows that every adherence to external, material things is not only another way to God, but also a lesser and lower way. Instead he emphasizes the summons to perfection. External signs are no longer necessary once the child in Christ has become a man.[19] Certainly he may not then consider himself superior to them in an absolute sense, and thus give offence to his weaker brother. But in the end the highest rule is: 'God is spirit, and he is moved by spiritual sacrifices ... He is mind, the purest and the simplest of minds. Therefore he must be worshipped above all with a pure mind.'[20] All externals are of no avail if they do not reflect what is happening in the heart. 'Blessed ... are they who hear the word of God within. Happy those to whom the Lord speaks inwardly, and their souls will be saved.'[21] It is from this evangelical freedom, and not from slavery to external commandments, that Erasmus expects everything.

In expounding these views Erasmus feels himself to be the defender of the true freedom that Christ brought and protected against the Pharisees, the freedom Paul championed against the Judaizers who wanted to take the church of the first century back to Judaism. The church has the right to institute certain ceremonies and to prescribe rules. But it is to freedom, at least to inner freedom from all these laws, that Christ called us. The danger is great: if man honours Christ with visible things instead of invisible ones, and sees this as the summit of piety and condemns others, then he is drawn away from Christ by all these externals, he forsakes the law of freedom and falls back into Judaism. 'Judaism' here, as most often in Erasmus, does not refer to the ethnic group or its religion, but to a lower, external form of religion that was to be found among many Christians and that could be compared in the point of its service to forms with that of the Jews. This means self-righteousness and thus superstition; once more, man does not put his faith in God but in earthly things and thus in himself. Alas, not only the great mass of Christianity, but also its leaders – priests, theologians, bishops – have almost without exception fallen into this error.[22] The monkish clique seeks the summit of religion in the scrupulous observance of ceremonies. 'If anyone were to examine and question them about spiritual things, he would find very few who do not walk in the flesh. And from this derives this great weakness of souls, which tremble with fear where there is nothing to be afraid of and yawn with weariness where the danger is greatest. This is the reason, too, for that perpetual infancy in Christ.'[23] Erasmus does not deny that ceremonies are sometimes useful, but man must not be so punctilious about small things that he loses his sense of what is most important; he must not rely on externals, for that is corrupting;[24] God 'detests ... that one remain in the flesh of the law, and trust in something of no worth.'[25]

Where in particular does Erasmus find the material, the earthly? It should at least be clear that the external side of the life of the church belongs to it, as a few examples will show. Erasmus goes into detail about the veneration of saints. Ultimately, in his opinion, true devotion to the saints consists in emulating the best in them, the submission of Mary, the faith of Paul, the love of Peter. It is useless to have yourself buried in a Franciscan habit; if your way of life is quite different from St Francis', the habit will not save you. Venerate the bones of Paul? Far more important that you should honour the spirit that lives in his writings.[26] Erasmus has little use for amulets with a portrait of Christ, or the veneration of a fragment of the cross of Christ or of the sudarium. It is better to listen to the words of Christ. 'Nothing is more like the Father than the Son, the Word of the Father emanating from the innermost recesses of his spirit, so nothing is more like Christ than the word of Christ uttered in the innermost sanctuary of his most holy mind.'[27] The word, above all the word of Holy Scripture, is spirit, yet it is not spiritual enough. Even in Scripture it is necessary to distinguish between the letter and the mystery behind the letter. What would one have to say of the sometimes naive, sometimes repugnant tales of the Old Testament, if one were not to seek the deeper meaning of the story?[28]

Erasmus goes into the greatest detail on the Eucharist. There too the flesh is opposed to the spirit. Jesus even thought it of little use to eat of his body and drink of his blood unless it were eaten and drunk spiritually. The man who attends mass daily but nevertheless lives only for himself is still in the 'flesh' of the sacrament. No, the eating of the Eucharist shows that man is one spirit with the spirit of Christ, one body with the body of Christ. If one strives to attain this ideal, one is a living member of the church. In communion the death of our head, Christ, is completed, and therefore we should ask ourselves how far we too have become dead to the world.[29] This reasoning also means that the whole external ritual of the mass belongs to the lower, visible world. It has value only if it expresses an inward attitude, if a man offers himself to God, and if the sacrifice is thus also taking place in his heart. In these reflections Erasmus was not attacking the doctrine of the church; as he saw it he was attempting instead to raise the worship of Christ in the Eucharist to a higher level. For one must always strive for the higher, the invisible, the spirit.

In this context, Jacques Etienne has spoken of the 'religion of the pure spirit.'[30] The expression is well chosen. It is characteristic not only of the *Enchiridion*, but of the work of Erasmus as a whole. Later, Erasmus also applied the tension between flesh and spirit to dogma: the more the church laid down hard and fast rules, the more love cooled and gave way to compulsion and threats.[31] To the tendency to define ever more articles of faith, Erasmus opposed the call to live a holy life. This is the invisible, the spirit. Here too everything is set in the same context, man's ascent from the visible to the invisible world. In this ascent, the dogma of the church can only play a preparatory role. The essential goal is to become one with Christ.

Yet it is not enough to observe that Erasmus did not attack church doctrine. Eustachius van Zichem argued that the internal and the external belonged together, that God demanded outward observance too. Behind this argument lay his concern that the spiritual emphasis that Erasmus advocated and regarded as a purifying of religion would lead to total internalization, in which all outward forms would become unimportant. From there, Van Zichem feared, it was but a step to resignation, flight from reality, withdrawal within one's own soul. Erasmus had no wish to tread that path. On the contrary he desired, in his work, to confront the reader with the question: how can I, in this age, as a free person responsible for my actions, serve God in the spirit? In this connection it is fitting to cite the words by which Paul de Rovere had been so struck: 'Do not try to divide yourself between the world and Christ. You cannot serve two masters. There is no alliance between Christ and Belial ... There are only two paths, one which by the gratification of the passions leads to destruction, the other which by the mortification of the flesh leads to life. Why are you puzzled? There is no third way. Whether you wish to or not, you must enter on one of these two. Whoever you are, you must enter upon this narrow path, on which few mortals walk.'[32] Behind this admonition stands the opposition of flesh and spirit, but now applied to man in particular. Man has, as we have seen, a share in both worlds, and for that reason Erasmus calls him a third world,[33] which is drawn in both directions. The bodily, the animal part of man, which manifests itself in the genitals, conforms to the visible world. The highest part of man, the spirit, has a share in the divine world. Erasmus considers this twofold nature of man important enough to devote a chapter of the *Enchiridion* to it.[34]

Erasmus does not, however, see the body as evil in itself. On the contrary, the human being is unique precisely because he belongs to both worlds. Of course, the body is by nature the lower, but it is not worthless. In creating man God united both natures, soul and body, in a happy harmony with each other. In this harmony the soul dominated the body and the body willingly obeyed the soul.[35] But now, instead of harmony, discord and strife prevail. Here Erasmus deviates from the view of the Florentine Platonists, who on other points exercised a profound influence on his concept of man. They saw man as by nature an equivocal creature, so that the struggle was not directed against sin and its consequences but against man's baser inclinations. Erasmus clearly states that the discord in man arose through the action of the devil. Sin corrupted what had been good when it came from the hand of the creator. Erasmus himself compares the situation in which humanity finds itself with a state in which rebellion rages. The dregs of the nation, that is, the lower passions, have rebelled against their king, reason.[36] The highest quality in man, his reason, has remained unharmed and divine.[37] It is typical that Erasmus should see *ratio*, 'reason,' as the highest quality of man and that he should identify the brain as its seat. Elsewhere, however, he says that the creator engraved the eternal moral law in man with his finger, that is, with his spirit.[38] Thus Erasmus avoids a coarse rationalism, but at the same time it is clear that for him rationality and morality coincide. God has given everyone the understanding of good and evil, an awareness that has not been lost even through sin. In his spirit man knows what is good and what is evil, and thus there arises in him a struggle between the flesh and the spirit. All attention is devoted to this struggle. This tendency is connected with the goal that Erasmus set himself in writing the *Enchiridion*, to act as a pedagogue and as a pastor, to give instructions for the practice of the Christian life.

The goal of the struggle is fixed: in his spirit, man is divine and hence he must strive to become like God. How must he carry on the struggle? The first thing man needs, Erasmus expresses in the famous words: know thyself. He points out that this proverb was held in high honour among the ancients, who believed that it was of heavenly origin, and that all wisdom was contained in it. But the Scriptures too summon us to this difficult task: man must know himself as spirit and body.[39] Behind this demand for self-knowledge lies Erasmus' confidence that it is possible for man to better himself, provided he sees where the dangers lie. He sums up these dangers as blindness, the flesh, and the weakness of man, the remnants of original sin that remain with us even after baptism. First is blindness, the fog of ignorance that obscures the insights of reason. For Erasmus this was by far the greatest danger: the sin of our first parents had obscured the radiant, divine light; bad education, the wrong company, and so on have made this darkness even thicker.[40] For that reason also is knowledge so important, which together with prayer is the strongest weapon in the struggle against the devil. Prayer has the highest value, for it is conversation with God, but knowledge is no less necessary. Man must have two leaders, Aaron and Moses, as symbols of prayer and knowledge.[41]

Time and again Erasmus has been reproached with rationalism because of this expression. His critics overlook his explicit statement that by 'Moses' he means knowledge of the law, that is, of Holy Scripture. A few lines further on he explains at length that it is a question of 'fervent study of the sacred Scriptures.'[42] This is not to deny that there is an element of rationalism in Erasmus' thinking: that has already appeared above.

This whole chain of ideas clearly went back, for Erasmus, to the Bible, which speaks again and again of the struggle between spirit and flesh. In the Old Testament this struggle is represented by Esau and Jacob, Eve and Adam, Sarah and Abraham: the flesh is constantly shown at odds with the spirit. But Paul speaks of it much more clearly. In his Epistles he draws the distinction between flesh and spirit, slavery and childhood, the law of sin and the law of the spirit, the outward and the inner man, the earthly and the heavenly man. This is the same as Plato's teaching of the two souls in one man.[43] This much is clear: Erasmus read the Bible as a child of his time. Of course he took the concepts of 'flesh' and 'spirit' from Paul, but the significance he gave them rather suggests Platonism. Human freedom, dignity, and responsibility, ethical idealism, the central position of man in the world – Erasmus found all these ideas in the Bible. They are evident in his encouragement to man to think of the dignity of his destination: 'Remember ... that you were born and redeemed for one thing only, to enjoy forever the sovereign good. God fashioned this whole contrivance of the world so that everything would serve your needs.'[44] Man is 'a noble animal, for whose sake alone God fashioned this marvellous contrivance of the world; he is the fellow citizen of the angels, son of God, heir of immortality.'[45]

We have let Erasmus speak for himself at length and tried to read the *Enchiridion* as a contemporary might have read it. Now we must stand back and ask ourselves: What was Erasmus trying to achieve? Erasmus himself undoubtedly gave the best characterization of his book: it was a 'certain theory of piety.'[46] For him, the paramount task of the theologian was to provide such a theory. But what sort of a theory was it? Renaudet has pointed out that all previous attempts to reform the church had been content to revive asceticism and the study of traditional theology, to disseminate the writings of the mystics, and to restore the monastic ideal. Erasmus, however, showed the way to a reformation that would also be intrinsically new, and he pointedly opposed merely praising the old ways once more.[47] I quite agree with this observation. Many felt themselves to be deeply offended by the close of the *Enchiridion*, in which Erasmus warned against 'that superstitious tribe of monks' who lived 'as if there was no Christianity outside the habit. When they have made man's heart heavy with pure anxiety and inextricable subtleties, they bind him to petty human traditions, submerge the unfortunate entirely in a certain Judaism, and teach him fear, not love. Monkhood is not piety, but a way of life which is useful or useless depending on someone's physical and mental constitution. I do not advise you to adopt it, nor do I urge against it.'[48] Followers of the *devotio moderna* and those who had been touched by its ideals could make nothing of such words. For his part, Erasmus in the *Enchiridion* implicitly rejected the form of piety represented by the *Rosetum* of Jan Mombaer.[49] They were two different worlds.

Erasmus' pronouncements were something unheard of in his day: that there is no higher and lower within Christianity, no difference between clerics and laymen, that baptism is the only entrance to Christianity and the baptized are all equal, whatever way of life they chose for themselves. Thirty years later Erasmus aptly said, 'I wrote the *Enchiridion* so that good letters might be of service to piety.'[50] And this goal appears to have been realized, since his book appealed to those people who felt that good letters, the new culture, had something to say to them. After these words from the closing passage of the *Enchiridion*, Erasmus continued: 'To this alone I urge you: seek piety neither in food nor in your way of life nor in any visible thing, but in what we teach. Attach yourself to those in whom you find the true image of Christ.'[51]

The work was intended for attentive readers who were looking for a new way. It is no accident that its popularity was at its height in the same years in which Luther and Zwingli were trying, each in his own way, to provide for the same spiritual need. The foreword to the second Dutch translation of 1523 states this exactly. The translator points out that man, weak as he is, can hardly choose between light and darkness, good and evil. The *Enchiridion* can help him in his choice and the struggle that faces him. 'Thus this little book will teach him and instruct him in everything that might be of need to him, to become a perfect Christian man, in whatever state a man is or may come to be.' These words were after Erasmus' own heart, a perfect summing up of what he wanted to express in the *Enchiridion*.

'A perfect Christian.' It is sufficiently well known that a need for God was deeply felt at the end of the Middle Ages. A broad movement in the church wished to meet this need by multiplying the existing forms of worship, the familiar paths to God, all of which were within the church organization. These included more masses, more indulgences, deeper devotion, greater reverence for priests, increased emphasis on the distinctiveness of priests and monks. One well-known representative of this type of piety, Johannes von Paltz, went so far as to call priests 'gods and Christs.' Against this background the distinctive character of the piety Erasmus expressed is seen in its true light. It is not the piety of the masses, but of the individual. Its consolation for the conscience does not lie in the community worship of God in all the ways offered by the church. Erasmus saw in all this only earthly, material things that might be useful for the beginner, but were otherwise rather a hindrance than a help. Individualism permeates Erasmus' ideal of the Christian life. The young man described in one of the *Colloquies* does not feel himself a part of the community even during church services. He searches out a good preacher, and if the sermon still fails to please him, he reads passages in his New Testament with one of the Fathers as expositor.[52] Man stands before God as an individual and takes counsel only of God and his own conscience. Man's responsibility and ability to live his own life receive all the emphasis. This is the way of inwardness: the objective world is unimportant, the institutional framework is no help, the all too massive aids that the church offers do no good – only the heart, the disposition count. And for this reason also Christ holds so high a place: 'Be careful not to turn the eyes of the heart away from your model Christ. You will not go astray if you follow the lead of Truth.'[53]

Epistolae obscurorum virorum part 2, title-page
showing the 'obscure men' at work
Speyer: Jacob Schmidt 1517
Öffentliche Bibliothek, University of Basel

Defyderii Derafini Roterdami veteru maximecp infi
gnium paroemiaru id eft adagiorum collectanea: opus
qum nouu tum ad omne uel fcripture uel fermonis ge
nus uenuftadu infigniendutp miru in modu coducibile.
Id quod ita demu intelligetis adolefcetes optimi:fi hu
iufmodi deliciis et litteras veftras et oratione quotidia
nam affuefceris afpergere. Sapite ergo et huc tam raru
thefauru tantillo numulo venale vobis redimite:multo
preftantiora propedie accepturi:fi hec boni cofulucritis.
Ualete.

· In noie fcte trinitatis

Duobus in locis libellus hic proftat:In magiftri Iohanis philippi offi
cina:cuius quide tum induftria: tum fumptu nitidiffimis formulis
eftemaculatiffime impreffus:In uia diui Marcelli ad diuine trinita;
tis fignum:Rurfu in uia diui Iacobi ad Pellicani quem uocant notam:

Erasmus *Adagiorum collectanea* title-page
Paris: Jehan Phillipe 1500
Houghton Library, Harvard University

Beatus Rhenanus
Portrait in Nikolaus Reusner *Icones siue imagines*
Strasbourg 1587
Rare Book Division, The New York Public Library
Astor, Lennox, and Tilden Foundations

John Colet, dean of St Paul's
Bust in plaster, probably by Pietro Torrigiano
Owned by St Paul's School, London
and presently on loan to the Victoria & Albert Museum

ENCHIRI-
dion militis Christiani, salu-
berrimis præceptis refertum,
autore Des.Erasmo Rotero-
damo.   Cui accessit noua
miréq; utilis Præfatio. Et Ba
silij in Esaiam cómentariolus,
eodem interprete.
Cum alijs quorū Catalogum
pagellæ sequentis Elenchus
indicabit.

Erasmus *Enchiridion militis christiani* title-page
Basel: Johann Froben, July 1518
Gemeentebibliotheek, Rotterdam

uiendum fuit.Sed quid ego hæc tibi,pa
trono tam fingulari,ut caufas etiam nó
optimas,optime tamé tueri poffis? Va
le difertiffime More,& Moriã tuã gna/
uiter defende,Ex Rure,Quinto Idus Iu
nias.

ΜΩΡΙΑΣ ΕΓΚΩΜΙΟΝ.i.Stulticiæ laus
Erafmi Roterodami Declamatio.
Stulticia loquitur.

Tcũq; de me uulgo
mortales loquũtur,
(neq; enim fum ne/
fcia, q̃; male audiat
ftulticia etiam apud
ftultiffimos) tamen
hanc effe,hanc inquam effe unam,quæ
meo numine deos atcq homines exhila
ro,uel illud abunde magnũ eft argumé
tum,quod fimul atcq in hunc cœtũ fre/
quentiffimũ dictura prodij,fic repente
omniũ uultus noua quadam atcq info/
lita hilaritate enituerũt,fic fubito frõte
exporrexiftis,fic læto quodã & amabi/
li applaufiftis rifu,ut mihi pfecto quot
quot undicq pfetes itueor, pariter deo/
rum Home

eft in dignitate rerum
& fermonũ,cuius præ
cipua ratio habetur in
tragœdijs,comœdijs,
& dialogis. Quid
ego hæc tibi) ἀποσίώ
πκσιϛ eft. Patrono tã
fingulari) Patron⁹ hic
fignificat aduocatum
caufarum.Nã aliquan
do refertur ad libertũ.
Eft aũt Morus præter
egregiam optimarum
literarum cognitiõem,
inter Britannicarum le
gum profeffores, præ
cipui nominis.

DECLAMATIO

pte uo
cauit
decla
mati/
onem
ut int
telligas rem exercendi
ingenij caufa fcriptam,
ad lufũ,ac uoluptaté.
Porro Moriã fingit uel
terum more,ceu deam
quãdam,fuas laudes
narrantem,idq; deco/
re,quod hoc ftultis pe
culiare fit,feipfos ad/ Rifus ftul
mirari,decq feipfis glo torum
riofe prædicare. Ta/
men hanc effe.) Hanc
ᵈᵃκτικῶϛ accipiendũ,
ut feipfam digito oftê/
dat. Frontem expor

rexiftis) Frontem exporrigimus,cũ hilarefcimus.Contra mœfti frõte cõ/
trahimus,quære in Chiliadibus Erafmi. Ideorum Homericorum.) Facet
te uocat Homericos,qui cum non fint ulli in rerum natura,tamé ab Home/
B   rofingũ

Folly preaching
Drawing by Hans Holbein the Younger
in the margin of a copy of the 1515 (Froben) edition
of the *Moriae encomium*
Öffentliche Kunstsammlung Kupferstichkabinett, Basel

Illustration for Erasmus *Praise of Folly*
The Master of the Miracles of the Apostles
Nationalmuseum, Stockholm

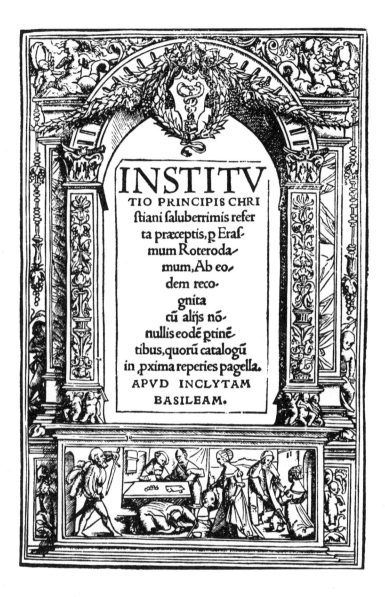

INSTITV

TIO PRINCIPIS CHRI
ſtiani ſaluberrimis refer
ta præceptis, p Eraſ-
mum Roteroda-
mum, Ab eo-
dem reco-
gnita
cū alijs nō-
nullis eodē ptinē-
tibus, quorū catalogū
in ,pxima reperies pagella.
APVD INCLYTAM
BASILEAM.

Erasmus *Institutio principis christiani* title-page
Basel: Froben, July 1518
Cornell University Library

Erasmus *Querela pacis* title-page
Basel: Froben, December 1517
Gemeentebibliotheek, Rotterdam

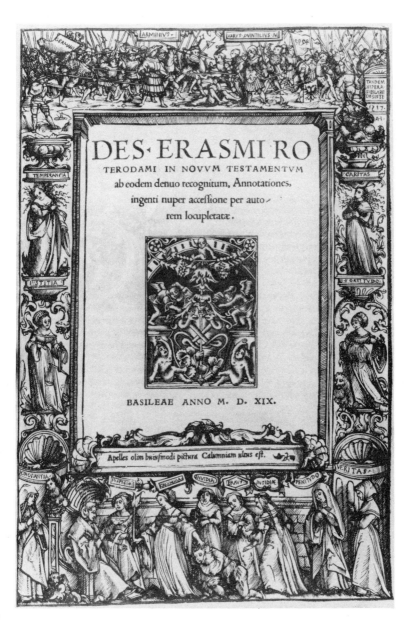

Erasmus' edition of the *Novum Testamentum* title-page
Basel: Froben 1519
The Philip H. and A.S.W. Rosenbach Foundation, Philadelphia

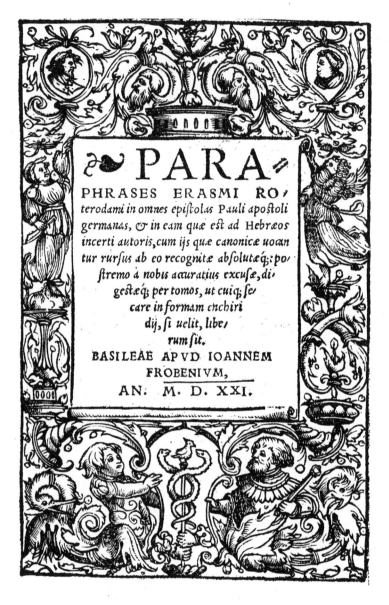

&ebranch; PARA⸗
PHRASES ERASMI RO⸗
terodami in omnes epiſtolas Pauli apoſtoli
germanas, & in eam quæ eſt ad Hebræos
incerti autoris, cum ijs quæ canonicæ uocan
tur rurſus ab eo recognitæ abſolutǽq;: po⸗
ſtremo à nobis accuratius excuſæ, di⸗
geſtǽq; per tomos, ut cuiq; ſe⸗
care in formam enchiri
dij, ſi uelit, libe⸗
rum ſit.
BASILEAE APVD IOANNEM
FROBENIVM,
AN. M. D. XXI.

Erasmus *Paraphrases in omnes epistolas Pauli* title-page
Basel: Johann Froben 1521
Centre for Reformation and Renaissance Studies,
Victoria University, Toronto

Johann Reuchlin
Woodcut portrait on page 23 of Part III of Heinrich Pantaleon's
Prosopographiae heroum atque illustrium virorum totius Germaniae
Basel 1566
Houghton Library, Harvard University

Jacques Lefèvre d'Etaples
Contemporary engraving
Courtesy of the Trustees of the British Museum

Martin Luther
Portrait by Lucas Cranach the Elder, 1526
Nationalmuseum, Stockholm

Ulrich von Hutten
Woodcut by Hans Weiditz, c 1495–c 1537
Kupferstichkabinett, Staatliche Museen, Berlin

Martin Bucer
Medal by Friedrich Hagenauer, 1543
Archives et Bibliothèque de la Ville de Strasbourg,
Cabinet numismatique

Huldrych Zwingli
Portrait by Hans Asper, 1531
Graphische Sammlung, Zentralbibliothek, Zürich

Philippus Melanchthon
Lucas Cranach the Younger
Kurpfälzisches Museum, Heidelberg

FAMILIA·
RIVM COLLOQVIORVM
FORMV/
LAE,
ET ALIA QVAEDAM,
PER DES. ERAS
MVM ROTE/
RODA/
MVM.

Erasmus *Familiarium colloquiorum formulae* title-page
Basel: Froben, November 1518
Gemeentebibliotheek, Rotterdam

Syß hand zwen schwytzer puren gmacht
furwar sy hand es wol berracht.

Die göttliche Mühle
Zürich: Christoph Froschauer, 1521

The *Praise of Folly*

ꙮ

Almost everyone knows the *Praise of Folly* (*Moriae encomium*) by its title. Few know the book itself. This is not a recent phenomenon. Erasmus himself prepared a commentary on it only a few years after the appearance of the first edition, an exposition that was to accompany almost all printings of the text from then on. He had to do so, for the work struts in buskins, it is stuffed with citations from and allusions to such classical authors as Homer, Plato, Virgil, Horace, and Pliny.

Yet the origin of the book was a very human one. In the summer of 1509, returning from Italy to England on horseback, Erasmus – as he tells us himself in the dedication that precedes the book – was unwilling to waste his time on idle gossip. He preferred to think of his studies, and rejoiced in the knowledge that after so many years he would be seeing his friends again. Among them, Thomas More, for whom the dedication was intended, held pride of place. More's name led him to *moria*, 'folly,' and the idea was born. Why not a praise of folly, dedicated to the man who was the last fool in the world? More liked a jest.[1] After a journey of two months Erasmus arrived in England, lodged with More, fell ill, and to cheer his spirits worked on his idea for a week, without books or other aids, as he later, unconsciously playing up to his role, felt compelled to relate.[2] Two years later the little book appeared as a co-production of two Paris publishers in an unattractive and poorly corrected edition.

The Folly was ready, as her latest translator into English, Clarence Miller, says, 'to begin her brilliant career as one of the most popular and controversial prima donnas of Western literature.'[3] M.A. Screech has drawn attention to the differences between the original text of

1511 and the edition that Erasmus produced around three years later in November 1514. Apart from all kinds of minor points, Erasmus inserted four extensive passages into the text, as a result of which the composition was to some degree revised, and the content given more point. In this discussion of the *Praise of Folly* I shall begin with the first edition and then examine the changes made in 1514.

Is the *Praise of Folly* a game, begun in boredom and carried through as a distraction from pain and illness? Erasmus speaks of it rather dismissively, calls it a 'game,'[4] and speaks of 'jests,' 'jokes,'[5] but clearly of a joke which has its serious side. In an apologia he says that 'in the guise of a game' he had the same goal in view as in the *Enchiridion*. The question arises from an unreal dilemma, not very appropriate either to folly or to Erasmus. He recalls, immediately after the comparison with the *Enchiridion*, Horace's phrase 'to tell the truth with a smile,' and the role of the fool, who was free to mock faults that were not too serious.[6] 'Perhaps it may seem inappropriate to include Christ in this list,' he promptly continues. That is Erasmus to the core. He can only express his deepest emotions dispassionately, as in this sentence, or behind the mask of irony, as in the *Praise of Folly*. But the book remains a game. Erasmus even names his predecessors in classical antiquity, Lucian with his ironic eulogy, and others. Historians have offered comparisons with the carnival and the French *sermon joyeux*, a short mock-sermon held before the true sermon or before a stage play. The *Praise of Folly* remains a game. One of the foremost characteristics of the game is, of course, that it is deadly serious.

What is the distinctive feature of this burlesque eulogy? That the speaker speaks of himself. Some examples of this are known from classical antiquity, as of poverty praising herself. But here it is Folly, foolishness, who speaks in her own praise, and that gives everything said a double meaning. If Folly praises folly, then folly is heaped upon folly, and it is soon no longer clear where yes becomes no: 'I hear your applause, and in fact I've always felt sure that none of you was so wise or rather so foolish – no, I mean so wise – as to think ...'[7]

But enough about Folly. It is better to listen to her. 'Whatever is generally said of me by mortal men, and I'm quite well aware that Folly is in poor repute even among the greatest fools, still I am the one – and indeed, the only one – whose divine powers can gladden the hearts of gods and men.' With these words Folly begins her address, and her audience sit and listen with laughter. This is the theme of the first part of the *Praise of Folly*:[8] Folly rules men and gods, but this is fortunate. Her father is money, her wet-nurses were Drunkenness and Ignorance, her maids of honour are Self-love, Flattery, Forgetfulness, Idleness, Pleasure, Madness, and Sensuality. With the aid of these faithful servants she has brought the whole world under her sway. Folly shows us in detail that everything happens by her leave: war, the government of the state, friendship, love – everything comes from her hand. She is many-facetted: the foolishness of the nobles' hunting parties, the vanity and flattery of women, the inexperience of youth and the childishness of old age, even the good cheer and fun at a festive banquet would be inconceivable without her.

The author casts a sharp eye around him. Are philosophers of any use in war? No. Then one needs 'stout and sturdy fellows with all the daring possible and the minimum of brain.'[9] Why are stupid people happy? 'To begin with, these people have no fear of death ... They are neither tortured by dread of impending disaster nor under the strain of hopes of future bliss. In short, they are untroubled by the thousand cares to which our life is subject.'[10] Hear Folly on chauvinism: The English boast of their good looks, their musical talents, and fine food, the French pride themselves on their culture, the Parisians boast of being the best theologians in the world – the grapes were still sour! – the Romans dream of the restoration of their ancient empire, the Germans are proud of their tall stature and their knowledge of the black art.[11] More than mere power of observation is evident in the remark: 'The two main obstacles to learning by experience are a sense of propriety which clouds the judgment and fear which advises against an undertaking once danger is apparent. Folly offers a splendid liberation from both of them.'[12]

Folly also exercises her influence in the field of religious practice. Everything falls under the same verdict: exaggerated mania for building, dicing, the belief in all kinds of miraculous tales, which yield an income to the priests and penitential preachers, the belief in certain saints: 'A man will soon become rich if he approaches Erasmus on the proper days with the proper bits of candle and the proper scraps of prayer.'[13] Indulgences, reciting particular prayers, the special patron saints of a given area, the specialized aid of saints – Appollonia for toothache, Hyacinth for the pangs of childbirth, Anthony for theft – it is all pointed out relentlessly.[14]

Is there a leading idea? Towards the end of this first part it is expressly stated. 'But it's sad, people say, to be deceived. Not at all, it's far sadder *not* to be deceived ... Finally, man's mind is so formed that it is far more susceptible to falsehood than to truth.'[15] But we find the idea worked out in more detail earlier:

> If anyone tries to take the masks off the actors when they're playing a scene on the stage and show their true, natural faces to the audience, he'll certainly spoil the whole play ... Now, what else is the whole life of man but a sort of play? Actors come on wearing their different masks and all play their parts until the producer orders them off the stage, and he can often tell the same man to appear in different costume, so that now he plays a king in purple and now a humble slave in rags. It's all a sort of pretence, but it's the only way to act out this farce.
>
> At this point let us suppose some wise man dropped from heaven confronts me and insists that the man whom all look up to as god and master is not even human, as he is ruled by his passions, like an animal, and is no more than the lowest slave for serving so many evil masters of his own accord. Or again, he might tell someone else who is mourning his father to laugh because the dead man is only just beginning to live, seeing that this life of ours is nothing but a sort of death. Another man who boasts of his ancestry he might call low-born and bastard because he is so far removed from virtue, which is the sole source of nobility. If he had the same sort of thing to say about everyone else, what would happen? We should think him a crazy madman ... It's a true sign of prudence not to want wisdom which extends beyond your share as an ordinary mortal, to be willing to overlook things along with the rest of the world or to wear your illusions with a good grace. People say that this is really a sign of folly, and I'm not setting out to deny it – so long as they'll admit on their side that this is the way to play the comedy of life.[16]

This impressive passage forces one to ask: what role is Erasmus playing at this moment? Is Folly speaking the truth? Is outward appearance to be preferred to naked truth? Erasmus was anything but a stormer of heaven. And yet it is as if he were depicting himself in this way as the fool who cannot be content with the shadow, but asks for the reality.

The second part of the *Praise of Folly* turns to a traditional theme, criticism of the various classes and groups of society.[17] Schoolmasters, poets, rhetoricians, the writers of learned and insignificant books, jurists, dialecticians, natural philosophers, theologians, monks, princes, courtiers, popes, cardinals, and bishops – none of the representatives of the social and intellectual élite is overlooked. Folly speaks in her own voice much less persistently than in the first part. Not without reason does Erasmus remark towards the end of the passage that it is almost becoming a satire.[18] It is Folly's intention to take her seat with the other gods and to survey the earthly stage from on high.[19] Sometimes this detachment is in fact achieved, as when the natural philosophers are dismissed with a self-evident disdain as foolish, completely ignorant mountebanks and charlatans. 'Theirs is certainly a pleasant form of madness, which sets them building countless universes.'[20] In the treatment of teachers we find the same lofty condescension. Certainly some pity for the 'most unfortunate and wretched class of men whom I know' comes through, but Folly is more struck by their presumption, through which 'they do remarkably well at persuading foolish mothers and ignorant fathers to accept them at their own valuation.' They even want to pass for competent philologians.[21]

Elsewhere Folly is raised above the confusion but sees through the eyes of Erasmus. Thus she speaks of merchants: 'Although their lies, perjury, thefts, frauds, and deceptions are everywhere to be found, they still reckon themselves a cut above everyone else, simply because their fingers sport gold rings.'[22] Whoever reads the letters from Erasmus to his Antwerp banker Erasmus Schets from a later period almost feels some sympathy for Erasmus' namesake, so suspicious was the humanist of his admirer from the world of finance. Especially revealing is the passage on those who 'court immortal fame by writing books ... They add, change, remove, lay aside, take up, rephrase, show to their friends ... And their futile reward, a word of praise from a handful of people, they win at such cost.'[23]

Folly steps out of her role when she turns to theologians, monks, and the princes of the church. Detachment vanishes; mockery and mischievousness yield to anger and rage. In short, Folly has to make way for Erasmus. First the theologians come under fire, although it would be more reasonable to give a wide berth to such a 'supercilious and touchy lot.'[24] They are accused above all of concerning themselves with the most impenetrable mysteries and thus of posing absurd questions: 'Could God have taken on the form of a woman, a devil, a donkey, a gourd, or a flintstone? If so, how could a gourd have preached sermons, performed miracles, and been nailed to the cross?'[25] A cheap criticism of the centuries-old scholastic method, which in fact cannot be dismissed as foolish. True, but it is more to the point to recognize that a new method of theological thought was announcing itself here, a method that did not want to start from questions in the existing theological system but from the text of the Bible. This is the context in which Erasmus rebukes the theologians: 'You can imagine their happiness when they fashion and refashion the Holy Scriptures at will, as if these were made of wax,'[26] an image which was not new, but in which Erasmus was to have a school of followers. Nor is his attack on the barbarous Latin of the scholastics mere condescension. 'They insist that it detracts from the grandeur of sacred writing if they're obliged to obey the rules of grammar,'[27] but in the new method of theological reasoning the text, and thus grammar, is given its own importance.

Erasmus has even more to say about monks and friars.[28] They are stupid, but they pride themselves on this as a sign of their piety. The mendicant friars are a true plague. The most important things in their eyes seem to be all the precise rules on clothing and daily routine; everything is strictly regimented. Here Erasmus speaks from experience, as he himself had only fairly recently laid aside the monastic habit. Most of all he was irritated by the sermons he had heard from the regular clergy: foolish display of theological nonsense, varied by silly tales. He is vexed by their crude and boorish delivery. Only towards the end does Folly interrupt with her comment: 'Now I think you must see how deeply this section of mankind is in my debt, when their petty ceremonies and silly absurdities and the noise they make in the world enable them to tyrannize over their fellow men, each one a Paul or an Antony in his own eyes. For my part, I'm only too glad to leave these hypocrites, who are as ungrateful in their attempts to conceal what they owe to me as they're unscrupulous in their disgraceful affectations of piety.'[29]

By far the sharpest satire is reserved for the last passage of this section, which deals with the pope, cardinals, bishops, and the lower clergy. Everything hinges on honour, power, glory, rights, pomp, and show; there is an army of scribes, copyists, and every other functionary you can name; interdicts, excommunications, papal bans are wielded; popes seek their glory in war. 'Here even decrepit old men' – Erasmus meant Pope Julius II, whose wars in northern Italy he had experienced – 'can be seen showing the vigour of youths in their prime, undaunted by the cost, unwearied by hardship, not a whit deterred though they turn law, religion, peace, and all humanity completely upside down.'[30] And through every rank of the church it is money – the harvest of money, as Erasmus called it – that plays the chief role. It is noteworthy that in these passages Erasmus deals with his subject in two ways. He argues from the symbolic significance of the priestly cloth: the white of the alb is the unstained way of life, the crook watchfulness over the flock, and so on. The symbolic meaning of priestly dress had been fixed for a long time and was a hackneyed theme in the handbooks. Erasmus also opposes the present practice of the church to that of the apostolic age: 'The cardinals might consider how they are the successors of the apostles and are expected to follow the example of their predecessors, and that they are not the lords but the stewards of the spiritual riches for every penny of which they will soon have to render an exact account ... Then the supreme pontiffs, who are the vicars of Christ: if they made an attempt to imitate his life of poverty and toil, his teaching, cross, and contempt for life ... what creatures on earth would be so cast down?'[31] This motif was not new either. It was, however, the first time that Erasmus used it, and soon the nostalgia for former times, for the golden age of the earliest Christianity, was to be one of the determining facets of his thinking.

In the last part,[32] Folly is to list the authorities whose words and deeds bear witness to her power. One would expect a number of passages from more or less well known authors, for that is what the expression 'authorities' suggests in the first place. At first this is the case, and above all the quotation from the *Disticha Catonis* sounds happily ambiguous: 'To play the fool in season is the height of wisdom.'[33] But almost immediately Folly asks leave of the theologians to buttress her argument with quotations from the Bible, which counts perhaps for more among Christians than other authority. This is in itself a transition, for up to now the Bible has not played any special role. Now Folly will appear as a theologian, she hopes, under the inspiration of Duns Scotus. In fact, what follows is a selection of biblical texts from Ecclesiastes, Proverbs, and the Epistles of Paul to the Corinthians. On the last, and in particular on 1 Cor 3:18, she builds up her argument: 'Whoever among you thinks himself wise must become a fool to be truly wise.'

Then follows a fabulous conjuring trick. Why do the fools please God? A first answer is: For the same reason that princes hate people who are shrewd, but are glad to surround themselves with fools.[34] Is this Folly speaking? It does not help if one turns the argument on its head. On the contrary, it proceeds without a break: 'Christ also loathes and condemns those "wiseacres" who put their trust in their own intelligence.'[35] So people who rely on their own intelligence are set against the children, the women, and the fishermen for whom Christ clearly cared most. The important thing is to be small, to put oneself in God's hands, to be free from care. It was not by chance that Jesus preferred to ride on an ass, the symbol of stupidity. And yes, Jesus himself was in some sense foolish when he assumed human nature. Erasmus concludes: 'To sum up (or I shall be pursuing the infinite), it is quite clear that the Christian religion has a kind of kinship with Folly in some form, though it has none at all with wisdom. If you want proofs of this, first consider the fact that the very young and the very old, women and simpletons, are the people who take the greatest delight in sacred and holy things, and are therefore always found nearest the altars, led there doubtless solely by their natural instinct.'[36]

Erasmus knew of another sort of fool as well. 'Those who have once been wholly possessed by zeal for Christian piety' are the real fools, who squander their possessions, who are insensible to insult, and who submit to injustice. It is as if their spirit is already elsewhere, and not in their body. A second layer of folly, thus, if the absolute demand of the gospel is fulfilled absolutely.[37]

After a couple of abrupt sentences, the train of thought takes another turn.[38] The happiness Christians seek is – no offence meant – a particular sort of folly or foolishness. As in Plato's well-known myth of the prisoners in the cave, who saw nothing but shadows and laughed at the one man who had seen reality, so the great mass of Christians, who remain attached to material and visible things, laugh at the one who strives for the spiritual, the invisible. The idea familiar to us from the *Enchiridion* is here worked out in one of its aspects. The person who flies from the material and seeks the purely spiritual no longer belongs in this world. He is like one of those madmen whose souls have succeeded in escaping from their bodies, or the dying who, in the face of death, already speak as if they were in spiritual rapture. The body means nothing to them, coarser feelings die away, even natural love is overcome. If the mass is thus opposed to the individual, they call each other fools, 'though in my view the epithet is more properly applied to the pious, not the common man.'[39]

There is a final stage. In heavenly bliss the human soul, released from the body, will be absorbed into the divine spirit, the highest good to which everything tends. This blessedness is enjoyed by some here, albeit only a tiny droplet, a mere flavour or odour. 'Those who are granted a foretaste of this – and very few have the good fortune – experience something which is very like madness.' When such a person comes to himself again, he only knows that he was happy and wishes that he could suffer this form of madness for eternity. 'And this is only the merest taste of the happiness to come.'[40] Then Folly stops suddenly and concludes with a few sentences.

In November 1514 an edition of the *Praise of Folly* appeared with important additions in the second and third sections. In the second part Erasmus expanded the passages on the theologians and monks so much that the composition was not improved. In the third part, too, he added lengthy insertions, but there the revisions are more skilfully disguised. The new passages all refer to the church and its leaders, above all to the theologians and preachers, so that it was only in this new edition that the work was given a clear point.

The new passages contain some masterly genre pieces. The reader sees the pedantic preacher before him. Behind a show of learning he unveils the deepest holy secrets in the three cases of the name Jesus: *Jesus, Jesum, Jesu*; the letters at the end show that he is *summum, medium et ultimum*, the first, middle, and last. An even greater secret lies in the middle letter of Jesus, in Hebrew called *sin*, which sounds in Scots – the language of the eighty-year-old Scotist who gave the sermon – like 'sin,' from which Christ has redeemed the world.[41] Erasmus' irritation at such a sermon is matched by his aversion to a theological dispute – 'I have often been present,' says Folly – when a grim old man – 'whose arrogance made it clear that he was a theologian' – gave so-called theological arguments in favour of killing heretics. Had Paul not commanded us to avoid heretics, that is, to kill them? Just listen to the Latin: *devita*, 'avoid,' becomes *de vita*, 'remove from life.'[42] There are examples of biting satire in a couple of razor-sharp words. Ecclesiastes (1:17) has said that he wanted to learn wisdom and folly, and deliberately named them in that order: in processions is it not the most important dignitaries who appear last? At any rate, they listen to the words of Jesus, that the first shall be last.[43] There are also examples of very subtle mockery. In Jesus Sirach 41:18 (15) it says: 'Better is a man who hides his folly than a man who hides his wisdom.' Naturally, say Folly, for man only hides valuable things like gold and precious stones.[44] She observes that 'it's the generally accepted privilege of theologians to stretch the heavens, that is, the Scriptures, as tanners stretch a hide':[45] they make of it whatever they like. The double meaning becomes apparent only when one recognizes the allusion: 'God stretches out the heavens like a hide,' says the Latin translation of Psalm 103 (104):2. It is thus clear which rights the theologians arrogate to themselves; the sixteenth-century reader, unlike most commentators of our time, could still hear this echo between the lines.

Elsewhere the humour is rather coarse. 'For my part,' says Folly, 'I follow the large, fat, stupid, and popularly most highly thought of theologians with whom the majority of scholars would rather be in the wrong, by Zeus, than hold a correct view along with your experts in three tongues.'[46] In the new passages, these men of three tongues, those who know Hebrew, Latin, and Greek – the humanists – make their appearance. In this case it is Erasmus himself to whom belongs 'the second place in this flock, if not the actual leadership,' who dares to rebuke no less a man than Nicholas of Lyra, *the* exegete of the Middle Ages, for having given a false exegesis of a statement of Paul. No wonder, in fact, for in St Paul the words of Holy Scripture are given another meaning than they had in their original context.[47] Thus: If Paul cites the Old Testament, he often gives words a new sense. You just have to take the risk, so many thought.

In another passage, Erasmus refers expressly to the distinction between the new generation and the old. After a long tirade against the scholastic theologians, he continues:

> You may suppose that I'm saying all this by way of a joke, and that's not surprising, seeing that amongst the theologians themselves there are some with superior education who are sickened by these theological minutiae, which they look upon as frivolous. Others too think it a damnable form of sacrilege and the worst sort of impiety for anyone to speak of matters so holy, which call for reverence rather than explanation, with a profane tongue, or to argue with the pagan subtlety of the heathen, presume to offer definitions, and pollute the majesty of divine theology with words and sentiments which are so trivial and even squalid.[48]

What is in question here is nothing less than the proper method of exegesis of the Bible and of theological reasoning in general. This is more than a technical question. Erasmus was angered by the exegesis of Nicholas of Lyra, who interpreted Jesus' words instructing his disciples to set out with only a pouch and sword in such a way that the pouch meant everything a man needs for his livelihood and the sword everything that could serve for his defence. 'And so this interpreter of the divine mind fits out the apostles with spears, crossbows, slings, and catapults, and leads them forth to preach the crucified. He also loads them up with coffers and trunks and packs – lest they might perchance have to leave the inn without breakfast.'[49]

'To preach the crucified.' Here in four words, Erasmus expresses the contradiction that became characteristic of his thought, and that is not found so acutely in the original version of the *Praise of Folly*. It is the contradiction between former times and the present, between the church, the servants of the church, and theology of now, and the way of life and doctrine of Christ and his apostles. Erasmus develops this contradiction on two important points. Speaking of monks, he had expressed his contempt for the foolish regulations concerning ceremonies and clothing. He now elaborates this passage. On the day of judgment they will appear, boasting of all their self-imagined merits. But Christ will interrupt them and say merely: 'Where has this new race of Jews sprung from? I recognize only one commandment as truly mine, but it is the only one not mentioned.'[50] He is much more detailed in his treatment of scholastic theology. He had already made it ridiculous, with its abstruse questions. Now he holds it up for comparison with the apostles, who did not conquer the world for Christ with such a message. They would not even have understood it. 'Paul could provide a living example of faith, but when he says "faith is the substance of things hoped for, the evidence of things not seen"[51] his definition is quite unscholastic. And though he provides the finest example of charity in his first letter to the Corinthians, chapter 13, he neither divides nor defines it according to the rules of dialectic.'[52] Erasmus is tireless in working out this contradiction. Did the apostles know of transubstantiation? Did they know how Mary had remained free from original sin? Did they realize the precise meaning of all the nuances of the doctrine of baptism? Against the confusing and useless complexity of today stands the clarity and the simplicity of the past.

The new edition of the *Praise of Folly* betrays something of Erasmus' mood in 1514. We saw that it was the time of his first great triumphs in Germany. More important, it was in that year that a new Erasmus stands before us, an Erasmus with a clear programme of life. This comprised scholarly work, in the first place the publication of the New Testament and of the works of Jerome. Erasmus had had these intentions for a long time; in the *Praise of Folly* we find him taking the first steps towards their realization. Not only do we come across passages foreshadowing the annotations to the New Testament that he was to publish in 1516, but here for the first time grammar and rhetoric form the basis of scholarship and oust dialectic from its place. It also means the ideas in the field of society and the church –the domains were still the same – that he was to propagate from this time forward. That becomes clear in the edition of the *Adages* of 1515, the *Complaint of Peace* of 1517, the later editions of the New Testament from 1519, and the *Colloquies* from 1522. The 1514 edition of the *Praise of Folly* is a first witness to Erasmus' programme in this respect also. In it the reader finds, in a nutshell, various elements of his ideas of renewal, particularly in the discrepancy he depicts between his own day and that of Christ and the apostles.

In 1515 the *Praise of Folly* appeared from the press of Froben in Basel, who was to become Erasmus' printer *par excellence*. The edition was important because it was the first to contain the commentary needed to explain the work for the reader who was insufficiently acquainted with classical antiquity. This appeared under the name of the Dutch humanist Gerardus Listrius, but parts of it were by Erasmus himself, certainly in its later enlarged versions. It was in the margin of a copy of this edition that Hans Holbein made his famous drawings.

Apart from the *Colloquies*, no work of Erasmus enjoyed greater success. During his lifetime thirty-six editions appeared, produced by twenty-one different printers. However difficult the task, translations and a legion of imitations were also published. In the Latin editions the commentary of Listrius was often included, and very often also a detailed letter in which Erasmus defended the work against the attacks of the Dutch theologian Maarten van Dorp, who taught at Louvain.[53] Later attacks from Paris and Spain were of a different kind: by then, the aversion to the *Praise of Folly* displayed by the theologians of the old church must be seen against the background of the Reformation. Significantly, the substance of Luther's criticism was the same as that of his own most violent opponents. It could no longer be just a game.

Erasmus and the *Praise of Folly* belong together: the book offers an unsurpassed expression of the spirit of its author. There is no subtler man than he, no more subtle book than this. As his creation does, so the author looks down from Olympus. Or is Erasmus depicted in this way too distant? Holbein places Folly with her fool's cap in a professorial chair – or perhaps it is a pulpit. A chalk drawing, probably by a Dutch contemporary, presents another version. Folly is still a woman, but without the fool's cap, seated on her throne. Before her, her audience: a monk, a bishop, an artisan. Among the group is Erasmus, a finger raised in admonition.[54]

SEVEN

Christian Philosophy

🙏

'If ever there was a golden age, then there is a good hope that ours will be one.' So Erasmus wrote in a letter to Pope Leo x in April 1517.[1] He summarizes his reasons for such high hopes: Christian piety is being restored; literature, which had been forgotten and corrupted, is regaining its place; the unity of Christianity, the cradle of both godliness and culture, was assured for all time. In the years between 1514 and 1518 Erasmus repeatedly expressed this hope. For Erasmus personally, these too were golden years, and the future looked promising. He was released from his vows and received an appointment as a counsellor of Charles v and thus also the promise of an annual salary (although he was to observe bitterly that it was seldom paid to him).[2] His financial situation improved considerably. He was a celebrity in Germany, and his correspondence, a sign of the fame he had won, grew to an extent he could not have imagined. The greatest luminaries of the age recognized him as one of their own. He corresponded with cardinals and dedicated his edition of the New Testament to the pope, passing over his old patron William Warham, the archbishop of Canterbury. In short, he penetrated into the centre of the civilized world.

In the same years he also published the works which most clearly reflected the ideals that inspired him and induced his optimism. All these concerned the three fields which he summarized in a letter to the pope, godliness, literature, and the unity of Christendom. In this chapter these writings are first dealt with separately in brief. They were inspired by a single spirit; a single conception underlay them, in spite of their differences in theme. Therefore it is possible to treat the vision that these works reveal as a unit. This conception is described in the second part of this chapter.

In 1515 a new edition of the *Adages* appeared.[3] Erasmus was particularly pleased with his work. In the foreword he explained that the edition of 1508 had been a tremendous improvement on the first edition.[4] Now he had again excelled himself, and thus the applause would be great.[5] In this respect he had no reason to complain. The Venetian ambassador in London wrote that he read the book every day 'with the greatest pleasure and chuckling' and that Erasmus' commentary interested him more than the proverbs themselves, although in general he preferred the classics to the modern authors.[6] His secretary was even more enthusiastic. He devoted two hours a day to this 'golden and truly divine work,' and felt it necessary to write to Erasmus that, in his opinion, the humanist was 'far the most learned man who ever was, is, or ever will be.'[7] By comparison Ulrich Zasius was more sparing with his praise. He stated that Germany had not seen a more learned man in 'six hundred years and more.'[8] But he was a jurist, a star in his subject. The difference from the previous edition was not in the number of proverbs treated: Erasmus added only 150 items. Nine long entries were, however, inserted in which the discussion of the proverb turned into an elaborate essay on a social phenomenon. They attacked tyranny, described the evils of war, pleaded for reforms in the church, and defended the ideal of *bonae litterae*. Several of these essays were issued separately, and also in vernacular translations. Margaret Mann Phillips speaks of the 'Utopian edition,'[9] and with reason. There were points of agreement between Thomas More's *Utopia* and Erasmus' *Adages*. They share the same social concern, the same indignation at the shamelessness of the powerful and the suppression of the humble, although even in these works the difference between the statesman and the idealistic but rather naive independent intellectual is visible.

In 1516 followed the *Institutio principis christiani* (*The Education of a Christian Prince*), dedicated to the future emperor Charles v, a 'mirror of princes' like the many that had already been written.[10] Erasmus composed it when he heard that he was to be appointed to the wide circle of Charles' advisers and that an annual salary would be allotted to him. Such an appointment was conferred as an honour and entailed no obligations. The *Institutio* is a typical occasional piece, and one certainly need not weigh its every word on scales of gold. Yet it contains some ideas that are central in Erasmus' thought. The most important appears in his dedication. Following Plato, he demands that the state should be ruled by a prince who loves philosophy, 'not that philosophy, I mean, which argues about elements and primal matter and motion and the infinite, but that which frees the mind from the false opinions of the multitude and from wrong desires and demonstrates the principles of right government by reference to the example set by the eternal powers.'[11] In the work itself, 'being a philosopher' is equated with 'being a Christian.'[12] For both the philosopher and the Christian strive for the highest good.

In the same year appeared the first printing of Erasmus' edition of the New Testament. This undertaking and Erasmus' activities as an exegete of the Bible are discussed in chapter 8. Here I merely want to mention two of the so-called introductory works, the *Paraclesis* of 1516 and the *Ratio verae theologiae* of 1518. In part, these go into all the questions that concern the text and the interpretation of the Bible, but they also reveal the world of ideas in which Erasmus lived and the ideals that guided him in his biblical exegesis.

In 1517 Erasmus issued his *Querela pacis* (*Complaint of Peace*).[13] That too was an occasional piece, written, as Erasmus himself said, 'on instructions from Jean Le Sauvage,' chancellor of Burgundy, in support of the plans for the conclusion of a treaty between the rulers of the Empire, Spain, France, and England for the assurance of peace in Europe.[14] In the end the treaty was never signed, and one can even say that the work was no longer up to date when it was published. Yet it was a great success: twenty-six printings during Erasmus' lifetime, two German translations in 1521, one in French, translations into other vernaculars, including several into Dutch, the first of which appeared in 1567 in the midst of the troubles of the early years of the revolt against Spain. In our century too, there has continued to be great interest in it. In 1955 the first Russian translation appeared, and the *Querela pacis* plays a great part in anthologies of texts about peace and studies of the question. It is indeed an impressive piece, starting from Christ as the founder of peace and ending in a eulogy to the new young princes of Christian Europe. The editor in the new Amsterdam edition rightly points out that the optimism of the conclusion is not the key to the whole work.[15] There is a penetrating criticism of church and society and a deep mistrust of man, left to his own devices. Ultimately, peace is only to be found in Christ, who makes Christians into brothers and unites Christians with non-Christians in true unity.

Finally, we turn to the introductory dedication to the 1518 edition of the *Enchiridion*.[16] It is a relatively short piece, which may nevertheless serve as a summary of Erasmus' thinking in the golden years: all the themes are touched on, and the ideal of a truly Christian society dominates the little work.

All the titles mentioned were published by Froben in Basel. Although Erasmus had originally promised the *Adages* to the Paris publisher Josse Bade, the copy was entrusted to Froben through a misunderstanding – one may assume a misunderstanding organized by Erasmus.[17] From then on Froben printed all of Erasmus' important books. Froben even provided the author with a house in Basel where Erasmus settled in 1521 and lived for many years. The cooperation was beneficial to both men, for it provided Erasmus with the calm he needed to work without being disturbed. And work he did in those years. Even if one bears in mind that part of the material had already been prepared in England, and that the same themes recur in different contexts, his output in these years is still almost incredible. When the famous Paris humanist Guillaume Budé cautiously warned him in 1516 not to occupy himself with trivialities, Erasmus proudly summed up everything he had published: the *Enchiridion*, the *Adages*, and the *Institutio principis christiani*. He had not spent his time on trifles; on the contrary, he had been accused of being too daring because he ventured to treat controversial subjects. The *Enchiridion* showed that he was not afraid to proclaim different opinions against all the authorities. The *Adages* were full of detailed literary investigation, certainly, but the longer essays showed that he ventured into the territories of the philosopher and theologian and allowed himself to be drawn further than was proper. The *Institutio* gave instruction on a subject that no theologian would dare to undertake.[18] In these years Erasmus was conscious of his strength and his boldness. He had a mission to fulfil.

Where is the unity in Erasmus' thought? In the previous chapters we have already touched on some important facets of it. If we think of the *Praise of Folly* it is clear that criticism of the existing order occupies an important place, a criticism that was directed at society as a whole, with the reproach that man constantly preferred the shadows to the reality of things. It is aimed in particular at the church, the theologians, and the regular clergy. We saw too that behind this criticism lay a nostalgia for the past, the age of Christ and the apostles. A third trait was seen to be the contrast, particularly fully discussed in the *Enchiridion*, between the flesh and the spirit, the visible and the invisible.

It should be clear that these facets are interrelated. But first of all one must look for the central theme, the idea that was decisive for Erasmus and led naturally to all the rest. He himself liked to describe this as 'Christian philosophy' or 'the philosophy of Christ' or 'heavenly philosophy.' What did Erasmus mean by these terms? They have been the cause of many misunderstandings. According to Renaudet they were characteristic of Erasmus' evangelical positivism, which mocked philosophy and theology. Renaudet argues that Erasmus is the man who wants to offer a morality founded on the gospel and defends a freedom that leads to a complete spiritualization, as opposed to any reduction of the faith to formulae and all obligatory ecclesiastical practices. The unusual term 'Christian philosophy' shows that he is concerned with the teaching of a master, who is divine and nevertheless familiar, close. For this teaching Erasmus turned especially to Plutarch and Cicero, but corrected them according to the gospel.[19] Louis Bouyer by contrast has rightly pointed out that the term goes back to the Greek Fathers of the church and was a deliberate archaism on the part of Erasmus. He rejects Renaudet's interpretation emphatically.[20] Others have also shown that the term 'philosophia Christi' was by no means foreign to mediaeval monastic tradition.

Erasmus probably used the phrase for the first time in the *Adages* of 1515. There he explained the saying 'The sileni of Alcibiades,' which goes back to Plato but did not become proverbial until Erasmus himself made it so. Erasmus explains that it refers to something that at first sight is ludicrous and contemptible but on closer inspection proves to be admirable. It appears, he says, that the sileni were grotesque images that could be opened to reveal the image of a god within. Such a silenus was Socrates, with his ridiculous exterior, simple language, and modest means – but open this silenus and you find a god rather than a man. The same was true of Antisthenes, Diogenes, and Epictetus. But was Christ not a very special silenus? Born to poor and unknown parents from a humble house, he won a few poor men as his disciples and led a life of hunger and misery that ended on the cross. But when he wishes to reveal himself to the purified eyes of the soul, what unspeakable wealth we find:

> What exaltation in such humility, what riches in such poverty, what unimaginable strength in such weakness, what glory in such shame, what a perfect rest in such troubles – and finally, in his so bitter death, the abiding source of immortality. Why have the very people who boast of his name such an aversion to his picture? Of course, for Christ it would have been easy to win the mastery of the whole earth and to conquer what the rulers of Rome had striven for in vain, to surround himself with a greater bodyguard than Xerxes, to surpass the riches of Croesus, to impose silence on all the philosophers, and to suppress the so-called wise men. But this was the only pattern he sought for, and which he held before the eyes of his disciples and friends, that is, of Christians. He chose this philosophy above all, which completely differs from the rules of the philosophers and from the principles of the world, the one and only among all others which was to bring what everyone tries to acquire one way or another – happiness.[21]

This long quotation shows that Erasmus used the word philosophy in the sense of a way of life, or perhaps more accurately an outward expression. It is not a matter of a particular doctrine or system. Erasmus wanted to indicate who Jesus was and what Jesus brought about. He gave happiness, and here Erasmus chose the same word that at the end of the *Praise of Folly* indicates the eternal joy of heaven. There are other marked agreements. Is the church, with its outward show of pomp, in conformity with the life of its founder? Its servants exercise power, its ceremonies set their stamp on society, its scholars dominate the universities; it controls social and economic life. Everyone is a member of the church, the bishops are mighty, the pope is exalted above all peoples. 'A great part of humanity forms a silenus turned inside out,' says Erasmus cuttingly.[22] All these people, with their imposing titles, their learning, their pomp and their magnificence, put on a brilliant outward show, but what do they look like on the inside? This state of affairs is wholly at odds with the natural order of things. In the seed lies the life force of the tree – and how small it is! Gold and jewels lie hidden deep in the earth. Air and water are the most important elements but the hardest to grasp. Man is no different. His spirit, his most divine and immortal part, is invisible. Breath, the most vital part of the human body, cannot be grasped. And the most ungraspable of all for human senses is God, who is exalted above all our knowledge or comprehension.

Behind these views lies a deep need for the genuine and unadorned, a longing for humanity, a world, and above all a church that would have the courage to be once more what they ought to be. Sometimes, says Erasmus, there is an unknown little man, in the eyes of others a simple soul, half fool, in whom this is truly to be found. They have lived before: the prophets, of whom the world was unworthy; John the Baptist, who scorned all earthly honour; the apostles, who were mocked by everyone. But more strongly than in any man, we find it in Christ, who 'had no form nor comeliness ... he was despised and rejected of men' (Isa 53:2–3).[23] Thus Erasmus set himself against a church that had assumed worldly pomp. He rejected with disdain all display of triumphalism. Against the *Christus imperator*, 'the triumphant Christ,' he placed the suffering servant. In the *Ratio*[24] Erasmus explained in broad terms how Christ had overcome the world: not by war, not by the syllogisms of the philosophers, not by riches or honour. Erasmus draws a lively picture of a Jesus who went about with the despised, who became a man in order to save humanity, who mixed freely with sinners in order to cleanse them, who was always willing to approach people on their own level. Here too, he was the Servant of the Lord from Isaiah, who would not break the bruised reed and would not put out the smoking flax. 'It was with these means above all that Christ and after him the apostles overcame the stubbornness of the Jewish people. He conquered the pride of the puffed-up philosophy of Greece. In this way he defeated the ferocity of so many nations invincible in battle.'[25] Erasmus' heart went out to that Jesus who was tenderness and humility personified, who overcame by mildness, and who triumphed not through armies but through death. We have seen that the expression 'philosophy of Christ' was in no sense an abstraction for Erasmus. He was concerned very concretely with Jesus as he had revealed himself to the world. Of his divinity, Erasmus leaves no doubt. The charge that for Erasmus Jesus was not the Son of God does not hold water. He was, however, struck by the real, the authentic in Jesus, and the result of this is that he concentrated, not on the Jesus who is enthroned on high above humanity, but the Jesus who stands alongside it.

Erasmus also applied the term 'philosophy of Christ,' particularly in the *Paraclesis*, to Christians and to Christianity. It is the goal for which we all have to strive. Christ is our teacher, appointed as such by the Father himself. '"This," he said, "is my beloved Son, with whom I am well pleased. Hear him." What does "Hear him" mean? Without doubt, "This is the only teacher, you are pupils of him alone."'[26] This teaching is not a question of intellect, for it is love that is decisive. For this reason Erasmus admonishes parents to take care that their children's world be filled with Christ's doctrine. 'What a man learns in the earliest years of his life he never forgets. Let the first babble be "Christ," let infants be taught from his Gospels. I would like to see Christ so prominent in education that even the children love him. I ask: speak of Christ in such a way that the children too like him. Then let them immerse themselves in this, until by insensible growth they have become full-grown men in Christ.'[27] Erasmus calls on us to imitate Christ in his poverty and humility, in his love and self-denial. If we call ourselves Christians, we must abide in Christ.

With this interest in mind Erasmus pleads on several occasions for as simple as possible a summary of the quintessence of the Christian faith. In both places, in the *Ratio*[28] and in the foreword to the 1518 edition of the *Enchiridion*,[29] the aim is to give the novice a guide. In the *Enchiridion*, the background is this: Erasmus finds the New Testament a rather difficult book; sometimes he has to sweat to discover the meaning. In the *Ratio*, his stimulus was current theology with all its hard questions and even harder problems, which destroyed the enthusiasm of the untrained. In this work Erasmus also gives a summary of his thought. Everything should be concentrated on Christianity, which must live as Christ lived. In the foreword to his *Enchiridion* he says briefly:

What concerns the faith should be set out clause by clause, as few as possible; what relates to life should also be imparted in a few words, and those words so chosen as to make them understand that Christ's yoke is easy and comfortable and not harsh; to make them understand that they have acquired fathers and not despots, shepherds not robbers, and are invited to accept salvation and not dragged by force into slavery. They are human beings, as we are; there is neither steel nor adamant in their hearts.[30]

In the context of these words it is evident that Erasmus saw his own book as an attempt in this direction. Now, however, it appears from the foreword that he was thinking of a group of men who should receive an official commission from the pope. It is obvious that these words betray a certain view of what a theologian should be, a picture that Erasmus was to sketch more explicitly in the *Ratio*. As opposed to the typical contemporary theologian, he asks for one who will not spend his time on all manner of foolish questions, but will explain Holy Scripture, will speak of faith and piety, who will shed tears and incite people to turn their thoughts to heaven.[31] Thus the philosophy of Christ becomes Christian philosophy, both for the theologian and for the merest novice, and a hymn of praise can be sung to it. In fact the *Paraclesis* is nothing else from beginning to end. 'Only be eager to learn, then you are already far advanced in this philosophy. It offers the Spirit as teacher, and this imparts itself most willingly to the simple ... it adapts itself to all equally, it makes itself small with the small, adapts to their measure, feeds them with milk, bears them, embraces them, supports them, does everything until we become full-grown in Christ. It assists the lowest, but is also admirable for the highest. Yes, the further you penetrate into its treasures, the more you are awed by its majesty.'[32] This imitation must be taught to everyone. Above all princes, bishops, priests, and educators of the young have a great task before them.

The goal is a society in which Christ is the centre. In the foreword to the *Enchiridion* Erasmus depicts it as a hierarchic whole; it must be a well-ordered world, in which each class of people and each individual occupies its proper place. There are different circles around Christ. Closest to him stand the priests, bishops, cardinals, and popes, whose task is to pass on the doctrine of Christ to those nearest them. In the second circle are the princes of the world, who serve Christ in their own way by maintaining public order and keeping wrongdoers within bounds. In the third circle are the common people, who also belong to the body of Christ. This scheme seems very medieval, but Erasmus breaks away from the static element when he states that there ought to be growth towards Christ. In this growth process, the natural order is disturbed, which is a good thing. The ordinary people form as it were the legs, feet, and genitals of the body. But a foot can become an eye. On the other hand, the classes that stand closest to Christ run the greatest danger of degeneration.[33] No wonder that it is precisely the clergy and the princes who commit the gravest errors: the corruption of the best is always the worst. In the *Institutio* we find a fine passage in which Erasmus works out this idea for the prince. The prince, as Plutarch had already said, is a kind of living image of God. A bad prince, Erasmus adds, is the image of an evil demon, in whom we find the alliance of great power with the highest evil, as in the good prince we find the union of goodness and power. A Christian prince must therefore not be puffed up with pride, not arrogant if he hears that he is the image of God: 'Let the fact make you all the more concerned to live up to that wonderful archetype of yours; and remember that, though following him is very hard, not following him is a grave scandal.' God is the highest power, the highest wisdom, the highest goodness. This triad the prince must realize, as far as his powers permit him; power without goodness is tyranny, without wisdom it is a disaster, and not a properly ordered realm.[34]

If Erasmus sees society as so thoroughly Christian, then the obvious question is how he saw the non-Christian citizens of the society of his day, in practice, what he thought of the position of the Jews. For Erasmus it was self-evident that they should enjoy normal civil rights, but his view of them was negative. Jewry was a religious group, and an obsolete one, that had remained attached to an external ceremonial even after the coming of Christ. The Jews had chosen the body, the flesh – and that was the reverse of what they ought to have done in this age. In the *Ratio* we find a detailed passage about the Jews, who rejected Christ and offered stiff-necked resistance to the salvation that Christ offered them. Erasmus formulates the distinction between Christians and Jews briefly and clearly: 'The Jew boasts of his good deeds; the sins of his past are not held against the repentant heathen'[35]: the Jew is the eldest son from the parable of the prodigal son. In his opposition to the Jews Erasmus has in mind, in the final analysis, those Christians who also reduce religion to the service of forms and who are rightly called Jews or Pharisees. He concludes the passage on the Jews in these words: 'Each century knows its Pharisees, each century runs into danger if it abuses God's goodness.'[36] Erasmus cannot be accused of hatred of Jews or of anti-Semitism, but the identification of society with Christendom does imply a latent threat to the Jews; the characterization of the Jewish religion as obsolete and dangerous can easily lead to anti-Semitism.

How much room is left for a realistic approach to the facts? The monarchies of the sixteenth century were tending towards absolutism. There were perpetual wars, which became more violent through the emergence of national states and national feeling, wars that were blessed by the princes of the church. The century also saw a beginning of territorial expansion and colonialism, and continual conflict with the Ottoman empire. There are marks of these historical realities in Erasmus' works from these years, especially in the *Institutio principis christiani* and the *Querela pacis*. It is striking that the idea of Christ as the centre of society, whether explicitly stated or implied, always forms the framework of Erasmus' thought. He had a tendency to approach reality from an idealistic point of view, and to condemn it from that viewpoint. This is the strength and at the same time the weakness of his reflections. The moral appeal is a powerful one, and founded on a religiously determined view of reality, but it leads to resignation when reality becomes too brutal.

Two motifs determine Erasmus' thought: the freedom of all men and peace. Since all men are free, princes must not treat their subjects as slaves. In the *Institutio* Erasmus first explains that nature has created all human beings free, even according to the opinions of the heathen. Thus, he reasons, it is not fitting that a Christian should exercise tyranny over Christians, that he should, against all law, make slaves of those whom Christ has redeemed from all slavery, who share in the same sacraments, who have Christ as their lord in common with him. Does this mean that a heathen ruler has more power than a Christian prince? No, he answers, the latter certainly has rights over his subjects, but they rest on another foundation. The subjects are not his property, for it is their consent that first makes him their prince. They will obey willingly, for they obey freely.[37] This in fact obscures real problems, for the question of the right of resistance is not raised, and cannot be raised: consensus, the agreement of his subjects, has given the Christian prince an authority that tends towards the absolute.

The second motif is that of peace. The *Querela pacis* is an impressive working out of this concept. Erasmus knew that princes made use of the national feelings of their subjects: 'The Englishman hates the Frenchman, just because he is a Frenchman. The Briton is the enemy of the Scot, simply because he is a Scot ... Why don't you wish him well as another man and a fellow-Christian?' Paul had not wanted divisions to appear among Christians. 'Are we then to treat the simple word "fatherland" as a serious reason why one nation should be bent on exterminating another?' In these pronouncements being human and being a Christian are continually intermingled. Then the argument takes a clear step forward: 'Why do they not rather think of the fact that this world is the common fatherland of all – if the concept of fatherland unites; that all men are descended from the same ancestors – if blood relationship makes us friends; that the church is a single family, to which all belong equally?'[38] In this sequence we feel the tension in Erasmus' thought. Being a Christian means being identified by such concepts as unity and harmony. The reality is that cannon were invented by Christians. They were also given the names of the apostles; probably Erasmus was thinking of the twelve pieces of artillery that Henry VIII had had cast for his campaign against France in 1513 and that had been given the names of the twelve apostles. If we wish to convert the Turks to Christianity, we must first become Christians ourselves. Nowhere is there a bloodier war than that between Christians, and that is exactly what Christ detests most of all.[39] 'What is most absurd of all, the cross is displayed in both camps, in both battle-lines, and the sacraments are administered on both sides. What anomaly is this, when the cross fights the cross and Christ makes war on Christ!'[40] Erasmus' repugnance to these practices helps us to understand the classic passage at the beginning of the book, in which Peace says: 'Whenever I hear the word "man" I rush to him, for this being is related to me above all others, confident of being able to find rest there. Whenever I hear the name of "Christian" I hasten all the more, in the hope of surely being able to rule there.'[41] Alas, among Christians there is more strife than anywhere among the heathen!

We find a breakthrough in the sequence in the famous adage added in 1515, *Dulce bellum inexpertis*, 'War is sweet to those who do not know it.' It is a detailed treatise, which was reprinted separately many times, in Latin and in translation. In the closing passage Erasmus discusses the war against the Turks,[42] a favourite occupation of his age, although more in words than in deeds until the moment, in the second half of the 1520s, when the Turks marched on the West. Erasmus was very suspicious. He felt that pure imperialism was at stake, and that it took no account of the fact that a majority of the population in those lands was Christian or semi-Christian. Let the Dominicans and Franciscans convert them instead! Erasmus flatly rejected war. Christendom was in a bad way if it had to be defended by such means. In this context he made several remarkable observations, in which the boundary between Christians and non-Christians became vague. If you remove from your imagination the Christian name and the cross, then 'we fight like Turks with Turks.' Furthermore: 'those whom we call Turks are for the most part half Christian, and perhaps they are closer to true Christianity than many of us.' We send soldiers who do not believe in the resurrection or in eternal life to fight 'little heretics who doubt whether the pope has jurisdiction over the souls who are in torment in purgatory.'[43] The boundary is crossed on both sides: the Christian who acts in an unchristian way or scorns the essence of the faith is no Christian, and the Muslim is close to Christianity. Erasmus clearly has no difficulty with the eastern Christians. The word translated as 'little heretic' shows that he did not take this difference seriously. In all this the unity of the human race all over the world plays a great part. The idea appeared frequently in the Renaissance:

there was a conviction that the world was not populated by individuals.

In Erasmus this idea of unity was worked out in another way too. In harmony with his interest in classical antiquity, he was enthusiastic about the unity of humanity through all the ages. This idea too represents the crossing of a boundary. Erasmus faces the question how it was possible that the great minds of antiquity could have said things that would certainly have been not unworthy of a Christian. In the *Paraclesis* he writes: 'We can find a great deal in the books of the pagans that agrees with [Christ's] doctrine.'[44] He also gives the examples: the Stoics, Socrates, Aristotle, Epicurus, Diogenes, Epictetus. Nor is he concerned with their words only, but also with their deeds. Not a few of them fulfilled a good part of Christian doctrine in their lives. Erasmus also gives his grounds for such a statement. As he sees it, the Christian faith is not an exotic or impenetrable matter, nor is it Christ's intention to restrict it to a few. On the contrary, it is entirely in harmony with the disposition and nature of man, and therefore penetrates into the hearts of all men. 'What is the philosophy of Christ, which he himself calls "being born again," except the renewal of nature, which was created good?'[45] Because the gospel answers to the best in man, it is not strange that the best men and women have spoken words and performed deeds that answer to the gospel.

But we would put this statement in the wrong context if we took no account of the point at issue, which is not to set a high value on the classics, but the reverse. Erasmus expresses his astonishment that Christians devote so little attention to the words of Christ and the Gospels. Christ is the all-dominating figure. Nor can it be otherwise. For only the doctrine of Christ is a whole, and only in him do teaching and life coincide. He enjoined innocence, tenderness, and poverty, but he also was what he bade us be. 'Perhaps you find things in the writings of Plato and Seneca that do not differ greatly from the commandments of Jesus. You will find things in the life of Socrates which to some extent agree with the life of Christ. But this closed circle and the unconditional harmony in every respect you will find in Christ alone,' says the *Ratio*.[46]

Erasmus expresses similar ideas concerning the course of sacred history. He discusses this in the *Ratio* in the context of the proper exegesis of the Scriptures.[47] One must bear in mind the different periods at which the history was accomplished, and not merely transpose pronouncements from one period to today. First came the age of the Old Testament with its commandments and prohibitions, which have lost their validity for us. Hatred of the enemy, wars, polygamy, and such things were permitted then, sometimes even commanded. Then followed the age of John the Baptist, a time of preparation for the light that was to come. He did not yet attain what would make a man a Christian, for that was reserved for Christ. John taught that the soldier might not do violence to anyone and must be content with his pay, but not yet that one should do good to one's enemy. Perhaps the first preaching of the apostles, who on Christ's orders were silent about him, also belonged to this period. Then came the age of the nascent church, with its strict commandments: to take the cross onto oneself, to leave father and mother, to sell all one's goods. To that age also belonged the injunction to the heathens who had been converted that they should abstain from all meat slaughtered by suffocation and from blood, a useful rule to meet the 'insuperable stubbornness of the Jews,' but now completely superfluous. Paul wanted bishops to rule their wives and children well, but today not even subdeacons may marry. There are more differences: then the prescribed feast days did not exist, nor perhaps did secret confession. If it were only as salutary as it is generally practised, adds the critical Erasmus. After Emperor Constantine in the fourth century followed yet another period. New laws were introduced by the church, some of which, if we do not take into account the distinctions between the various periods, appear to be at odds with the commandments of Christ. Erasmus does not name these commandments at this point, but he does so adequately elsewhere. He appears to be concerned with all the pointless regulations of the church dealing with externals. He did not reject such laws absolutely, but it is clear that his heart yearned for the third period, that of the primitive church with its strict commandments. He saw a final period approaching, in which a degenerate church would have fallen away from the original power of the Christian spirit. In the world around him he already saw its portents.

Or had the last period already dawned? In these years 1513 or

1514 Erasmus wrote his dialogue *Julius exclusus e coelis* (*Julius Excluded from Heaven*),[48] which was to appear in print a few years later. Erasmus always denied, implicitly rather than in so many words, that he was the author, but it is generally assumed that this fierce satire was his work. The theme – the recently deceased Pope Julius II haughtily demands admittance to heaven, but is rejected by Peter – gave Erasmus the opportunity to contrast the present pope and church with the earliest church and its pope, a device which, as we have seen, he used quite often. But now another technique comes into play. The tone becomes extremely violent, because the whole conversation is an example of linguistic confusion created by Erasmus. Peter and Julius speak totally different languages. When Peter utters the word 'church' he is thinking of the Christian people, united by the spirit of Christ; Julius corrects him, saying that this word means church buildings, priests, the curia, and above all himself as head of the church. When Julius says that the church is now flourishing as never before, Peter asks: through warm faith? through sacred learning? through contempt for the world? For Julius, these are empty words; he is thinking of palaces, horses, servants.[49] Naturally Julius appears as his bellicose self, and finally he threatens Peter with an invasion of heaven!

The aim of Christian philosophy is to change the heart: 'Let this be your first and only goal, this your longing, strive for this only, that you let yourself be changed, drawn along, inspired and transformed in that which you teach ... Do not believe that you are making progress if you dispute more acutely, but only when you become aware that you are gradually becoming another person,' says the *Ratio*.[50] For this reason we must approach this philosophy with a pure heart and renounce all desires that arouse discontent, so that Christ, the image of eternal truth, is reflected in us as in still water or a shining mirror.[51] This sounds quietist, and in spite of Erasmus' generally more activist nature, this too was part of his personality. Time and again he contrasts the old theology with the new: 'I would rather be a pious theologian with Chrysostom than an invincible one with Duns Scotus.'[52] In such a comparison, the New Testament is opposed to Aristotle and dialectic. But Erasmus goes deeper when he states, in the *Paraclesis*, that the true theologian 'in his expression, in his glance, in his life teaches that one must despise wealth, that the Christian must not rely on the aids of this world.' He continues in this style and then adds: 'If, I say, someone inspired by the spirit of Christ preaches all this, inculcates, admonishes, invites, summons his hearers to it, then he is a true theologian, even if he is a peasant or a weaver.'[53] The change of heart, the imitation of Christ is the essential point.

Erasmus saw this imitation of Christ realized in the virtues of humility and love. In this he was building on a long tradition, which had received a new impulse in the later Middle Ages. That was especially the case in the emphasis on *humilitas*, which in Erasmus is often fused with the heritage of antiquity, in particular the encouragement to 'live a retired life.' Sometimes he penetrates more deeply. In the *Institutio principis christiani* Erasmus thinks it foolish for a prince to hold up Alexander the Great, Julius Caesar, or Xerxes as his models.[54] (In the *Adages* he adds Croesus to this list.) He poses the question whether it befits a pope to emulate such rulers, 'who are no more than robbers on the grand scale,' rather than Christ, who openly declared that his kingdom was not of this world.[55] The words about rulers as robbers are an allusion to Augustine's words on rule without justice; the names of Alexander and Julius recall the last two popes Alexander VI and Julius II.

Love is given great emphasis as well as humility. It is nothing less than the highest love with which Christ wished to inspire us, that is, the fire that he came to cast upon the earth. When Jesus spoke with his disciples shortly before his death, burning, ardent love echoed in his words. It was a love stronger than death, which made the disciples risk their lives, and which at Christ's command distinguishes us from other people.[56] Erasmus gives the command to love one another polemic point by contrasting it with the many commandments of the church concerning ceremonies, eating, drinking, fasting, and so forth: 'Christ proclaimed aloud that man is not created for the sake of the Sabbath but the Sabbath was established for the sake of man – and you want to attach so much importance to your laws that a man must die rather than deviate an inch from them.'[57] Here Erasmus sees love submerged in human commandments that bind the conscience.

Erasmus' writings from the crucial years 1514 to 1518 are distinguished by a clear tendency. Erasmus pursued a definite ideal with respect to society and church. He saw the church and theology of his day as obstacles on the path to God. The heart of his religion was Jesus Christ. The goal of his work was to make of Christians Christians in reality and not in name only, and to show them the way to the great example, the great teacher. Only in this way can the world again do justice to God's intentions. Of course his project was bound to appear rather one-sided. That will be discussed again when we turn to the 1520s. At this point it is enough if we realize that this programme, designed and propagated before the names of Luther and Zwingli were known to anyone, attracted people and gave them new hope.

EIGHT

The Bible and
the Fathers of the Church

🔆

For one thing I found crystal clear: our chiefest hope for the
restoration and rebuilding of the Christian religion ... is that all
those who profess the Christian philosophy the whole world
over should above all absorb the principles laid down by their
Founder from the writings of the evangelists and apostles, in
which that heavenly Word which once came down to us from
the heart of the Father still lives and breathes for us and acts
and speaks with more immediate efficacy, in my opinion, than
in any other way. Besides which I perceived that that teaching
which is our salvation was to be had in a much purer and more
lively form if sought at the fountain-head and drawn from the
actual sources than from pools and runnels. And so I have
revised the whole New Testament (as they call it) against the
standard of the Greek original, not unadvisedly or with little
effort, but calling in the assistance of a number of manuscripts
in both languages, and those not the first comers but both very
old and very correct.

These words, addressed to Leo x, appear in the dedication of
Erasmus' edition of the New Testament in 1516.[1] In seventeen lines
Erasmus characterizes his entire enterprise. Later we shall come
back to his words. They are characteristic of the works to which we
turn our attention in this chapter. The most important of them was
his edition of the New Testament, then the editions of the various
Fathers of the church, the Paraphrases on the books of the New
Testament, and the commentaries on several psalms.

In March 1516 the *Novum instrumentum* appeared. It was given this name because the word *instrumentum*, unknown in this context, more specifically denotes a written document, in Froben's edition a folio of more than a thousand pages, in twelve hundred copies. The book consists of a dedication, followed by the preliminary matter, the *Paraclesis*, *Methodus*, and *Apologia*, respectively an encouragement to read the New Testament, pointers to the fruitful reading of it, and a defence of the undertaking.[2] Then follow in two parallel columns the Greek text and a Latin translation by Erasmus himself. Finally come the *Annotations*, notes on the text, which take up almost as much space as the Latin and Greek texts put together.

The edition had been a long time in the making.[3] It had begun around 1500 with Erasmus' plans to master Greek and to devote his life to the *sacrae litterae*. It soon became evident that these intentions would lead, among other things, to the exposition of the Bible. In 1501 Erasmus was working on a commentary on the Epistles of Paul, but this work never led to a publication. In 1505 he published Lorenzo Valla's *Adnotationes*. Was he also occupied at about the same time with his own Latin translation of the New Testament? This has often been assumed, but Andrew J. Brown has recently shown convincingly that there are no grounds for such an assertion. Not until 1512 do we hear once more of biblical study, when Erasmus compared the texts of old Greek and Latin manuscripts of the New Testament that differed from each other on certain points. In the years between 1512 and 1514 he made brief notes using this material.

By the time Erasmus left England for Basel late in the summer of 1514, he had formed the intention to do something with the many annotations on the text of the New Testament that he had collected in the preceding few years. He probably wanted to publish the text of the Vulgate with his own annotations, or perhaps the notes on their own. On the advice of 'scholarly friends, to whom I sometimes defer more than I should,'[4] he changed his plan soon after his arrival in Basel: he expanded the notes, rapidly produced a translation of his own, and added the Greek text to it. It does not seem impossible that the printer Johann Froben also had a hand in the eventual plan of the edition. Since 1514 the Spaniards had been occupied in printing a polyglot, that is, an edition of the Bible in which the text in various languages was printed in columns, the New Testament in Greek and Latin. This enterprise had become known in Germany; hence Froben was in a hurry and wanted to bring out a particularly impressive piece of work. In the end it was 1521 before this Complutensian Polyglot (so called from its place of publication, Alcalá, in Latin *Complutum*) was released for circulation.

In the course of 1515 the manuscripts went to the printer, and in six months of working like a slave, Erasmus accomplished the enormous task, with the aid of some expert correctors, Nikolaus Gerbel and Johannes Oecolampadius, the latter especially for the Hebrew. Here Erasmus was in his element. The printers worked from four-centuries-old Greek manuscripts and from the Latin text and annotations of Erasmus. All this had to be made ready and put together. In this work Erasmus was following his great model, St Jerome. Just as the saint had partly corrected existing translations and partly supplied new translations for his contemporaries, so Erasmus did for the people of his own day, who had other requirements. The main thing was the new Latin version with its supporting annotations. The Greek text was added to give the few experts the opportunity to check Erasmus' translations. Erasmus rejected Gerbel's plan to print the Greek and Latin texts successively so that the experts could, if they wished, buy a copy without the Latin. Henk Jan de Jonge has rightly drawn attention to the true character of Erasmus' edition.[5] It did not in the first place aim to be the first edition of the Greek New Testament, but 'the New Testament translated by me,' as Erasmus expressed it.[6] Since the seventeenth century the edition of the Greek text has been considered the more important element, but for Erasmus it was the less important.

Publication was accompanied by an extensive press campaign. As early as 1514 Maarten van Dorp, in the same letter in which he made known his objections to the *Praise of Folly*,[7] had also spoken out against the projected publication of Erasmus' annotations.[8] In his opinion the existing Latin text could not contain any inaccuracies, because the church, which used this Bible, could not err. Moreover, the western church had shown more care than the eastern for the faith and for the uncorrupted preservation of the text of the Bible through the ages. Erasmus gave a detailed answer in

1515,[9] and this found its way into the following editions of the *Praise of Folly*, a stroke of well-aimed propaganda.

The book was received with enthusiasm. There is no better witness of this than a letter from the famous French scholar Guillaume Budé to Erasmus. He received the 'glorious' book in Paris on Saturday and read the introductory matter on Sunday morning. Immediately after his meal, he visited his friend François Deloynes; Budé found him in a state of high excitement. Deloynes had found in the work, which he had just received from the printer, still unbound, a eulogy of Budé in one of the annotations.[10] Some days later Budé thanked Erasmus most graciously for this.

But there were bitter attacks too. Preachers warned from the pulpit against a man who dared to alter the Our Father and the Magnificat,[11] who was the Antichrist in person,[12] and so on. Little resistance could be offered to this kind of assault. Others protested in writing: the Louvain professor Jacques Masson (Jacobus Latomus), the Englishman Edward Lee, and Erasmus' most skilful adversary, the very competent Spanish biblical scholar and collaborator on the Complutensian Polyglot, Diego López Zúñiga. In all these polemics, two often intertwined questions were constantly raised. On the one hand philological questions on a particular reading, translation, or explanation, on the other hand alarm at the method followed, the treatment of the Bible as a literary work, which could only lead to a breach in the authority of the church and traditional theology. There is no point in following this criticism and Erasmus' defence – for he never silenced his critics – in detail. The underlying questions will be discussed later.

Erasmus' edition was a success, as is evident from the rapid succession of printings that followed. As early as 1519 the second edition was published, now under the title *Novum Testamentum*, and this title was retained in the editions of 1522, 1527, and 1535. The introductory sections underwent quite considerable alterations in the various editions. In the second the *Methodus* was greatly expanded into the *Ratio verae theologiae*,[13] which also appeared separately on several occasions. The consequence of this was that it was no longer included in the third edition. From the fourth edition, the *Paraclesis* was also omitted, so that the introductory material of the 1527 and 1535 printings consisted only of the short *Apologia* and the *Capita argumentorum*,[14] which Erasmus had added to the second edition and subsequently retained. The composition of the work itself remained broadly the same in all editions. In the fourth, the Vulgate text was included in a third column, but was omitted again in the fifth edition. Erasmus regarded the second edition almost as a new piece of work, and one with which he was very satisfied.[15] Apart from these great editions, the Latin text was also published separately, and Erasmus was not averse to this.[16] In this way his translation was widely disseminated, and became even better known through translations into various vernaculars. Gerbel also published the Greek text separately.

If we look at the various parts, it is fair to say that Erasmus did not devote a great deal of attention to the Greek text. In England he had used Greek manuscripts that were not available to him in Basel. In Basel he had to be content with the material available there, a total of seven manuscripts.[17] Two of these were sent to the printing house, one for the Gospels and one for Acts and the Epistles, with some corrections derived from the other manuscripts. For Revelation he used the manuscript of a commentary from which the text was distilled. This, however, proved to lack the last six verses of the last chapter. Erasmus retranslated these verses from Latin into Greek, as he himself stated, and not without some errors. The manuscripts that formed the basis were all rather recent, and all belonged to the same text form, one which he wrongly considered the most ancient and best. The correction must have been carelessly carried out, for the text contained many errors, above all in verb forms. The second edition showed improvements, but also new errors. In preparing the third edition Erasmus took great pains with the Greek; after that, there was little change. In the second and third editions he also incorporated various new manuscripts. Only in the fourth edition were the last verses of Revelation corrected. The so-called *comma Johanneum*, 1 John 5:7b–8a, in which the Trinity is stated explicitly, has become famous. Erasmus did not find the words in the Greek manuscripts and therefore omitted them. This earned him severe rebukes: he was accused of being an Arian, an opponent of the church's doctrine of the Trinity. In the third edition Erasmus included the passage in his work. A manuscript containing it had, it appeared, surfaced in England. True to his own rule Erasmus now included it, although he had a suspicion that the Greek manuscript had adopted the reading from the Vulgate. The reality was even worse than he suspected: the manuscript with the words, translated in fact from the Vulgate, had been produced around 1520, with the exclusive aim of embarrassing Erasmus.[18] The Greek text of the New Testament that Erasmus presented set the tone for the following centuries. In principle all later edition until the nineteenth century went back to Erasmus. However, its importance for his own day was quite different. We know that Zwingli transcribed the Epistles of Paul in Greek from Erasmus' New Testament, and that it was only in this way that he acquired a reasonable knowledge of Greek. There must have been many more like Zwingli.

Erasmus' Latin text served to make clear to the reader how the Greek text of the New Testament read. It was intended to be an aid to the study of the Bible. Its aim was not to offer an outstandingly elegant rendering of the Bible.[19] Erasmus wanted to preserve the simplicity of the language of the apostles, but within these limits to write good Latin.[20] Nor did he want his version to supersede the Vulgate; that must remain in use in the liturgy and in schools.[21] Erasmus probably did not realize how deeply the alteration of a hallowed text affected many of his contemporaries. And it was an alteration, in spite of all protestations to the contrary. The mere assertion that through his translation one could come closer to the original text, to God's own word, in itself was enough to disqualify the Vulgate. Erasmus' assurance that sometimes the Vulgate text was better than the Greek could not possibly outweigh this suggestion of spotless authenticity. This was unmistakably the work of another spirit than the somewhat revised Vulgate text which Lefèvre d'Etaples had offered in 1512, in his exposition of the Epistles of Paul.

In the first edition Erasmus' translation was fairly conservative; in the second, as he said himself, he ventured further.[22] After that there were few further changes, apart from minor corrections, though until the fourth edition he continued to make use of new manuscripts he came across.

A few specimens may reveal his method of work. I begin with a harmless example. Matthew 7:1 says, 'Judge not that you be not judged.' The Greek verb *krinein* also allows the translation 'Condemn not, so that ye be not condemned.' In the then usual Vulgate text the passage read: 'Judge not and you shall not be judged. Condemn not and you shall not be condemned.' In the edition of 1516, Erasmus translated: 'Judge not so that you be not judged.' His annotation explained that the words 'condemn not and you shall not be condemned' do not appear in any Greek manuscript at all, nor are they in the oldest Latin ones; probably someone had originally put them in the margin, and from there they had crept into the text. In the edition of 1519, he translated 'Condemn not, so that you be not condemned,' but left his annotation as it was, merely adding that someone has given the exegesis that 'judge' here meant the same as 'condemn'; this is possible in Hebrew, and Paul too uses the word in this sense. It would have been more consistent if he had stuck to the translation of 1516. The whole affair shows that he was exactly aware of possibilities and problems.

Other examples are less harmless. Thus from the first edition Erasmus added to the text of the Lord's Prayer in Matthew 6 the words of praise, 'for thine is the kingdom, the power, and the glory, forever. Amen.' In an annotation he explained that he found these words in all Greek manuscripts and that they were expounded by 'Vulgarius' (more of him in a moment), so that they must have been in Vulgarius' text as well. But they were lacking in all Latin manuscripts and also in all other expositors. They must therefore, Erasmus concludes, come from the liturgy. In the second edition Erasmus had discovered that Chrysostom too knew of the words of praise, but his verdict is sharper: a scandal! That people dared to add to the words of Christ! If anyone should maintain that the words of praise were uttered by Christ, he must also assert that the whole western church has been missing a good part of the Lord's Prayer until now. Remarkable: in his edition the words now are printed in small print, probably to show that there is some doubt about them.

A question of translation pure and simple that involved Erasmus in great difficulties was his rendering of the angel's greeting to Mary. 'Greetings, thou favoured one,' Erasmus translated in Luke 1:28, from the second edition, while the first edition follows the Vulgate: 'full of grace.' The difference was considerable: is it Mary with her grace who stands in the foreground or God, who confers grace on her? His remark in his annotations, that the greeting of

Gabriel 'had something of a declaration of love, as it were betrayed something of the lover,' did not improve matters. Vigorous protests followed from Edward Lee, and finally Erasmus deleted these words from his annotation, on the advice of Maarten van Dorp.

A famous translation is that of *logos*, 'word,' in the beginning of the Gospel of John. The usual translation is *verbum*, but from the second edition Erasmus chose the word *sermo*. (In the first edition, he says, 'superstitious fear' had held him back.) It was a happy choice. Christ was not just a word of the Father, a single word or short utterance, but the continued speech of God. Moreover various Fathers of the church had translated it in that way. A storm blew up. London, Brussels, and Paris echoed the accusation that Erasmus did not shrink from correcting the Gospel of John and putting doctors of theology back in their school benches.[23]

If we look at these cases, it becomes clear why in 1523, in a survey of his writings up to that date, Erasmus distinguished the edition of the New Testament as the high point of his activities as an editor[24] and did not rank it with the translations from Greek. This does not contradict what was argued earlier in this chapter. The New Testament is both: a translation of a Greek text, but also the annotated edition of a Latin text.

This brings us to the *Annotations*. Erasmus did not want to supply a commentary, a continuous explanation from beginning to end, but explanatory notes on passages he felt needed explanation. In 1516 these were exclusively short notes of a philological nature intended to justify his translation. Over the years much material was added, especially in the second and third editions. In the first place, Erasmus constantly corrected his remarks, sometimes as a reaction to criticism. He then often entered into discussion with his opponents, and defended himself unceasingly. Finally he took over more and more material from predecessors whose work he used, medieval exegetes, and above all the Fathers. Some examples of his annotations have been mentioned above, and there would be little point in multiplying them. Some general remarks will be more useful.

It is striking that the character of the annotations did not change essentially as the material expanded. They continued to play an auxiliary role, supporting the text. This did not prevent Erasmus from dilating at length from time to time. He used the material offered by medieval exegesis, the *Glossa ordinaria* of the twelfth century, and the *Postillae* of Nicholas of Lyra from the fourteenth century, often without stating his source. He thought the Fathers more important. As early as the first edition he repeatedly brought them on stage. In the subsequent editions it was this material in particular which was enormously expanded. This expansion paralleled other activities. Thus the various editions of the New Testament reflected the preparations for editions of the Fathers of the church. The noteworthy expansion of the annotations on Romans in the editions of 1527 and 1535 is undoubtedly the outcome of his preparatory work for the *Hyperaspistes*, in which he defended his opinions on the relation between divine grace and human freedom against Luther.

Erasmus did not use his material uncritically. Of course he made mistakes, sometimes grave ones, and to a certain extent these were caused by indiscriminately taking over the data of others. One of the most famous examples was the so-called Father 'Vulgarius,' who appeared in the first edition, indeed on the title-page, as the author of a commentary on the Gospels. Erasmus took the name from the binding of the manuscript at his disposal, because the beginning of the manuscript had been so badly damaged that the author's name had become illegible. Only later did he discover that it referred to the twelfth-century archbishop Theophylact and that 'Vulgarius' meant 'from Bulgaria.' But one also finds excellent discussions, especially when he exposes the dogmatic prejudices behind a particular exegesis or shows how far the medieval exegetes strayed from the truth because in expounding Greek their lack of solid knowledge forced them to rely on their imagination. A certain malicious sarcasm is not unknown. Thus he remarks first that it is astonishing that Latin Christianity should prefer the Greek word 'hypocrite' while there is a good Latin word. 'I cannot omit,' he says 'for the fun of it, to mention what Nicholas of Lyra adds, for you would never imagine that he could be so foolish. He says "hypocrite" comes from *hypos*, that is, "under" and from *krisis*, "gold," because under the gold, that is, under the honesty of the outward way of life, is hidden the lead of falsehood. Now let them tell us that it makes no difference whether or not you know Greek!' A schoolboy's knowledge would have shown the difference between *krisis*, 'division,' and *chrysos*, 'gold.' This is an annotation on Matthew 6:16. At verse 2 Erasmus had given a learned treatise on 'hypocrite,' the primary meaning of which is 'actor.' Just look, he says, how well that fits: the hypocrites want to be seen by people.

The significance of the *Annotations* thus lay in the fact that they went back to the Greek text in order to justify the translation, contrary to the practice of the Middle Ages, and that they continually used the Fathers of the church without deviating from textual analysis into deeper and more spiritual exegesis. Yet Erasmus also employed this work in the service of his beloved ideals. From the second edition, his own thoughts on theology, church, and society appeared in the *Annotations*. Sometimes there was only a brief but biting remark in the middle of an otherwise purely philological passage. Occasionally his comments grew into short essays, as had been the case four years earlier in the *Adages*. A typical example was the annotation on Matthew 11:30, 'My yoke is easy and my burden light.' In the first edition the exegesis occupied two lines, in the second almost a hundred. It had grown into a dissertation on the goodness and love of Christ as opposed to the strictness and harshness of all the human institutions that now prevail in the church. In Romans 5:12 a complete treatise on original sin emerged from what was at first sight a purely technical question of translation. At 1 Corinthians 7 we find a detailed essay on marriage and divorce, a burning question of the time, in which the church recognized virtually no grounds for divorce. At the same time Erasmus raised the question of church laws in general, which deviated from those that had applied in early Christianity. In an annotation on 1 Corinthians 15 he dealt with problems concerning the resurrection of the faithful, and on 1 Timothy 1 he addressed the foolish questions theologians posed in the doctrine concerning God, Christ, and the power of the pope. Some of these discussions were later published separately in translation; they were reprinted several times and found a wide circle of readers.

I do not intend to deal with the introductory writings. The previous chapter made many citations from them, and the rest of this chapter will do likewise. I consider only one aspect which is of importance for all Erasmus' work in the field of biblical study, the so-called allegorical exegesis. He treated this in the *Ratio verae theologiae*, the introductory work which offered a hermeneutic, that is, an attempt to give rules for the correct exposition of the Bible, following Augustine's work, *De doctrina christiana*. It was eagerly read. Heinrich Stromer saw a man reading it avidly, and that during the discussion between Luther and Eck at Leipzig in 1519.[25] The book apparently interested him more than the dispute, which concerned the foundations of faith. In the *Ratio* Erasmus defended spiritual or allegorical exegesis at length, as he had done before in the *Enchiridion*.[26] In the Middle Ages, more systematically than in antiquity, two senses of Scripture were distinguished: the literal sense, which investigated the wording of the text and the meaning of the writer, and the spiritual, which asked what was the significance of the biblical passage for Christians and for the church. The spiritual sense, also called the allegorical sense, was subdivided into the allegorical sense in the strict meaning of the word, which showed the value of the passage for the faith; the tropological sense, which set forth its significance for the actions of a Christian; and the anagogical sense, which made clear what a Christian hoped for. Might one not have hoped that Erasmus, interested as he was in sober literal exegesis that asked what the text meant, would reject this distinction? Yet this was not the case. Erasmus rejected the arbitrary and eccentric spiritual exegesis he found in his contemporaries, but he did not reject the method as such. It was indeed the only way, he thought, to unlock a definite meaning from the Old Testament. Christ and Paul are our examples; they have already applied the method: think of the way in which Paul in Galatians 4 uses the story of Hagar and Sarah. It is a question of the deeper spiritual content of the Scriptures and not of the letter alone. At this point, the wider framework of his preference for spiritual exegesis becomes clear. The distinction between a literal and a spiritual sense in Scripture is entirely in keeping with the tension between flesh and spirit that permeates mankind and the world.[27] Erasmus was aware that the method had hidden dangers. He urged moderation in its use and said expressly that it should never be used to buttress pronouncements on the faith, but to encourage, to console, and to reprove.[28] In this context he insouciantly applied the word 'play,' a term he had borrowed from St Jerome: playing in the field of the

Scriptures. It says something that his preference was for the allegorical exposition in the strict sense of the word and for tropological exposition, for they concerned faith and Christian life, which together were *par excellence* the subject-matter of theology.

Besides the New Testament, Erasmus' editions of the most important Fathers of the church deserve our attention. It all started with the study of St Jerome. As early as 1500 Erasmus had been thinking of an edition of Jerome's works. In 1516 they appeared in nine large and handsomely printed volumes. In the foreword we can detect how important Erasmus thought his work was. What great pains he had had to take and still was not able to produce a completely pure text. But it had been worth the effort: no one takes us further into the Holy Scriptures, no one was better informed of all the learning of his time, no one proclaimed the doctrine of Christ better than Jerome.[29] Erasmus pursued his study of the Fathers. Origen stood even higher than Jerome as a master of allegorical exegesis, as in general Greek authors were to be preferred to Latin ones.[30] It was not a coincidence that Erasmus held Jerome and Origen in such honour – two authors who, like him, wanted to achieve a synthesis of Christianity and ancient civilization.

Erasmus carried through an impressive programme: editions of Cyprian, Arnobius, Hilary, Ambrose, Augustine (in ten volumes), editions and translations of Chrysostom and Irenaeus, translations of Origen. Rudolf Pfeiffer has pointed out that Erasmus accomplished mountains of work in an age when it was difficult to find manuscripts and collate them.[31] Criticism from later editors has therefore not always been fair. Erasmus was not striving for perfection, but wanted to lay a foundation for those readers who were interested in the language and content of the Fathers of the church. He wanted a theology that welcomed everything good, wherever it came from. This applied to the service rendered by the philologists as well. 'Theology is rightly the queen of the sciences, but she will possess more glory and learning if she includes such useful handmaidens, with proper friendliness, among her servants.'[32]

Erasmus also wished to be helpful at the level of the practice of Christian life. He had shown this in the *Enchiridion*, but he also sought a method of serving people seeking God that would be directly linked to the Bible. It was with this end in view that he published the *Paraphrases* on the various books of the New Testament and the exposition of eleven of the psalms.

The *Paraphrases*[33] are a popular exposition of the books of the New Testament, with the exception of Revelation, which was unsuitable for this treatment. They form a continuous exposition, an explanation in which the text of the Bible is paraphrased and expounded. In Erasmus' own words: 'the art of saying things differently, without saying different things.'[34] They appeared, starting with Romans, between 1517 and 1524, in handy little volumes, later in slightly revised and collected editions. The *Paraphrases* were the works which were closest to Erasmus' heart; in the midst of all the unrest and strife working on them calmed his unease and gave his conscience rest.[35] They were repeatedly reissued, and from 1521 until well into the seventeenth century were translated into a variety of vernaculars. The work was particularly popular in the Netherlands, and in England it was prescribed by law in 1547 that every parish church and every clergyman who did not possess a doctor's degree were to be in possession of a copy of the translation. Nor was Erasmus untrue to his aims in these works. Starting from the text of the Bible, he mentions, as it were in passing, all kinds of abuses in the church. An eloquent example is offered by his explanation of Matthew 16:19, where Christ gives Peter the keys of heaven, 'for it is fitting that he is the foremost in authority who is foremost in his witness of faith and in love.' Thus Erasmus wished to explain the Scriptures, unconstrained, and not squeezed into the harness of doctrinal decisions and tradition.

Between 1515 and 1533 Erasmus wrote commentaries on eleven psalms.[36] On the one hand they offer few surprises: we find in them the same criticism, the same ideals, that we meet in his better-known works. Two of them go directly into the questions of the day: the exegesis of Psalm 28 (29) of 1530 into the burning question of the war against the Turks, that of 1533 on Psalm 83 (84) the question whether the breakup of Christendom into several churches could still be averted. Both these commentaries were often reprinted. It is however striking that Erasmus explicitly proceeded from the fourfold sense of Scripture, and, following Origen's example, worked out the allegorical and tropological senses in particular detail. In the *Paraphrases* he also used this method, but much more cautiously and discreetly.

What was Erasmus aiming at in the *Paraphrases* and the commentaries on the psalms? It becomes clear if one remembers the objections he urged against many sermons he had heard: much parade of pseudo-learning, but no food for the heart. It was Erasmus' aim to contribute, through this exposition of the Bible, to the renewal of preaching and devotional literature. Let us look at Psalm 2 as an example. Erasmus briefly sets out the main content of this psalm; it is not just a piece of the history of the gospel, but the full story of the redemption of the human race, because Christ has become man, overcome the heathens and philosophers, and so on.[37] Then he shows, *in extenso*, where all this is found in the psalm. It is facile to say that such an exegesis is displaying imagination rather than giving an introduction to the psalm. It was Erasmus' goal to show the preachers of his day how they could make use of passages from the Old Testament in preaching to the people. The same also applies to the New Testament, but there historical exegesis was much more important, because it had greater practical use.

Erasmus worked on various levels. In his New Testament and the editions of the Fathers of the church, he supplied the scholar with the material to gain a deeper knowledge of the bible and theology. In the commentaries on the Psalms he offered preachers an example of how to make fruitful use of them. In the *Paraphrases* he showed both cultivated and simple folk the way to Christ.

In conclusion we can say that the positive achievement of Erasmus in the field of the study of the Bible and the Fathers can only be evaluated correctly against the background of his objections to the customary theology. Erasmus was convinced that theology was a unit. In his time, that unity had been breached; the study of the Bible, systematic theology, and devotional reading had become separate from one another, and that in itself was wrong. Moreover, he had grave misgivings about the way in which all three genres were practised.

Erasmus objected that the method of studying the Bible was totally antiquated. It stressed the study of the literal sense – but how was this possible if its practitioners did not know Greek? How was this work meaningful for modern people if its practitioners were not even skilled in Latin, swore by the Vulgate, and rejected a new translation? People have changed, explained Erasmus in the *Capita argumentorum*: they laugh if the deacon mispronounces Latin words in the liturgy. It would contribute to the dissemination of the gospel if it were translated into a purer idiom, so far as that is possible.[38] Why did exegetes not use the great ancient expounders of the Scriptures, and why did they not go back to the sources?

Erasmus' objections to the systematic theologians, that is, the scholastics, were even greater. He accused them of a use of language that would not do, and that created unnecessary obstacles to understanding. He was even more averse, if possible, to their whole method of work. The true old theology started with the Scriptures and remained with the Scriptures. The scholastic theologians posed questions that had nothing to do with the Bible and were completely absurd. Against this criticism it has been objected that Erasmus in various places expresses his admiration for the work of the great masters. Christian Dolfen in particular has followed this line in a well-documented book. He has rightly observed that Erasmus spoke in terms of praise about Peter Lombard and Thomas Aquinas; he would not have wished to see scholasticism disappear entirely. But Erasmus used the concepts of the scholastics only when he was forced to, in warding off attacks from scholastic theologians or from Luther. The same criticism Erasmus made of the scholastics' use of language can be applied to their method. The younger men had not seen that times had changed, that they were *epigonoi* who had nothing to say to a contemporary audience. 'If they have given a proof of their capacity in this nonsense, they become *baccalaurei*, without ever having read the Gospels or the Epistles of Paul,' he says in the *Ratio*.[39]

Erasmus' criticism was directed against devotional literature and sermons as well. In the *Enchiridion* he tried to do something for the better-educated people of his age, but, he says in the *Ratio*, he had often felt ashamed when listening to a sermon. 'I see how simple people, who hang open-mouthed on the lips of the preacher, yearn for food for the soul, eager to learn how they can go home better people. And then such a pseudo-theologian ... shows off his knowledge of some stupid and complicated subject from Duns

Scotus or Ockham. He shows off what he has learned at the Sorbonne, and with that showing off he is chasing popular favour.'[40] Thus theology also fails to fulfil its mission in the area of pastoral practice.

What was to be done to remedy this? In the answer to this question we come to the ultimate goal Erasmus set himself. Briefly and programmatically expressed: Erasmus strove to unite *bonae litterae* and *sacrae litterae. Bonae litterae* included the study of ancient civilization and the way of life connected with it. Only the man who immersed himself in the world of the classics became a genuinely cultivated person. Theology, however, had degenerated; its practitioners spoke a secret language about unreal questions. The result was that the modern human being was alienated from the Christian faith. In the circle of the humanists, scholastic theology was looked down on and disparaged: whoever loved true culture must turn aside from theology. Erasmus wanted to bridge this gulf. He wanted to reunite Christianity and culture, so that a cultured person could also be a Christian with a good conscience and not live in two distinct worlds.

The first steps towards a restoration of this unity would be taken at the level of technique. Philology must put itself at the service of theology. But just as, for Erasmus, commitment to *bonae litterae* meant more than mastering a technique, so the unification of *bonae litterae* and *sacrae litterae* required more than the application of a method. The problem went deeper than that. Erasmus started from the unity of humanity. God did not conceal himself from previous generations, but his spirit was working long before Christ's coming to earth. We have gone into the questions which this raises.[41] Here it is enough to recognize that this renewal of an idea which appears as early as the oldest Christian theology formed the basis of Erasmus' ideal of the unity of all culture. Because God had given, in the classics, a moral and an intellectual preparation for the full revelation in Christ, classical culture was fully usable. But it ought to be used in theology also. Erasmus thus shifted the emphasis to the *sacrae litterae.* The study of classical literature was like a school for recruits: one must concern oneself with it as a passer-by and not as a resident. Using an image borrowed from Augustine, Erasmus considered it as the treasures of Egypt with which the tabernacle was adorned.[42]

In concrete terms this means that Erasmus wanted to put the philological methods developed in humanism at the service of biblical scholarship and of theology in general. Opponents represented him scornfully as no more than a teacher of grammar, and Erasmus adopted this name.[43] He was convinced that he was rendering an important service to Christianity. In the *Capita argumentorum* there is a remarkable passage in which he tackles his opponents' argument that the Greek of the New Testament was not perfect and that consequently the Latin translation did not need to be couched in polished Latin. Erasmus admits the first point, but argues that this is no reason to be satisfied with bad Latin. As with the episcopal robes of then and now, 'in every respect the lustre of the church has increased.' Then the apostles spoke a language that was understood by the lettered and the unlettered, just as Christ too spoke the vernacular, Aramaic. Must we therefore babble in childish language? No, we must avail ourselves of the language that is common to all those who understand Latin. If the aim is to reach the greatest number of readers, the Bible must be translated into French or German, but not into a Latin that is so bad that it is understood neither by the cultivated nor by the uneducated.[44] The educated reader needs a translation and exposition such as those available for works of classical antiquity. Biblical scholarship is linguistic scholarship, to summarize it in five words.

Let us think back to the quotation with which this chapter began. Clearly philological method is far more than an auxiliary technique in biblical exegesis. Living spring water compared to the troubled water of stagnant pools: the return to the sources – a good humanistic phrase – also becomes a return to the 'heavenly word which once came down to us from the heart of the Father.' It is also a return to the old theology. Erasmus' ideal was that 'the *bonae litterae* preach ... the honour of Christ the Lord and of our God.'[45] This coupling of classic culture and theology was what Erasmus found in the Fathers of the church. The old theology was the ideal, a golden age by comparison with the theology of recent times. 'It is an old idea, which they [his opponents in Paris] are hissing at as new, that the study of theology is allied to the knowledge of languages and of polite literature.'[46] Here is the origin of the patristic studies that occupied such a great part of Erasmus' life. It was not merely historical interest which drove him to undertake them. Rather it was the conviction that in these old masters, the synthesis the world needed was to be found. In the *Ratio* Erasmus says: 'Just compare them with each other, theologians like Origen, Basil, Chrysostom, and Jerome on the one hand and the modern theologians on the other. There, a golden stream, here scanty little trickles far removed from the fountainhead; there a brilliant garden, here thorns and thistles.'[47]

From the above it will have become clear that Erasmus also had in mind those people who did not themselves read these writings, but longed for the Bible no less than the learned. In one of the introductory writings to the New Testament we read an ardent plea for translations into the vernaculars: 'I would wish that all women read the gospel and the Epistles of Paul. If only they were translated into all human tongues, so that not only the Scots and the Irish but also the Turks and the Saracens could read and study them ... If only the peasant sang something from them at the plough, the weaver recited something to the measure of the shuttle, the traveller dispelled the tedium of the journey with such stories!'[48] Erasmus put forward a similar argument in another place, when in the printing of the *Paraphrase on Matthew* in 1522 a couple of leaves of the first quire turned out to be blank. That was impossible; the buyer would not pay for blank paper, and so Erasmus wrote a hasty piece, in which we find the remark: 'Often it is those who are wholly unimportant for the world who count most to Christ, and those whom the world thinks most learned are ignorant in the eyes of Christ.'[49]

NINE

In the Circle of
the Biblical Humanists

꙰

Once again we pick up the thread of Erasmus' life. What filled his days in the good years between 1514 and the beginning of 1519? We are extremely well informed: many letters have been preserved. In perusing them we must bear in mind that some were explicitly intended for publication and others were not.

The first thing to consider is his immediate environment. Between August 1514 and May 1516, Erasmus lived in Basel, apart from a four months' journey to the Netherlands and England in the early summer of 1515. From May 1516 he lived in the southern Netherlands, from 1517 in the university city of Louvain. In those years he made a journey to England in the summer of 1516 and one to Basel in the summer of 1518. In 1516 he was still complaining of his 'accursed penury,'[1] but at the same time he wrote of expensive gifts, a goblet and horses,[2] and in 1518 he boasted of invitations to Spain, France, various German cities, and England, invitations that came from three kings, two dukes, and nine princes of the church.[3] He had achieved something. Not only the numerous marks of honour bear witness to that, but even more the New Testament, the 'monument to bear witness to posterity that I existed,'[4] as Erasmus proudly remarked at the end of a letter in which he related how ill he had been on the journey from Basel to Louvain in 1518. He had probably just recovered from an attack of the plague, and, having turned fifty, felt himself an old man, for it was an age which few attained;[5] 'old age ... knocks at my door and indeed now presses close upon me.'[6]

The years he spent in Basel were the happiest of Erasmus' life.

Looking back on them he recalled: 'I can hardly say how much I like this Basel climate and the kind of people who live there; nothing could be more friendly or more genuine.'[7] He was thinking above all of Bishop Christoph von Utenheim, a cultivated and pious man, who had read the *Enchiridion* with care.[8] Shortly after his arrival in Basel, Erasmus listed the people he had already met.[9] In the first place he named Beatus Rhenanus, from Sélestat, who had already been living for some years in Basel and was to become Erasmus' most intimate friend, his *alter ego*.[10] Rhenanus was a very talented philologist, but also a man who was to perform several disagreeable tasks for Erasmus and finally to write his obituary soon after his death, in the edition of Origen's works, and in more detail in 1540 in the collected works of Erasmus himself. Then there was Gerardus Listrius, a fellow countryman of Erasmus, who was to write the notes for the *Praise of Folly*; Bruno Amerbach, son of the famous Basel printer Johann Amerbach and himself an outstanding philologist; Johann Froben, who continued the tradition of Johann Amerbach after the latter's death; and Froben's father-in-law, Wolfgang Lachner, associated with his son-in-law as publisher and bookseller. A few days after Erasmus' arrival the university officially welcomed him at a banquet. Erasmus referred by name to the rector, Ludwig Baer, whom he praised highly. In the twenties Baer was to read and criticize Erasmus' theological publications, such as *De esu carnium*, on the eating of meat during fasts, and *De libero arbitrio* (*The Free Will*), before Erasmus published them. In this circle Erasmus was to live from 1514 to 1516 and again from 1521 to 1529, and of this circle, the Basel humanists, he soon became the centre. Its members also included Henricus Loriti Glareanus, poet laureate, musicologist, and historian; Wolfgang Faber Capito and Caspar Hedio, both theologians, who at a later date were to become leaders of the Reformation in Strasbourg; Johannes Oecolampadius, later the reformer of Basel; and several others. They formed a loose group, the *sodalitas basiliensis*, devoted to study, but also to pleasure and gossip.

There were differences within this group, but it is true to say of many of them that they wanted to serve theology by the new philological methods. For the Amerbachs, for example, that is very clear. From the 1470s Johann Amerbach senior had, besides many other works, published the Fathers of the church in sound editions and handsomely produced folios. The edition of Ambrose that appeared from his press in 1492 had a typical foreword, in which his interest was clearly expressed. He gave his three sons a good education in the three languages.[11] Two of them, Bruno and Basilius, took on much of the responsibility for Erasmus' edition of Jerome, and in the foreword they wrote for the fifth volume, they expressed the ideal soberly and eloquently: 'Our father hoped that, if this old theology were to be revived, that hair-splitting tribe of sophists and that banal sort of theologians would have less to say, and we should much rather have genuine and true Christians. For study changes the reader, and we develop in the image of the authors whom we read daily.'[12] No wonder Erasmus at once felt entirely at home in this circle and that in turn he was very soon accepted and even honoured as its central figure. 'Erasmus is not to be measured by normal yardsticks. He has in a certain sense gone beyond the human level,' Beatus Rhenanus asserted in all serious-ness.[13] Not everyone went so far. But what are we to think of Huldrych Zwingli, the pastor of Glarus? Glareanus introduced him to Erasmus, and, after being received by the humanist, Zwingli was so enraptured that he wrote a letter of thanks casting himself at Erasmus' feet and assured him that even a rejection would be a mark of his favour.[14] It was in this atmosphere that Erasmus lived for two years.

Of course he had contacts beyond Basel as well. Some of these, as we have seen, were with important people: princes, bishops, and prelates. These contacts prove that Erasmus had become a celebrity. Then there were connections of another kind, with kindred spirits elsewhere. In these years there emerged what some writers have called an Erasmian movement, a network of relationships among scholars who had similar ideas, a group of which Erasmus was the focus. Various names have been given to it: Erasmianism, German humanism, Christian humanism. I myself prefer the term 'biblical humanism,' introduced by the Dutch church historian Johannes Lindeboom, because it indicates exactly what united those in-volved.[15] They set in train a process of renewal that was orientated towards the Bible and founded on the Bible. They wanted to make the achievements of modern philological methods, as the humanists had applied them to the study of classical texts for more than a century, bear fruit for the understanding of the Bible and the Fathers, and in so doing to revive theology. For this purpose they dismissed scholastic theology as wholly antiquated and sterile, preferring to go back to the sources, and set themselves the goal of renewing not only theology but the church also. The previous chapters have described Erasmus' share in the realization of these ideals, and now his place in the movement as a whole deserves attention. It should be remembered that the differences within it were considerable, that every trace of organization was absent, and that it involved people who discovered something of their own idealism in others. In this context, the question is: how did Erasmus behave towards people who developed ideas similar to his own?

In these years passions were aroused above all by the attack on Johann Reuchlin launched by the Cologne Dominicans and their tool, the converted Jew Johann Pfefferkorn. Reuchlin was one of the first Christians to know Hebrew. When Pfefferkorn called for the books of the Jews to be burned, in order to convert them, Reuchlin had, when asked, advised against it. This earned him the charge of heresy, an accusation that was fought out right up to Rome. At certain moments the conflict between Reuchlin and the Cologne theologians developed into a battle for and against the new studies. Ulrich von Hutten above all saw the attacks on Reuchlin in this light, and called on the humanists to take Reuchlin under their protection. The spear of Erasmus – he meant his pen – was worth more than six hundred anathemas from 'that Florentine,' Pope Leo x, who was a scion of the Florentine house of the Medici.[16] Erasmus took Reuchlin's part. In 1515 he expressly took him into his protection with the most influential cardinals of the curia, and the letters in which he did so were immediately published.[17] Yet he also admonished the genuine partisans of Reuchlin to observe moderation. He had little sympathy with the study of Hebrew writings outside the Old Testament, finding it a waste of time for Christians, and not without danger: Christianity was far above Judaism.[18] It was a negative interest that bound him to Reuchlin. If the latter were to be condemned, the sophists, as the victors, would make all the more frenzied efforts to strike at their other opponents, himself included.

In 1515 the first part of the *Epistolae obscurorum virorum* (*Letters of*

Obscure Men) appeared. A second part followed in 1517. These fictitious letters, written in a grotesque dog-Latin, are almost all addressed to one of the Cologne theologians. In them his friends and pupils complain of the mockery that has befallen them and make their plans for revenge; in short they are pilloried in all their contemptible absurdity. Erasmus had seen one of the letters before publication, and had amused himself over it with friends, until he knew it by heart and later recited it in Basel. When the first part was published Erasmus was greatly entertained, but deprecated this method of polemic.[19] On the publication of the second part he wrote a sharp letter of rebuke to Cologne,[20] partly because he himself had now been named: 'What a lot of harm they do, not only to themselves, but to everyone who has the cause of true learning at heart.' To Erasmus' dismay, this letter was published by the Cologne inquisitors as early as March 1518 – as if Erasmus wished to defend their cause! Even worse, Erasmus was also regarded at the time as the author of the *Epistolae obscurorum virorum*.[21]

At that moment Erasmus was already deeply involved in the controversy over Reuchlin. In 1517 Pfefferkorn had called Erasmus a runaway monk, a friend of the Jews, and one of the devil's captives in his *Streitbüchlein*, an attack on Reuchlin. Erasmus reacted at once, had Pfefferkorn's work translated into Latin, and sent it with an accompanying letter to his English patrons. He also sent six letters to the imperial court and to Cologne urging that measures should be taken against Pfefferkorn and the Cologne Dominicans: the bishops, the emperor, and the Cologne magistrates should impose silence on them.

These letters do Erasmus no honour. Pfefferkorn is depicted in them as 'a man utterly uneducated, of the most brazen impudence ... I would not cast the words "half a Jew" in his teeth if he did not behave like a Jew and a half ... Now for the first time he is playing the part of a real Jew, now that he has donned the mask of a Christian.'[22] These are the only truly anti-Semitic expressions we find in the oeuvre of Erasmus, but they are unequivocal. Erasmus' reaction when he felt himself threatened was to take over the insulting expressions Pfefferkorn had used of Reuchlin and turn them against Pfefferkorn. It is no coincidence that he never published these letters.

It is not known whether Erasmus had any success. In the spring of 1519 he was again publicly involved in the affair, this time thanks to the supporters of Reuchlin. They published a collection of letters from scholars to Reuchlin, which included five letters from Erasmus.[23] Erasmus cannot have been happy about this: he himself had not published these letters, nor did he do so later. His reaction followed in the autumn. At the last moment he inserted into a collection he had prepared of his own letters a detailed treatise addressed to Jacob of Hoogstraten, a papal inquisitor in three German provinces of the church who was very active in the Reuchlin question.[24] It is a long defence, which falls into two very distinct parts. First Erasmus, adopting the stance of an impartial judge, argues against Hoogstraten's attacks on Reuchlin. He himself, Erasmus says, had always advised Reuchlin and his supporters to be moderate. Reuchlin's friends had always defended him: he was peace-loving, the blame lay with his opponents. The same friends think very differently of Hoogstraten: some feel that he has been incited by others, others that he is eager for money and reputation. Erasmus had reserved judgment, but now, he says, he has read Hoogstraten's *Apologia*: 'May I tell you the effect it had on me? I speak with regret, but with perfect truth. I had had a higher opinion of you before I read you in your own defence.' He continues in this tone of proud and reserved good will. He will not pronounce on whether Reuchlin or Hoogstraten is right in the end: 'This task has not been entrusted to me, and if it were, I can imagine I should gladly refuse.' Then he suddenly changes his tone and gives Hoogstraten a furious scolding because he had dared, in his last work, to judge Erasmus' annotations on a passage of the New Testament heretical. Only at the end is the unfortunate inquisitor given the fatherly advice, in a somewhat milder tone of voice, to think of the dignity of his order, yes even of the order of theologians in general.

Erasmus' attitude in the affair was characteristic. He was pulled in two directions. He made it clear that he favoured Reuchlin, without identifying himself with him. Both sides sought publicity in letters and other writings. This mingling of detachment and involvement is entirely in harmony with Erasmus' character. It was also appropriate to the subject, which ultimately affected him only in its consequences, the defence of the *sacrae litterae*.

The situation was different in the case of the second conflict of these years, Erasmus' disagreement with Lefèvre d'Etaples, which burst out violently in 1516 and 1517. Among the French humanists, Lefèvre was an authority. He had published various works of Aristotle and had been working for ten years on the study of the Bible. In 1509 he had brought out his *Quincuplex Psalterium*. This was an edition of the Psalms in four old Latin versions and a revised Latin text composed by himself on the basis of the old translations, to which Lefèvre added a paraphrase of the Psalms and an exposition of difficult passages. In 1512 he had published a commentary on the Epistles of Paul, in which he had also printed his own Latin translation alongside the Vulgate. Though Erasmus knew him slightly, he was not a personal friend of Lefèvre, who was ten years his senior. He was even unaware that Lefèvre was working on the Epistles of Paul until the book appeared.[25] In both works Lefèvre had discussed in great detail the correct reading of Psalm 8:6. The customary version, *Minuisti eum paulominus ab angelis*, 'Thou [God] hast made him [man] a little lesser than the angels,' was in his opinion incorrect. For these words of the psalmist did not refer to man in general, but to the God-man Christ, of whom one might not say that he was lower than the angels. The Hebrew text read 'lesser than God.' The same was the case in Hebrews 2:7, where the words from Psalm 8 were cited and applied to Christ. Lefèvre, who started from the assumption that this Epistle was written by Paul, and originally in Hebrew, asserted that Paul also had written 'lesser than God,' and that only in the Greek translation had these words been altered to 'lesser than the angels,' as had also happened previously in the Greek translation of the Old Testament verse in Psalm 8. It seems to be a purely technical question of exegesis, but for Lefèvre it was much more than that. Christ was not less than the angels, even in his human nature, and he adjured his readers, 'by Jesus and his dear and blessed name,' to follow henceforth without fear in the liturgy the version he proposed.

He had not convinced Erasmus. In an annotation on Hebrews 2 in the first edition of his New Testament, the latter had dealt with Lefèvre's argument. In his opinion, Lefèvre's starting point was erroneous. The earthly Jesus did stand far below the Father, and below the angels; humiliated, hungry, thirsty, and finally crucified.

The whole difficulty was to be solved by translating the word *paulominus* not as 'a little' but as 'for a short time,' a translation that the Greek original text of Hebrews unquestionably allowed. The words 'a short time' then meant the short time Christ lived on earth. During that time, he stood beneath the angels.

Soon afterwards a new edition of Lefèvre's commentary on the Pauline Epistles appeared. He replied to Erasmus' argument in detail, and vehemently dismissed it as godless and insulting to both Christ and God. In so doing he turned a difference of opinion into an attack on Erasmus' orthodoxy. Erasmus' reaction was not long in coming. In August 1517 he issued a lengthy and brilliantly written apologia,[26] defending his orthodoxy and discussing the exegesis of Hebrews 2. Although he announced it as a friendly work,[27] the polemic in certain passages is deadly in its irony. The reactions show that the biblical humanists deeply regretted the controversy, which played into the hands of their adversaries. Lefèvre did not reply further.

The conflict was more than an academic dispute that had got out of hand, and it exposed far-reaching contradictions on two levels. In the first place, the two opponents had different images of Jesus. Lefèvre felt that it was godless to speak of Jesus' humiliation. He thought it was ridiculous for Erasmus to interpret the words of Psalm 21 (22):7, 'for I am a worm and not a man,' as an expression of Jesus about himself: that was the way the godless Jews spoke of Jesus. His Jesus was the exalted one. Erasmus saw him as the man of sorrows: 'We do not scorn him if we speak of his humiliation; his cross, his stripes, we honour with reverence; his mockery is our glory.'[28] He wished to recognize Lefèvre's image of Jesus as legitimate also, but thought that it anticipated the glory to come: 'And although Christ is admirable in both respects, could it perhaps be that his humility appeals to us more because admiration of his greatness concerns rather the life to come [the eternal glory]?'[29] Erasmus' own spirituality thus played an important role in his exegetical choice. Jesus was the crucified, on whom he had meditated in his *Enchiridion*, and whom he nowhere found so true to life as in the New Testament.

In the second place, there was a difference in the two men's approach to biblical study. Erasmus also started from the assumption that Psalm 8 spoke of Jesus, and his interpretation of this psalm was formed within a christological vision. Yet it is clear that in this debate he, unlike Lefèvre, was a philologist. He was willing to ask whether Psalm 8 always referred to Christ, and he did not think it a decisive argument that Paul thought so, asserting that Paul occasionally dealt in a curious way with the Old Testament. Was the Epistle to the Hebrews by Paul in any case?[30] Erasmus reproached Lefèvre with reasoning in the same way as had the adversaries of Reuchlin and those who attacked Lefèvre's own commentary on Paul.[31] In the field of exegesis we must be ready to learn from each other, dare to admit our errors, and not hurl accusations of godlessness.[32] Erasmus continues with an impressive summary of the errors into which Lefèvre had fallen. He had, so he rebukes Lefèvre, already pointed out several of these faults in his edition of the New Testament. Why had Lefèvre not deleted those things, which 'scholars will not read without laughter or irritation'?[33] After calling attention to a whole series of blunders, Erasmus delivers the coup de grace: 'If only you had refrained altogether from this field of translation and making annotations. It was, as I said before, not your métier. You were capable of greater things. This task, however humble it might be, demanded a knowledge of the two tongues. I need not say what capacities you have in this respect: your writings bear public witness to it.'[34] Not very friendly, but it hits the mark. This is the voice of a new way of dealing with the Bible, of exegesis. Sober craftsmanship stands in the foreground, in contrast to the old method of meditative contemplation, which characterized Lefèvre.

When Erasmus wrote this apologia he had been in the Netherlands again for just under a year. During 1517 he went to live in Louvain, at first with a friend, later in the College of the Lily, where he was to remain until the end of 1521. In the first year he felt himself increasingly at home in the academic milieu. He matriculated, and he sometimes took part in the activities of the university. Two things above all occupied him continually. The first was of course the New Testament, of which he was preparing a second edition. Besides that, Erasmus devoted a great deal of his time to organizing the teaching of the three languages at Louvain. Jérôme Busleyden, a member of the Great Council of Mechelen and a friend of Erasmus, had left large funds in his will to appoint three professors and to provide bursaries for eight students. It was a difficult matter to lay the money out well. At first the executors wanted to use the funds to expand one of the existing colleges of the university, on condition that the three tongues be taught there. The opposition of the faculty of letters frustrated this plan. Those involved then decided to fund a college that would be virtually independent of the university and to recruit teachers for it. Erasmus was intimately involved in this enterprise, especially in the search for teachers. His expectations were very high. The theologians, however, were afraid that these studies would impair the authority of theology. In his biography of Erasmus Beatus Rhenanus not unjustly compared the College of the Three Tongues, from which countless men had already come forth skilled in the three languages, to the Trojan horse.[35] The college took up much of Erasmus' energy in these years, and later too he continued to give advice from time to time.

These activities also helped to embitter the atmosphere during 1518. In the early months of 1519 the growing tension led to a few skirmishes between Erasmus and some of the theologians, not dangerous but annoying. A great stir was caused by an attack of the professor Jean Briart (Atensis), vice-chancellor of the university, on the occasion of the conferment of the degree of licentiate in theology on a Carmelite in February 1519. In his address Briart declared that it was heretical to praise marriage at the expense of celibacy. To all those present it was clear that these remarks were directed towards Erasmus, who in March 1518 had published an *Encomium matrimonii*, a eulogy of marriage, written more that twenty years earlier. In March another professor in the faculty of theology, Jacques Masson (Jacobus Latomus) published a *Dialogus* stoutly arguing that a knowledge of the three languages was not absolutely necessary for the theologian. He, like Briart, avoided mentioning Erasmus by name, pointing rather at the young German humanist Petrus Mosellanus, who had brought out an ardent defence of the study of languages in August 1518, a lecture delivered before the University of Leipzig. Yet a great deal of Masson's pamphlet was unmistakably aimed at Erasmus, and in particular at his *Ratio*, first published in autumn 1518. Meanwhile, the attacks of the English scholar Edward Lee on Erasmus' New Testament, which had begun earlier, grew more violent.

All this made Erasmus' position at Louvain more and more uncomfortable. Of course, he did not remain silent. He immediately published defences against Masson and Briart; the controversy with Lee did not reach its climax until the following year. In their content, these disputes are neither world-shaking nor on issues of principle. Erasmus had good grounds to claim, in his defence against Briart, that he did not reject celibacy absolutely. His clash with Masson was by no means a head-on confrontation, and it offered Erasmus a chance to clarify his statement that the true theologian incites to piety and is himself pious.[36] Both Masson's dialogue and Erasmus' reply seem at first sight to say the same thing: Masson too considered piety a prerequisite in the practice of theology. Yet there remains a difference. For Masson piety was an objective matter; it concerned a. state that a person reached, that is, orthodoxy, a particular religious doctrine. For Erasmus, piety was warmth, inner conviction, and this he felt was an indispensable prerequisite in theology: 'It appears to me, to say honestly what I think, untheological to speak of religion without feeling';[37] a theologian may not approach the Bible using his reason alone, he must 'feel, be deeply affected by what he reads in the divine Scriptures.'[38] These expressions are a necessary complement to the remarks Erasmus addressed to Lefèvre d'Etaples. Just as sober analysis is necessary, so too are the heart and ecstasy.

Yet what took place in Louvain was more than a succession of disagreeable but unconnected and trivial incidents. In this unedifying polemic we see the beginning of resistance to Erasmus and his method of practising theology. The enthusiasm of the years between 1514 and 1516 began to run into the sands of the opposition that Erasmus' onslaught on paralysis in theology and sterility in the church had provoked. The golden age was losing its lustre. Although Erasmus distinguished his work from that of Reuchlin, the same forces that had set themselves in motion against Reuchlin were now being roused against him.

It is in this context that the name of Luther appears. In Erasmus' first reference to him he remained anonymous. In March 1518 Erasmus reported to Thomas More, 'I send you Pace's book, the Conclusions on Papal Pardons, and the Proposals for a Crusade against the Turks.'[39] Erasmus disliked the first of these because his name was mentioned in it too frequently.[40] The third was an official advice, compiled by a broad commission in Rome chaired by the pope and issued in November 1517, proposing a war on the Turks with 80,000 men. In Erasmus' view the real aim of this scheme was not to launch a crusade but to drive the Spaniards out of Naples.[41] But he read Luther's Ninety-five Theses with approval: 'The Roman curia has abandoned any sense of shame. What could be more shameless than these constant indulgences?'[42] Luther's work was just one of the many ephemeral writings of those years.

TEN

The Luther Question

Luther had slipped into the scholarly world, one of many who were critical of the church and theology. He soon found supporters, especially in humanist circles, in Basel as elsewhere. In May 1518, when Erasmus travelled to Basel to see the second edition of the New Testament and a new impression of his *Enchiridion* through the press, it appeared to him that Luther's name was enjoying some notoriety. Interest in him was still unsuspecting; in Basel – and not only there – he was regarded as a kindred spirit. 'Luther pleases all the cultivated people in Zürich, just as the *Ratio* of Erasmus does,' was Zwingli's first remark on Luther.[1] In saying this, he was typical of the humanists: he named Luther in the same breath as Erasmus. In the early years it was the humanists above all who were interested in Luther, often seeing him as one of themselves.

At first sight it seems as if Erasmus shared this viewpoint. The earliest statement of his position with regard to Luther intended for a wide public is noteworthy. In 1518 the new edition of the *Enchiridion* appeared, with an important preface that was nothing less than a programme of reform for the church.[2] It includes a passage on the quarrels between Isaac and the Philistines over the wells dug by Isaac, which Erasmus applied to his own day. 'And if some Isaac or one of his household should dig and find a pure source, at once they are all protests and objections because they know this source will be an obstacle to their gains and block their ambitions, even though it makes for Christ's glory. It is not long before they throw earth into it and stop up the source by some corrupt interpretation, driving away the man with the spade, or at least so befoul the water with mud and filth that he who drinks from it gets more dirt and filth than liquid. They do not wish those who thirst after righteousness to drink from the crystal spring.' At the end Erasmus speaks even more clearly: 'And he who endures men who are all sham – cruel domineering men who teach not what makes for religion but what bolsters their own tyranny – displays the patience of a Christian only as long as the commands they issue make him only unhappy and not ungodly too. Otherwise, he will do better to meet them with the Apostle's answer on his lips: We ought to obey God rather than men.'[3] This was plain speaking, even without mentioning Luther by name.

But that is only half the story. Erasmus also addressed himself to Luther through Wolfgang Faber Capito, an early supporter of Luther and at this date still a disciple of Erasmus. In conversation he told Capito that he had a favourable opinion of the Ninety-five Theses, but that he was afraid the matter would end in disturbances.[4] Luther should imitate the apostles in their caution and above all take care not to insult the pope. It was his intention that Capito should pass this on to Luther, and so he did. Erasmus also took direct action. When he heard that Froben was considering publishing a number of Luther's works, he tried to dissuade him, but did not succeed.[5] In November Froben brought out a collection of 490 pages, including the most important works published by Luther to that time. The collection was very well received. According to Froben himself he had never before published a book that sold so well; it was exported to the Netherlands, England, Spain, and France. Erasmus, however, was annoyed that Froben had rejected his advice. From the Netherlands, where he had returned in September, he sent new warnings, this time to good effect. The collection was reprinted several times, but not by Froben.

Erasmus' attitude was not inconsistent. He approached the issue, like the Reuchlin affair, as a directly interested outsider. He thought the early works of Luther legitimate, although from the beginning he found something in them that was not to his taste. In terms of content, he agreed with Luther, but he found his attitude too sharp, too offensive: 'How I could wish that you always kept an escape route open, especially when you are attacked in discussions,' his spokesman Capito wrote to Luther.[6]

But could this attitude be maintained? On his return to Louvain, Erasmus found his difficulties increasing. In the spring of 1519 the charges against him were still rather vague, but gradually they hardened: he was accused of collaborating with Luther. It was asserted that Luther's doctrine was based on that of Erasmus, who was supposed to be the real driving force behind him; Luther's books were supposed to have been written by Erasmus. Erasmus spoke of 'most groundless suspicions,' which were not even taken seriously by his accusers themselves.[7] It was a turbulent year in the university city. Especially after the inquisitor Jacob of Hoogstraten arrived in Louvain with the condemnation of Luther by the University of Cologne in his pocket, the mood became highly charged. In November 1519 the University of Louvain also condemned several pronouncements of Luther. Then the enemies of Luther turned their fire on Erasmus. In the winter of 1519–20 his position grew almost impossible. He was loudly attacked in sermons, and there was even an informal instruction from the heads of the faculty of theology to set up an inquiry into Erasmus' books.[8]

Were these suspicions well-founded? The answer must be in the negative, but at the same time one must say that they were not entirely wide of the mark. Erasmus himself might see the differences between his efforts and those of Luther, but it is understandable that his adversaries were aware only of the similarities. Erasmus and Luther both set themselves against traditional theology, both called for a purified church, and both protested against abuses. Contact between them would have been natural. In fact there had been some contact, but it had remained rather distant. In April 1519, Erasmus had written to Luther's prince, Elector Frederick the Wise of Saxony, relating to him something of the uproar in Louvain, letting it appear between the lines that he did not regard Luther as a heretic. The letter ended in a call to protect Luther.[9] Luther himself, however, was demanding more by that time. In a gracious letter, written in a finely polished humanist Latin, he asked, 'And so, dear Erasmus, kindest of men, if you see no objection, accept this younger brother of yours in Christ.'[10] This was too much to ask. 'As for me,' Erasmus answered, 'I keep myself uncommitted, so far as I can, in hopes of being able to do more for the revival of the *bonae litterae*.'[11] He reported to Luther the storm raised by his books in

Brabant and his own position: he had always protested against a condemnation of Luther without a proper investigation of his works. He also gave Luther some unsolicited advice: polite modesty achieves more than intransigence; caution towards the pope and the princes was to be recommended. It was a generous letter, but a refusal. Luther held out a hand, but Erasmus rejected it; his task was elsewhere. The difference in tone between the letter to Elector Frederick and the letter to Luther is noticeable. Erasmus was convinced that Luther had to be protected, and he was willing to advocate this; if Luther were crushed low, his enemies would at once seize their opportunity to turn on the biblical humanists. On the other hand, Luther had to behave in such a way that he could be taken under protection.

Erasmus would have made it considerably easier for himself if he had declared himself against Luther at this time, and written against him. In spite of all the pressure exerted on him, he stubbornly refused to do so. On the first occasion on which Erasmus publicly set out his attitude to Luther, in a letter added to an edition of his very popular *Colloquies*,[12] he balanced on a razor's edge. 'I wish well to the good things in him, not the bad ... I am neither prosecuting him nor counsel for the defence nor judge ... Not but what I fail to see any cause of scandal in wishing him well quite apart from that inquiry. He is, as even his enemies allow, a man of high character; and he has a warmth of heart which although when exasperated, not without just cause, flared up too far, might yet, if diverted to other ends, prove a capital instrument in the cause of Christ.'[13] The passage is as complicated as it is subtly formulated: it is a refusal on both sides, to Luther himself and to Luther's enemies, a refusal that Erasmus could maintain as long as the dispute over Luther did not dominate all else. That was precisely what Erasmus wanted to avoid.

In the later months of 1520 this policy became impossible to maintain. As early as the summer Erasmus' unease had deepened. He received a visit from the headstrong Ulrich von Hutten, an adept of Luther as he had previously been of Reuchlin. Hutten wanted to resist Rome with fire and sword, and asked for Erasmus' cooperation.[14] From the other side, Erasmus received an emphatic warning from the imperial court not to meddle in the Luther affair.[15] Worst of all was the bull *Exsurge Domine*, in which forty-one errors of Luther were officially condemned. Erasmus found the bull completely foolish. Now it was clear what Luther's enemies were aiming at: 'One man's undoing would be a small matter; but if they are successful in this campaign, their insolence will be past all bearing. They will not rest until they have overthrown all knowledge of languages and all humane studies ... I am having nothing to do with this miserable business ... It grieves me to see the doctrine of the gospel so lost to sight.'[16]

Erasmus still attempted to ward off the evil. In September he wrote to the pope himself. On the one hand, he made a careful distinction in this letter between Luther's case and his own, which 'have nothing in common,'[17] and affirmed his own loyalty to Rome. At the end he stated his real goal. Firstly, Luther ought to have been refuted, and only then should he have been condemned. 'A free and generous mind loves to be taught but will not take compulsion.'[18] A bold step: after Luther had been threatened with the papal ban, Erasmus spoke in his praise and passed a damning verdict on the bull!

It was too late. At the end of September Girolamo Aleandro, formerly a fellow student of Erasmus and now papal nuncio, brought the bull to the Netherlands, and on 7 October the University of Louvain gave its adherence to it. On 8 October Luther's books were publicly burned. On 9 October the Carmelite Nicolaas Baechem (Egmondanus), who taught theology at the university, preached a sermon in St Peter's church, in which he first attacked Erasmus and then explained that Erasmus had shown great favour to Luther, and that Luther had fallen into his errors out of a 'passion for novelty.' 'Cleave to the old ways,' he adjured his hearers, 'shun that which is new, hold fast by the ancient gospel.' The implication was clear: Luther had borrowed his errors from Erasmus' 'New' Testament! A few days later the scene was repeated: 'These men too will come to the stake one day, unless they desist,' he exclaimed.[19] Erasmus was enraged and complained in vain to the rector of the university.[20] Perhaps it was at this time that an incident took place that Erasmus spoke of years afterwards. Immersed in a discussion with friends, he forgot to bare his head before the crucifix in the churchyard. The reaction of one theologian was 'I should dare to swear that he is a Lutheran.'[21]

For the first and last time Erasmus tried to influence the course of events around Luther through personal intervention. If Luther were to be condemned by the German princes as well as the pope, he would be lost beyond help, and their common enemies would triumph. During October Erasmus travelled to Germany where Charles v, after his coronation at Aachen, was to hold discussions with the German princes at Cologne. Since 1516 Erasmus had been a counsellor of Charles v, but without any special duties. Through a number of intermediaries, Erasmus circulated among the princes a plan that he had made jointly with a Dominican from Augsburg, Johannes Faber. It pleaded for arbitration. Charles v, Henry viii, and Louis ii of Hungary should each appoint some independent scholars from their own countries who would hold joint discussions with Luther and make a binding pronouncement. In this way, Erasmus thought, the pope could be gracious and Luther obedient.[22] In fact implementation of this plan would have meant that the pope would not only be gracious but also cede his powers to others. In Cologne, Erasmus had a personal interview with Frederick the Wise, at the latter's request. The elector had just received the papal request to burn Luther's books and to hand over Luther himself. Before he gave his answer, Frederick wanted to speak to Erasmus. A meeting was hastily arranged. The elector began the discussion by asking why Luther had been condemned. Erasmus gave the answer that was to become famous: Luther had sinned gravely, he had struck out against the bellies of the monks and the crown of the pope.[23] But there was more to it than this *bon mot*. Erasmus also deprecated the vehemence and the arrogance of Luther.[24] In this conversation and in his written advice to Frederick the Wise, formulated immediately afterwards, Erasmus pleaded for arbitration. In a lengthy talk with Aleandro, it became clear to Erasmus that such a plan was not to be realized.[25] The nuncio called on him finally to abandon his resistance to the bull. He would do better to come to Rome, and then he could count on a good bishop's see!

About three weeks later Erasmus was back in Louvain. The winter months were difficult. Nicolaas Baechem prayed for his conversion in a public lecture,[26] he was accused of causing the unrest among the people,[27] and the theologians made it clear to him that he could only avert suspicion from himself by writing against

Luther.[28] Yet all this could not make him change. The crisis proper
came when he read Luther's *De captivitate babylonica* (*On the
Babylonian Captivity of the Church*) in which Luther repudiated four of
the seven sacraments and a church that used the sacraments to
tyrannize over people and their consciences. This book was a frontal
attack on Rome, and it made any form of arbitration impossible.
Luther himself had frustrated any attempt to restrain him, as
Erasmus repeatedly asserted.[29] While he had originally wished to
attend the Diet of Worms, at which Luther's fate was to be decided,
Erasmus now excused himself, for it had all become pointless.
Luther's influence remained: 'No one would believe how widely he
has made his way into the minds of many nationalities, and how
deeply he has taken root through his books, which are circulating in
all directions and in every language.'[30] He was, however, lost to
Christianity; he did not want to be saved, and through his behaviour
he had made every attempt at reform suspect.

Where did Erasmus stand at this moment? We can find a clear
statement of his position in a letter, which he never published
himself, to Richard Pace, an English humanist and diplomat whom
he had known for more than ten years:

> The spirit in which he has written I find quite astonishing; at
> the very least he has laid a heavy burden of public hostility on
> all lovers of the humanities. Much of his teaching, many of his
> denunciations are admirable, if only he had not spoilt his good
> qualities with intolerable defects. Even had all he wrote been
> religious, mine was never the spirit to risk my life for the truth.
> Not everyone has the strength needed for martyrdom. I fear
> that, if strife were to break out, I shall behave like Peter. When
> popes and emperors make the right decisions I follow, which
> is godly; if they decide wrongly I tolerate them, which is safe. I
> believe that even for men of good will this is legitimate, if there
> is no hope of better things.[31]

These are the words with which Erasmus has given the greatest
offence. They are indeed typical, not as proof of his cowardice, but
rather as an example of an unusually honest self-analysis. Erasmus'
words are also in tune with his deeds. In the summer of 1521 he

refused to write against Luther when he again received an urgent call from Rome to do so. He later stated his reason frankly: Luther was a necessary evil, the best that was possible at this moment.[32]

In the later part of the year Erasmus' position in the Netherlands grew more and more difficult. The atmosphere was threatening. In December the prior of the Augustinian monastery at Antwerp, Jacob Proost, the man of whom Erasmus had written that he was almost the only one to preach Christ and neither human fables nor his own profit, was to be arrested.[33] In February the town clerk of Antwerp, Cornelius Grapheus, would suffer the same fate. Erasmus could remain unharmed, but on the condition that he allowed himself to be enlisted in the battle against heresy. That could mean a literary attack on Luther, which is what Erasmus initially named as the task allotted to him.[34] Later he wrote frankly that he must either leave or do the hangman's work.[35] This does not sound improbable. He had to remove himself from this environment in order to regain his independence. At the end of October 1521 he left for Basel. There he was to stay until 1529.

Erasmus' departure from the Netherlands is almost symbolic of the failure of his attempts to have the Luther question handled in a proper way. In the first years he had tried to calm the monks and theologians who were fulminating against Luther. When this failed, in late 1520, he had hoped to effect a reconciliation between Luther and Rome through the princes. That too came to nothing.[36] Only one course was left: to wait until a better opportunity presented itself. Basel, still quiet, offered the chance to play the role of Gamaliel. The expression is Erasmus' own: just as that scribe gave the advice not to persecute the first Christians but to wait until time should tell whether God was on their side, so Erasmus advised with regard to Luther.[37]

A year later the calm before the storm was over. In the mean time Pope Leo x had died and was succeeded, surprisingly, by Adrian vi, the only Dutchman ever to become pope and a good scholastic theologian, not unfavourably inclined towards Erasmus. As early as Adrian's enthronement in August 1522 Erasmus had sought contact. Towards the end of 1522 he wrote again, this time in very concrete terms: 'The world looks to you alone to restore calm to human affairs. If your Holiness instructs me, I will make so bold as to give you in a secret letter my own proposal, if not prudent, at least loyal, for putting an end to this evil in such a way that it will not easily sprout again. Not much is gained by suppressing it by brute force in such a way that it soon breaks out again in more perilous form, like the scar of a wound that has not healed.'[38] This letter and the pope's reply to an earlier, noncommittal letter from Erasmus crossed each other. The pope's letter was undoubtedly honourable to Erasmus. It was also clear. The pope saw a twofold task before Erasmus. The most important was to write against Luther; in this way he could free himself of every suspicion, contribute to peace in Christendom, and convert the heretics: 'Can you then refuse to sharpen the weapon of your pen against the madness of these men, whom it is clear that God has already driven out from before his face ...? Arise therefore to bring aid to God's cause, and employ your eminent intellectual gifts to his glory, as you have done down to this day.'[39] A second task was to come to Rome. Some time later Erasmus also received an answer to his second letter:[40] he could give advice, and he must come to Rome. The latter was what Erasmus was unwilling to do in any event. It would have deprived him of all his freedom of action. He gave his advice in a letter that he did not publish until 1529, and even then only in part.[41] He recommended a general amnesty, some limits on the freedom of the press, and real reforms. All this sounds well, but what might perhaps have had some chance of success in 1519 or even in 1520 was no more than a pipedream by 1523. An amnesty would mean setting aside the papal bulls and the imperial edicts; the printing press was no longer to be bridled; and, so far as reforms were concerned, Erasmus' published letter broke off at the very point where it became concrete – or did not do so. He received no reply, and from this he deduced that Adrian VI had other plans.

Erasmus did not confine himself to these contacts with the pope. In various works of the years 1522 and 1523 he pleaded for moderation, restraint in the desire to fix everything in binding dogmas of the faith, and mutual tolerance. His voice was too soft. Perhaps one should say rather that his ideal was too indefinite, it reckoned too little with an age in which sharp lines were being drawn to have any chance of prevailing. What had seemed revolutionary only a short time earlier had now been overtaken by events. His diagnosis was correct in many respects, but the proposed cure could no longer work. We find the diagnosis in three sentences from a letter of March 1523 to Georgius Spalatinus and through him to the elector Frederick the Wise: 'I am not worried about Luther, but two things concern me greatly. If Luther were to be overthrown, no god and no man would ever again be able to deal with the monks. And second, Luther cannot be made away with without the loss at the same time of a great deal of evangelical purity.'[42] It is worth noting that Erasmus put out feelers to the Lutheran movement in this letter, when for two years there had been no contact whatever. But the content is more important. Erasmus expressed in precise terms the reasons for his obstinate adherence to a policy of reconciliation. If Luther went under, every attempt at reform was doomed.

The contact Erasmus wished for did not materialize. Luther's answer – if one wishes to describe it as such – was a letter to Oecolampadius, once one of the Basel biblical humanists and now the head of the Reformation party in the city, in June 1523. Luther spoke very negatively of Erasmus: he hoped that Erasmus would give up his work on the New Testament; like Moses he would die in the fields of Moab, and not bring the people into the promised land.[43] Naturally the letter soon found its way to Erasmus.[44]

The final breach came about in the summer of 1523 through the intervention of Ulrich von Hutten. He had been in Basel in December and January, reduced to penury after the total failure of his war against the curia, and seriously ill. Although Hutten was insistent in his wish to speak to Erasmus, the latter stubbornly refused to see him. He feared that receiving such a compromising guest would expose him to great difficulty from those who were already quite convinced that he was a Lutheran. For Hutten, the rejection was symbolic. Just as Erasmus now showed him the door, so he had always turned aside from the losers and gone over to the winners. In this mood Hutten wrote his *Expostulatio* (*Complaint*), published at Strasbourg in June or July. The strength of Hutten's conviction gives his pamphlet its great persuasive force. He discusses Erasmus' attitude to Reuchlin, Hoogstraten, the Louvain theologians, Aleandro, the pope, and Luther, and in each case he comes to the same conclusion: Erasmus had intrigued and dissembled, he was untrustworthy and ready to go along with the victorious party. That is his picture of Erasmus: a great mind, but no character; Erasmus knew the truth, but knowingly and deliberately opposed it out of cowardice and weakness.

Erasmus was beside himself and spoke of 'inhumanity, shamelessness, bragging, and poison.'[45] His *Spongia* (*The Sponge*)[46] appeared at the beginning of September, a few days after Hutten had died (an unfortunate coincidence of circumstances, since it made Erasmus seem to want to fight a dead man).[47] He followed Hutten's pamphlet point by point, but devoted more than half of the work to refuting the charge that he had originally been for Luther and had now taken the part of his opponents. He explained that he wanted to be himself, and not to be enrolled against his will among supporters or opponents: 'In so many letters, in so many writings, in so many declarations, I continually proclaim at the top of my voice that I do not wish to get involved with either party.'[48] He wanted to carry out his own life work, to promote good literature and to renew pure theology, whether Luther agreed with it or not.[49] He had always worked to achieve one goal: 'Steadfastness is not always saying the same thing, but always having the same goal before your eyes.'[50] At the end he called on Christians to live in harmony even when they differed in opinion. Disputes and exchanges of insults on the one hand, bulls and the stake on the other, achieved nothing.

Erasmus knew that it was no longer any use. His position between the parties had become untenable. Hutten had made it impossible. Yet he continued to hesitate: should he turn against Luther in print? At the beginning of September he promised the king of England that he would,[51] and two months later he first mentioned his theme, freedom of the will.[52] In February 1524 a first draft was ready.[53] But publication was to be delayed until September – apparently not all the hesitation had been overcome. In May he received a haughty and provocative letter from Luther. Clearly, Luther wrote, it was beyond Erasmus' powers to place himself resolutely on his, Luther's side. If he was weak and of limited gifts, then he should at least refrain from attacking Luther and remain a spectator in the drama. Luther promised that in that case he too would not attack Erasmus.[54] Publication had now become unavoidable. In September 1524 *De libero arbitrio* (*The Free Will*) appeared simultaneously in Basel and Antwerp.

In this account of Erasmus' relationship with Luther nothing has been said so far about his judgment of Luther's opinions. Has the most important aspect of the conflict between them, then, been ignored? Luther might formulate the question in this way, but Erasmus would not. From 1519 Luther appears on virtually every page of Erasmus' correspondence – his life in these years was to a great extent determined by Luther – and yet there are only sporadic references in the letters to Luther's doctrines. Erasmus mentions a doctrinal statement of Luther's for the first time in March 1521: 'Where do I suggest that whatever we do is sin?'[55] The thesis that even the best works of men are sins was fundamental for Luther. Erasmus, however, did not take it seriously. He wrote rather ironically of the violent attack on 'some unimportant matters,'[56] and then this statement follows as an example.

The Lutherans saw things differently. At the beginning of 1522 Erasmus knew that the Lutherans had branded some expressions from his paraphrase on Romans 9 as Pelagian.[57] For true followers of Luther, this was the most serious accusation possible, since it meant that Erasmus acknowledged the possibility that man could accept or reject God's grace of his own free will. This put Erasmus in company with almost all the teachers of the Middle Ages, whose great fault, from the Lutheran point of view, had been that they granted man a certain autonomy in his relationship to God, allowing him a possibility of choice. The charge did not come out of the blue. As early as 1516 Luther had approached Erasmus, via Georgius Spalatinus, with some comments on his exegesis of Paul's letters in the *Annotations* on the New Testament. Erasmus had denied that Romans 5:12 was concerned with original sin, and he had explained the expression 'justification by the law' or 'justification by works,' which Paul in Romans and Galatians had opposed to 'justification by faith,' as the justification man thinks he has on the basis of his observance of the ceremonies prescribed in the law of the Old Testament.[58] This explanation of course is entirely consistent with Erasmus' views. Just as Paul at that time remonstrated against the Jews and some Christians who expected to be saved because they obeyed the law of God, so Erasmus attacked his contemporaries who put the ceremonial, the external, in the foreground.[59] Such a view was an abomination to Luther. In his opinion, Paul in these passages was also directing his attack at those people who tried to fulfil the Ten Commandments in their loyalty to the law, in order thus to win salvation. It is clear that Luther's exegesis of this central part of Paul's letters is directly related to his pronouncement that everything that man does is sin. Even the best of human works, if faith is lacking in their performance, have nothing to do with true righteousness before God. Only if God has justified us in his grace can we perform good works in the true sense of the word.

It is already clear from these observations that there is scarcely any common ground in these two ways of thinking. What was a central tenet of the faith for Luther Erasmus thought 'unimportant,' and elsewhere he speaks of a paradox, a deliberately too acutely formulated statement, which must certainly not be taken literally.[60] Nor did he take the accusation of Pelagianism entirely seriously. He consulted several theologians about it,[61] but found it a decisive argument, in the final analysis, that he had written these words of his *Paraphrase* in 1517 before he had ever heard of Luther.[62] As if Luther objected to an attack on himself, and was not vehemently criticizing a line of thought!

Only in 1523 did Erasmus make a more detailed statement about the freedom of the will. Even if it were true that there was no freedom of the will whatever, he would not wish to proclaim that baldly and openly to the people. Ultimately these were philosophical questions, already raised before Christ, about an 'impenetrable abyss.' He would be afraid to worsen the already excessive laxness of humanity by impressing it on them that everything depended on God.[63] Two months later he wrote to Zwingli on the 'patently absurd riddles' that Luther raised – and then he listed the core ideas of Luther's doctrine of sin and justification. He thought it pointless to quarrel over exactly what Luther meant by them.[64]

These are the only specific statements of Luther that Erasmus mentions. In view of the paradoxical and non-doctrinal character, as he saw it, of these utterances, he did not regard Luther as a heretic in spite of all the pronouncements of the church authorities. Precisely in March 1524, after he had already completed the first version of his work against Luther, Erasmus published in the new edition of his

Colloquies[65] a dialogue between a Lutheran and a Catholic. In the course of the dialogue it appears that the Lutheran adheres in every point to the Apostles' Creed and therefore considers himself orthodox.[66] The Catholic partner in the conversation agrees. Erasmus' intention is clear. He wanted to show that there was no difference between Luther and the church concerning the essence of Christian doctrine, and that Luther thus could not be considered a heretic.

Nevertheless Erasmus and Luther lived in different worlds of thought. Then why did Erasmus give himself so much trouble over Luther, and why did Erasmus' enemies so persistently link him with Luther? The answer is that the two men were closer to each other than they were willing or able to admit. Martin Bucer, in 1518 a Dominican monk at Heidelberg, later the great man of the Reformation in Strasbourg and one of the leading figures in the Reformation of southern Germany, is an eloquent witness. He was present at the Disputation of Heidelberg in 1518, at which Luther set forth his ideas clearly and precisely. A few days later, on 1 May, Bucer sent a report to Erasmus' friend Beatus Rhenanus. He was still completely under the spell of Luther, in a state of exaltation, so overpowering had he found him. And in the middle of his eulogy of Luther Bucer comments: 'He agrees in every respect with Erasmus. He even seems to excel him in this respect, that what Erasmus whispers, he teaches openly and frankly.'[67] Bucer said this before there was any talk of a heresy hunt, and he heard Luther expound all those theses which Erasmus was later to dismiss as paradoxes without understanding their import. He was not alone. Many of the biblical humanists were enthusiastic about Luther when he first became known to them, and in turn the first generation of leading theologians of the Reformation was made up predominantly of biblical humanists. In Luther's theology they found a deepening of ideas which they – wrongly – also felt were latent in Erasmus, or else they understood Luther's theology to be more superficial than it really was.

This implies that there was a common basis. Partly this lay in the method of biblical exegesis, less so for Luther himself than for his followers. The *Commentary on the Psalms* of Johann Bugenhagen, for example, is a typically humanistic piece of work, which attempts to offer an exegesis in the humanist style. The same is true of the commentaries of Philippus Melanchthon and even of his *Loci communes* (*Commonplaces*).[68] Thus Bucer probably found elements in Luther's handling of the Bible at Heidelberg that reminded him of Erasmus, whose work he knew well. The more important point of connection was criticism of all kinds of practices and abuses in the church. In the letter just cited, Bucer introduces Luther as the 'well-known scoffer at indulgences, towards which we have hitherto truly been not too little indulgent.'[69] It was under this banner that Luther won his early fame. In the following years too, criticism occupied an important place in his writings, reaching its climax in his *Commentary on Paul's Epistle to the Galatians*, which appeared in 1519. In this criticism Luther stood close to Erasmus and expressed in his own way, more sharply than Erasmus, objections that were widely held. This facet has been pushed into the background in recent Luther research, which has been interested chiefly in Luther's theology. Certainly his theology was in the long run more characteristic of Luther than his criticism of ecclesiastical customs and abuses. But for many of his contemporaries, including Erasmus, it was the other way around. This criticism was clear and placed Luther in a broad movement; his theology did not entail any separation since the offensive elements in it were regarded as paradoxes. Not that the biblical humanists agreed entirely with the criticism Luther voiced. As early as 1522 Erasmus spoke of people who were 'immoderately' or 'excessively' Lutheran and who posed the greatest danger to the Lutheran movement.[70] This was, of course, also a criticism of Luther himself, who Erasmus thought ought to observe moderation.

The extent to which Luther and Erasmus were felt to be exponents of a single movement in these years is evident from the output of the presses. In the years during which Luther's works were becoming popular and one printing followed another, the number of printings of Erasmus' works also reached its peak. Only in the second half of the 1520s did the number of editions of Erasmus' works begin to decrease; Erasmus was then outstripped by Luther.

ELEVEN

The Dispute on
the Freedom of the Will

🕉

'The die is cast, the work on the freedom of the will has appeared: believe me, a bold deed, as things now stand in Germany.'[1] In this way Erasmus announced to the king of England the publication of *The Free Will* (*De libero arbitrio*) in September 1524.[2] He was not proud of this work, and felt that he had been forced by the course of events to write against Luther: Luther himself had almost forced his hand, he had been under pressure from Rome and England, and in Basel an attack on Luther was expected of him. Was this work an attack? Immediately after its appearance Melanchthon praised Erasmus' moderation, without disguising the fact that there was a material difference of opinion. He thought it excellent that the question at issue should be studied in depth, and assured Erasmus of Luther's good will and of his intention to reply in the same spirit of reasonableness.[3]

Moderate or not, the treatise was an attack on Luther, even though Erasmus himself classified it as an apology, a self-defence.[4] He turned his fire directly on Luther's *Assertio* of 1521, but also disputed with Andreas Karlstadt[5] and Philippus Melanchthon,[6] sometimes playing Luther and Karlstadt against each other. He took care not to fall automatically into the camp of Luther's fervent adversaries. Unlike many, he did not choose a subject that would arouse strong emotions, such as Luther's onslaught on the structure of the church, its sacraments, or the position of the pope and the curia. He posed a much more academic question: to what extent has man free will in winning salvation? Must and can man do anything himself to attain salvation, or is he solely dependent on what God does? Erasmus prepared himself well for his task. He consulted a mass of patristic literature, above all Origen, Chrysostom, Ambrose, Jerome, and Augustine; of the medieval theologians especially Bernard of Clairvaux, Thomas Aquinas, and Duns Scotus; and of the modern authors Lorenzo Valla and in particular John Fisher's book against Luther.

True, in order to have a common basis for discussion with Luther, he wished to appeal exclusively to the Scriptures, but he needed the theologians mentioned to form and justify his own point of view and for the exegesis of biblical passages. Freedom of the will was without doubt a crucial issue, one on which Erasmus and Luther had taken widely divergent positions and on which Melanchthon had defended opinions that irritated Erasmus.[7] Nonetheless, it was an issue about which calm discussion was possible. After all the question went so deep that an unequivocal answer was not possible; in principle it would be better to be silent than to speak. At least that was what Erasmus thought.[8] For a year and a half he waited for an answer. When in February 1526 he finally received Luther's *The Bondage of the Will* (*De servo arbitrio*) of December 1525, it was clear at a glance that Luther's view of the matter was different. The statement 'that free will is naught,' the title of the able German translation that appeared as early as January 1526, was a matter of life and death for Luther. It became his most passionate work, and the moderation that Melanchthon had promised is nowhere to be seen. Luther gave vent to his anger all the more violently because applying himself to write had cost him considerable effort. He blamed Erasmus for this: Erasmus had not brought forward a single new argument, and his method of argument was so dispassionate that it had at first failed to inflame Luther.[9] Erasmus did not believe Luther had any grounds for complaint about this. On the contrary, he was annoyed by the treatment he received at Luther's hands: Luther depicted him not only as a good-for-nothing and a fool, but rebuked him for contempt of Holy Scripture, the destruction of religion, and enmity to Christianity.[10] In short Luther was a venomous beast.[11]

Within two weeks Erasmus' first answer was thought out, written, and printed. The first volume of the *Hyperaspistes*[12] (the word means 'shield-bearer' or 'defender'),[13] which answered the first part of *The Bondage of the Will* appeared in February 1526. Not until September 1527 was it to be followed by the second part,[14] after warnings from England to keep his promise.[15] Erasmus' reluctance to write was not less great than Luther's, but his self-control was greater. Unlike Luther, he did not descend to common vituperation, and he dared to show that he had been hurt by it. His work, however, is much too long and badly organized.

There is no point in analysing the polemics in detail. In what follows I shall deal first with the nature of the various writings, then with the way in which the adversaries went to work, and finally with the most important aspects of their arguments.

The title reveals the literary genre to which *The Free Will* belongs. It was called a 'diatribe' or '*collatio*.' A diatribe is a treatise, known since Greek and Roman times, in dialogue form on a moral or philosophical theme. A *collatio* is a collection of passages, here biblical texts, that treat the same theme or that supplement or contradict each other. In the *Ratio* Erasmus had advised the compilation of such a *collatio* on important questions so as to arrive at a reconciliation of contrasting pronouncements.[16] Indeed, we find elements of both diatribe and *collatio* in *The Free Will*.

The work is made up of three parts. The first consists of a long introduction, in which Erasmus discusses two problems: Is it sensible to deal with such a profound question? How can one reach an answer if Luther will only acknowledge the Scriptures as the norm but will not listen to others in explaining them?[17] In the second part of *The Free Will* Erasmus deals first with the biblical passages that support freedom of the will,[18] and then with those that argue against it.[19] This section is a *collatio* in the strict sense of the word. The third part contains the diatribe,[20] in which Erasmus states his own opinion on the basis of the biblical passages discussed. The voices for and against enter, as it were, into a discussion. Although Erasmus does not disguise his own opinion, the discussion remains open. At the start he assures the reader: 'So far we have been collecting biblical texts,'[21] and at the end, 'I have collected the material, may the verdict rest with others.'[22]

There can be no doubt of the character of Luther's work. It ends with these words: 'Truly in this book I have not collected texts from the Bible, but I have made and will make statements. Nor do I wish that the verdict should rest with anyone, but advise everyone to observe obedience.'[23] He makes *assertiones*, firm pronouncements; God's own truth is at stake. 'One should take a delight in firm assertion or one is not a Christian.'[24] This tone of impregnable certainty makes the book at times very irritating and on the other hand highly readable. Structurally it is weak: Luther replies to Erasmus point by point. What makes *The Bondage of the Will* impressive is Luther's total involvement in and certainty on the matter he is defending.

Erasmus' *Hyperaspistes* is pure self-defence. In the first part, published in 1526, Erasmus deals with Luther's expositions on the introduction to *The Free Will*, complaining incessantly (and rather querulously) of all the scorn and insults Luther had heaped on him. The second part, published in 1527, goes into Luther's arguments disputing the very moderate freedom of the will that Erasmus had upheld. *Hyperaspistes* is difficult to read. For one thing, it is too long. The first part is two and a half times as long as *The Free Will*, and the second part is six times as long. The treatise is also poorly constructed. Erasmus followed *The Bondage of the Will* point by point, and his arguments become wearisome as a result. Yet there are readable passages in *Hyperaspistes*, thanks to its conversational character, particularly in the second part. Erasmus is continually in conversation with his own book and with Luther's; he cites Luther, introduces him as a speaker, raises arguments against him and considers Luther's replies. Naturally Luther is not admitted to be right in a single instance. That was impossible in sixteenth-century polemic. Erasmus, however, took his opponent seriously, which Luther had not done. Luther had praised Erasmus' choice of subject: Erasmus had understood, the only one of Luther's adversaries to do so, what the central point was.[25] But throughout his book Luther had displayed only contempt for Erasmus, he had not accepted him as a partner in dialogue or even as a fully worthy adversary.

How did the two opponents set about their work? Georges Chantraine contrasts the inductive method of Erasmus with the deductive one of Luther.[26] Both are working out a theological problem, and both start from Scripture alone; the difference lies in the method they use. Erasmus reasons as an exegete in the tradition of the Fathers of the church. He takes as his starting-point a text from the Bible, which he explains philologically and where necessary provides with excursuses setting out in detail the theological implications of the text. Particularly in *Hyperaspistes* II, the discussion is punctuated with admirable passages of calm exegesis. Luther follows a dogmatic method. He starts from a systematic posing of questions, placing the biblical texts he uses in his explanation in a certain context from the very beginning.

It is desirable to contrast the two methods more distinctly. Erasmus and Luther had much in common, most importantly their conviction that 'the Holy Ghost ... cannot contradict itself,'[27] as Erasmus expressed it. Hence the two partners in the discussion are compelled to clear up, in one way or another, contradictory sayings of the Bible, for in the last analysis, the Bible can speak with only one voice. The ways in which they do so, however, are totally different. Erasmus allows the contradictions to stand for the time being. He does not try to reconcile them with each other, nor does he play them against each other, but concludes that on the basis of one and the same Holy Scripture people have reached different opinions depending on the goal they have in view: whoever is struck by the neglect of human beings to live as God asked them will lay the stress on the human will; whoever, like Luther, regards reliance on one's own achievements as the great danger will be inclined to attach little importance to human will. One must avoid both extremes and adopt a middle course in a finely balanced explanation, while one-sided emphasis on one side or the other will be necessary from time to time for pastoral reasons. This shifts the problem to the extent that Erasmus passes from contradiction in the Scriptures to contradictory exegesis of them. He says as much in so many words: there is disunity on the exegesis of the Bible.[28] Later he reverts to this point and states that for the parts of the Bible that appear at first sight to rule out all freedom of the will one must look for an exegesis that does not adhere to the letter: the biblical utterances in favour of freedom of the will are too numerous and too clear not to be taken as a basis. Even stronger: a complete denial of the freedom of the will would lead to absurdities; the acceptance of a certain efficacy of human will, while acknowledging that the effect of God's grace is much greater, can give their rightful place to the motives that led Luther to deny all effectiveness to the human will.[29] Luther thus has right on his side in his reading of the Scriptures provided that he admits that his view is not universally valid under all circumstances. In the present situation, it is a wholesome corrective, but if it is taken for the whole truth, it fails to give the core of the Scripture its full value.

Luther, like Erasmus, proceeds from the unity of the Scriptures. This unity is in their content: Christ. Once the stone of Christ's tomb had been rolled back and the highest secret revealed, nothing could be concealed any longer. Certain passages of the Bible may be incomprehensible, but the matter, the content of the Scriptures is clear. If people nevertheless regard the Scriptures as obscure, that is their own fault, their own blindness. 'Whoever covers his own eyes, or passes from light to darkness and hides himself, cannot accuse the sun and the daylight of darkness.'[30] The recognition that all salvation can only proceed from God, that every thought of the independence of man is utterly foolish, is part of the secret of Christ that has been revealed. Luther thus found a clear centre for his theology. All the scriptural texts that Erasmus cited in defence of the human will must necessarily have another significance. Then Luther is faced with the question of how it is possible that so many and such prominent men in the history of the church have taught that human will enjoys a certain freedom. For Luther this is one more proof of the rightness of his conviction. Through their opinion they have shown what man can do with his much vaunted free will. That men do not understand the Scriptures is not the fault of the weakness of their intellect, but of the way in which man is overruled by Satan.[31]

This difference in conception has direct consequences for the method which the two opponents follow. Erasmus can acknowledge that certain biblical passages seem to exclude all freedom of the human will. Naturally he tends to play this down as far as possible, but if this does not succeed, he can explain an apparently determinist expression by pointing to the *scopus* or goal of the statement: it is directed against excessive trust in human possibilities.[32] Luther does not do this and cannot adopt this method.

Finally, a description of the difference in content. In this connection, the main questions are: where do we find the distinctive characteristics of Erasmus, and what reason impelled him to embark on his debate with Luther? At the end of *The Bondage of the Will*, Luther offers his personal confession of faith: 'I truly acknowledge that even if it were possible I would not wish to have a free will or to have retained anything through which I could strive for salvation ... Then I would be forced to exert myself continually for something uncertain ... Even if I lived and worked forever, I should never know certainly in my heart how much a man must do to content God ... But now that God has withdrawn my salvation from my will and made it dependent on his will ... I live in complete certainty. For he is true.'[33] Luther sees himself as a sinner and as nothing else; a man is wholly determined by being a sinner. The entire existence of humanity is a flight from God. In God's eyes, nothing is left of our good intentions and works. In this context Luther speaks of the temptations, and dangers, of the evil spirits that afflict mankind and prevent anyone attaining salvation. But even without temptations and evil spirits, the uncertainty, the endless self-torment would remain.

Why did Erasmus object to this picture of humanity? One answer may be that his experience was different from Luther's. Huizinga observed that there was no Damascus in Erasmus' life, no moment at which he was so shocked that from then on everything stood in a new light. His development took its course without great eruptions. This cannot be more than a first answer; we must look for Erasmus' religious motive. In *The Free Will* he says: 'In the life of mortals there is abundance of weakness, vice, wrongdoing ... If anyone will take a good look at himself, he will lay aside all pride – even if we do not assert that man, even if he is justified, is nothing but sin – above all as Christ speaks of being "born again" and Paul of "new creation."'[34] These last words contain the heart of Erasmus' thinking. A pronouncement like Luther's does an injustice not to human dignity but to the place God in his grace has allotted to man. Man is a new creature; therein lies the reason for his existence. As a new creature he has the duty and also the possibility to serve God. Of course Erasmus also knew of lasting sin. In *Hyperaspistes* II he explains that man is weak rather than evil. True evil is found in some, but people are not naturally bad; they acquire evil by degenerating from bad to worse.[35] Sometimes it appears as if to Erasmus man were a Hercules at the crossroads, always choosing his path. Behind this lay the idea that God has chosen for man and leads the weak human being. In *The Free Will* Erasmus used an image to make clear how he thought of God's dealings with mankind. A father shows his young child an apple, helps the child to reach it, and finally puts the apple in his hands. The child has done nothing of which it can boast. The only thing is: the child could have spurned the apple and could have put up a struggle.[36]

No wonder Erasmus was deeply annoyed at Luther's exposition of Romans 3:20, 'law brings consciousness of sin.' Luther had argued that the law does indeed make one conscious of sin, but does not free from it. Developing this theme, he had explained the basic distinction between the law and the gospel: the gospel heals, points to Christ as the redeemer.[37] Erasmus erupts: Even a tyrant is not so foolish as to proclaim laws for the sole purpose of making people lawbreakers. Moses and Christ spoke quite differently of God's holy law, and Paul did not mean that the law makes me conscious of sin, but that it teaches me to recognize my sins as guilt.[38] In a personal letter to Thomas More Erasmus called this assertion of Luther's one of the two crucial points of his teaching.[39]

Erasmus did not intend in all this to magnify man's share in gaining salvation. At the beginning and at the end of the path to salvation – which is not, as it was in the view of the medieval theologians, determined by the sacraments – man is exclusively dependent on God's grace. As he treads this path, God's grace is the first cause, but human will is the second cause.[40] Why? Because otherwise human responsibility cannot be maintained. This is the nub: 'For whenever I hear that there is no merit in man at all, yes that all works, even of the truly pious, are sinful, whenever I hear that our will effects no more than clay in the hands of the potter, whenever I hear that everything we do or desire is brought back to unconditional necessity, I run up against many objections.'[41] Even if this were the truth, it was not to be revealed to everyone. For the masses, if they heard such a doctrine, would certainly give themselves up to a careless and godless life.[42]

For Erasmus, the responsibility of man corresponded to the trustworthiness of God; he was not a capricious God, who arbitrarily exalted man or cast him down. In *Hyperaspistes* II Erasmus spoke of a law 'deeply rooted in the human soul, so much so that even the heathen drew this consequence: God is to the highest degree just and good. If he is just, then he does not punish eternally those who have sinned without any guilt of their own but out of unavoidable necessity, nor does he punish the evil that he himself works in man. But in his goodness he does not give up anyone who does not give himself up.'[43]

It is striking that God's trustworthiness is also crucial for Luther: 'For God is trustworthy,' we read in him. He goes on: 'and will not deceive me. He is mighty and powerful: no devil, no temptation can overcome him or seize me from him.'[44] Luther had an eye for Erasmus' difficulties. Must no doubt arise in this way of the goodness and justice of God, who dooms men without their deserving it, who are born in godlessness and cannot help it? Luther took the consequences as far as they would go. 'Here we must bow down in reverence for the God who is full of compassion for those whom he justifies and saves without their being in any way worthy of it. And finally we must leave something to his divine wisdom. We must believe that he is just, when he appears unjust to us.'[45] In the letter to More mentioned above, Erasmus names this as Luther's second crucial point: 'through the sin of Adam, the whole human race was so corrupted that even the Holy Spirit works only evil in it.'[46] For Erasmus it was a riddle that a man could speak of God in such a way. In *The Free Will* Erasmus had held up to Luther all the scriptural texts in which God calls on man to be converted, including Ezekiel 33:11: 'As I live, says the Lord God, I have no pleasure in the death of the wicked, but that the wicked turn from his way and live.' 'Does the God of love regret the death of his people, while he himself brings it about?' adds Erasmus.[47] Luther's reply to this part of *The Free Will* is profound. He distinguishes the God who is preached from the God who is hidden. It is true that God does not wish the death of the sinner, but that is only true of God so far as he is preached and makes himself known to us. He is also the hidden God, whom we do not know and cannot fathom. The hidden God wants life and salvation, death and corruption depending on his unfathomable will.[48] God is righteous, certainly, but he is not righteous in our human way and by our human standard, otherwise he would not be God.[49] It is no accident that the notion of a path of salvation, along which man can progress in his dealing with God, is absent from Luther.

Erasmus could not possibly think of God in this way, and he was not the only one. A letter is preserved in which someone tells Erasmus of a conversation he had with one of Erasmus' admirers. The man, who was of high birth, asked whether Erasmus had ever expressed his opinion on Luther's thesis that God was the author of both good and evil. When the writer of the letter read out the passage in the *Hyperaspistes* that deals with this, the man showed himself profoundly grateful to Erasmus, for 'he had never been able to believe that God was so unjust and cruel that he would punish man for something to which he himself had forced and compelled the unlucky one.'[50] That is in fact precisely the core of Erasmus' aversion; God was not like that! For Luther it was blasphemy to think of God in such human terms. For Erasmus, it was blasphemy to think of God in such devilish terms: 'Who could manage to love with all his heart a God who made hell glow with eternal tortures in order to punish his own evil deeds in unlucky people as if he took pleasure in tormenting human beings?'[51]

The central issues for Erasmus were 'God's justice and compassion,' taken together because the two might not be played off against each other. The God he knew was not unrighteous in his compassion. Erasmus accused Luther of praising God's mercy to some so much that his God was no longer righteous towards others, only cruel: 'But I do not understand how people in full conviction can exalt the mercy of God to the pious so high that they make him almost cruel to others.'[52] Erasmus' God runs the risk of becoming banal. Yet it was not his intention to weigh the question of what God could be so carefully that reverence was lost. Much rather he accused Luther of 'judging with criminal boldness the decisions of God, which are inscrutable to man.'[53] At the beginning and at the end of *The Free Will* Erasmus refers to Romans 11:33: 'O the depth of the riches and wisdom and knowledge of God! How unsearchable are his judgments and how unscrutable his ways!'[54] He dared not think further, when he considered the differences between people: one highly gifted and as if created for good, another misshapen in body or indistinguishable from a beast – and then did Luther want to fathom God's purpose in this much more difficult question?[55]

Both men wanted to let God be God, both accused each other of making God into a sum in arithmetic, both in the end were speaking of the unspeakable.

The settlement of accounts was final. Luther felt only aversion for Erasmus, Erasmus completely failed to understand Luther. The breach between the two men is often represented as a breach between the Reformation and humanism in general. Bernhard Lohse rightly points out that this picture fails to correspond with reality in two respects.[56] First, linguistic study and exegesis of the Bible continued to be developed in the Reformation too. In this context it is more important that Luther's chosen position in the questions concerning freedom of the will was not adopted in its acute form by Protestantism. The Lutheran confessions of faith gave a much more cautious answer to the question than Luther himself. In the 1535 edition of his *Loci communes* Melanchthon, as he said himself, sided with Erasmus in various respects.[57] Later Melanchthon's position in the Lutheran churches was sharply attacked, among other reasons because of his views on the relationship of human will and divine providence. Nonetheless, the extremely acute formulation of Luther's position was adopted by Calvin rather than by Luther's own pupils. In fact, by rejecting Calvin's doctrine of predestination, they indirectly attacked Luther himself.

TWELVE

Between Scylla and Charybdis

❧

'I observe that it is my fate, that while I strive to be of service to both parties, I am stoned from both sides.' These words from 1525 reflect Erasmus' position in the twenties. A schism in the church had not yet come about, but the parties were lining up, and both pointed a finger of reproach at Erasmus. 'In Italy and the Netherlands, I am a Lutheran, in the whole of Germany ... such an anti-Lutheran that his fervent followers do not attack any mortal more violently than me,' the letter continues.[1] In this chapter we discuss the twenties from the viewpoint of the dangers which, in his own opinion, threatened Erasmus from both sides. To choose a middle path between Christ and Belial would be godless. 'But to hold the middle way between Scylla and Charybdis is in my view a sign of caution.'[2]

On one side stood above all Paris and Spain, where Erasmus was regarded as a Lutheran, as having laid the egg that Luther hatched.[3] On the other side it was not so much the followers of Luther in the true sense of the word. Erasmus seems to have written them off after 1525. He had more difficulties with the Reformation party in Switzerland. He often called these people 'Lutherans' too, but from 1524 he was aware of their differences from Luther. In *Hyperaspistes* I he mocks Luther for '[his] disintegrated congregation and [his] party which is everywhere "disparted."'[4] It was the leaders of the Reformation in Switzerland and southern Germany who now caused him the greatest difficulties: Huldrych Zwingli in Zürich, Johannes Oecolampadius in Basel, and Martin Bucer in Strasbourg. No wonder! In 1525 Erasmus wrote to his bitterest enemy in Paris, the professor Noël Béda: 'You see where I have written this, living between Zürich and Strasbourg, and in the city where Oecolampadius lectures in public.'[5] The three names mentioned have already appeared: the leading reformers in South Germany and Switzerland were kindred spirits, if not pupils, of Erasmus. That made things worse: they appealed more than once to his writings.

It began in the Lent of 1522, not quite six months after Erasmus had returned to Basel. In that year the fasts were repeatedly and ostentatiously broken in both Basel and Zürich. It was intended as a demonstration. The participants were concerned about 'evangelical freedom.'[6] Erasmus was embroiled in the affair at once, for some of the ringleaders appealed to the example he had given. Erasmus' health was poor, he hated eating fish, and therefore he had from time to time eaten poultry instead. That will have been the occasion for Erasmus to reach for his pen. In August he brought out *De esu carnium* (*On the Eating of Meat*),[7] a lengthy letter addressed to the bishop of Basel. The title is somewhat deceptive, for Erasmus was concerned with the whole question of the value of ecclesiastical laws, with special reference to the burning issues of the day: the rules of fasting, the obligatory celibacy of the clergy, and compulsory feast days.

Erasmus had already voiced his opinions on these three themes more than once in recent years. He considered that the prescription of fasts was more Jewish than Christian in character; he thought obligatory celibacy for the priesthood was undesirable if massive breach of the rule took place and was silently overlooked; and in his opinion the number of feast days – at that time about a hundred a year including Sundays – was far too high. At the moment the treatise was given an extra dimension in two respects. In the first place as a result of the situation. What had hitherto been winked at was now demanded on principle, on the grounds of the gospel, by Zwingli and his adherents. Erasmus condemned the events in Basel unreservedly: by acting in that way, people showed that they were not yet ripe for true evangelical freedom.[8] But the existing rules also formed a threat to the genuine freedom that Christ and Paul had preached. Moreover Erasmus showed his alarm at the social aspect. Fasting, especially, was a greater burden on the poor than on the rich, and the increasing number of feast days endangered their livelihood. On top of this, the church's hunger for money played a great part in the maintenance of the ecclesiastical ordinances and the issue of dispensations. These aspects which Erasmus mentioned were important in Switzerland, but not only there. All this made his work highly relevant. Its second interest lay in the broader context in which Erasmus placed the themes mentioned. He discussed the question how far any such ecclesiastical – and therefore human – ordinances could be binding. Could it really be in accordance with the will of God for the church to impose such commandments, under the threat of eternal damnation if they were broken? Erasmus saw a great difference between sin in the biblical sense of the word and the breaking of human rules.

Of course there was a certain view of the church behind this. For Erasmus the church was not a static entity; it had to adapt itself to the needs of the time. In the finest part of his work Erasmus paints a picture of the church as a community, the essence of which is defined by love. In this, he does not attack the hierarchic structure of the church in any respect. But the authority of the bishop, wholesome in itself, must not degenerate into tyranny over the faithful: 'They are sheep, but Christ's rather than the bishop's ... The people do not exist for the bishops, but the institution of bishops is there for the people ... Let the bishop rule over the people, but as a father rules over his children, or the husband over his beloved bride.'9 In this relationship, fatherly admonition, not tyrannical compulsion, is appropriate. Thus Erasmus does not look at the problem of the ordinances of the church in isolation. He is concerned with the problem of the church as a community, and the concrete question of certain ecclesiastical rules is subordinate to this.

De esu carnium is an appeal to both sides. Erasmus calls on the bishops to take the matter seriously and to lead the protest movement wisely and cautiously in the paths of the church. If the bishops reveal themselves as true shepherds of their flocks, no breach will be made in their authority, but the essence of the faith will be all the more clearly brought to the fore. Erasmus also addressed himself to the Reformation movement in Switzerland and called on it to show self-control. He shared its ideals of a purified church. He pleaded at this critical moment for staying within the existing hierarchical church. Hence he reacted with dismay when Zwingli, in his *Apologeticus Archeteles* (which followed similar events in Zürich) finally settled his account with the bishop: 'I beseech you by the glory of the gospel ... if you publish anything in future, it is a serious task, and you must take it seriously.'[10] Later he wrote that it was his *De esu carnium* which had first inflamed the wrath of the 'Lutherans' against him;[11] he will have had Zwingli and the reformers in Basel particularly in mind. As we shall see, it was no different with the irreconcilable enemies of the Reformation. Above all, the theologians of Louvain and Paris fell upon this work. As late as 1531, it was one of the most hotly disputed of Erasmus' publications, along with the *Praise of Folly* and the *Colloquies*.[12]

The situation became more serious in 1525 and 1526. A great deal had happened at Basel in the mean time and Erasmus felt considerably less at home in the city than he had before. Oecolampadius was attacking *The Free Will* in several ways, monks and nuns were leaving, monastic houses were being closed, and the young enthusiast Guillaume Farel, later a reformer of Geneva and Neuchâtel, had been in the city in 1523–4 and had launched such a ferocious onslaught on Erasmus that the victim pressed the magistrates to deny Farel further residence in the city – and with success. The greatest difficulties arose in 1525, when Oecolampadius began to discuss the Eucharist in his sermons. The year before Andreas Karlstadt had been in Basel. He was one of the first of Luther's followers at Wittenberg, but after a disagreement with Luther had come to this region as an exile. In a number of pamphlets he had defended the argument that the body and blood of Christ were not really and corporally present in the bread and wine of the Eucharist. Although Oecolampadius and Zwingli were not in agreement with Karlstadt on all points, they shared this view.

Erasmus had a premonition of approaching evil: 'this affair will turn into a great drama.'[13] He was not deceived. The controversy concerning the Eucharist, which exploded in full force in 1525, was to drive the Swiss and the Saxons apart and lead to the future separate existence of the Lutheran and Reformed churches. But the consequences were also to be great for Erasmus personally. Both Zwingli and Oecolampadius – this does not apply for Karlstadt – were his disciples in their view of the Eucharist, and developed further certain ideas of their master. For Erasmus, communion was in the first place an act by which the faithful created a community.

He also laid all the emphasis on the spiritual eating and drinking of bread and wine in the faith, thus pushing the physical aspect into the background.[14] As early as 1525 the rumours were circulating in Basel that Erasmus was going to write against Oecolampadius and, at the same time, that deep down, Erasmus fully agreed with Oecolampadius.[15] In fact Erasmus began a treatise, but soon gave up his attempt.[16] In 1525 and 1526 the situation became extremely disagreeable. Both in Basel and in Zürich the partisans of the Reformation made several attempts to force Erasmus to make a clear pronouncement. He could rightly say that he had never denied the corporal presence of Christ in the Eucharist,[17] but he had undermined this doctrine by regarding it as relatively unimportant: those who spoke of it were still bogged down in the flesh, while only the spirit, and so only the spiritual enjoyment of the Eucharist, was important.[18] Thus a considerable difference between Erasmus' views and that of Oecolampadius and Zwingli remained, but the intellectual background, the idea of the irreconcilability of matter and spirit, was the same.

The crisis came in September 1525, when Oecolampadius published a detailed and learned study of the Eucharist. For the sake of caution the book had been printed at Strasbourg. The magistrates of Basel had to pronounce on whether it was to be banned in their city. They called for the advice of four experts, including Erasmus, who replied: 'It is in my opinion a learned treatise, well arranged and worked out. I would add godly, if anything can be godly that is in conflict with the view and the unanimous feeling of the church. My judgment is that it is dangerous to differ in opinion with the church.'[19] Erasmus achieved a result to the extent that the book's sale was forbidden by the magistrates, as was the printing of other works by Oecolampadius.

But the rumour current in Basel, that Erasmus was not very happy with the request to give his advice, was certainly not without foundation. It was the first time that Erasmus had explicitly and directly voiced his feelings on the advance of the Reformation in Basel. What a difference with his 'no' towards Luther a year earlier! Then he had been under pressure from outside finally to state his own opinion; now he had received a commission from which he could not withdraw. Then, he had a subject of his own choice; now, one that he would certainly not have broached on his own initiative. Then, he had dealt with an inscrutable secret that had been rashly violated by Luther; now he approached a question that was close to his heart and that Oecolampadius had treated in the proper manner. Erasmus could agree even with his results. What held him back was the *consensus ecclesiae*, the unanimous feeling of the church.

Erasmus constantly returns to this point in connection with the Eucharist. To his confidant Willibald Pirckheimer he wrote, in a very personal letter: 'Oecolampadius' view would not displease me, if the *consensus ecclesiae* were not against it ... and yet I cannot be untrue to the *consensus ecclesiae*, nor have I ever been so.'[20] Later he wrote to the same correspondent that he would be in doubt if the authority of the church did not strengthen him. 'But I call the church the consensus of all Christian people all over the world.'[21] In this statement we have reached the heart of Erasmus' religious conviction. He sometimes uttered bitter criticisms of the forms in which the church appeared to him, he tolerated the church rather than loved it. But the concept of consensus was deeply rooted in him. At first sight it appears as if he was withdrawing into the tradition of the church, that is, to the past, or to the mass of the faithful of the day, as if the majority through time or over the world could pronounce the decisive word. James K. McConica, however, has made it clear that Erasmus had a deeper conception,[22] that of the community created by the Holy Spirit, in which the individual believer is incorporated. He shares this place with others. This does not excuse him from the duty to listen with his own ears to what the divine truth in the Scriptures says to him, but it does remove his isolation. The Bible is the expression of the continued speech of God with his people, which began with the apostles and the evangelists and has continued to our own time. Thus the faith is anchored in history, in tradition, but it is not swallowed up in it. It develops over time, and the individual believer participates in this dialogue, listening to what the Spirit has unveiled, in the past and now.

Erasmus' statements about the Swiss reformers' conception of the Eucharist show how much this concept guided his thoughts. In 1526 he was invited to attend the Disputation of Baden, a colloquy before the forum of the whole Swiss Confederacy. Erasmus did not go, but the concept of consensus again appears in the letter he wrote: he had never held an opinion in conflict with that which the Catholic church 'in its great consensus' (*magno consensu*) had defended.[23]

Would the champions of the old church be able to understand Erasmus' position? The attacks on him from that side in the twenties show that this was impossible; it had become 'all or nothing.' As early as 1522, Baechem, Erasmus' old adversary in Louvain, had even wanted to burn the new edition of the *Colloquies*, and resistance to this work arose again in 1524; some confessors had even refused students absolution at the Easter confession if they had read it. Though the faculty of theology at Louvain thought that was futile, its own continual agitation had provoked such a reaction. In 1525 the Louvain professor Jacques Masson demonstrated a high level of objective criticism in a book defending the right of the church to impose binding rules on its subjects, but the satires directed against Erasmus naturally made a greater impression.

More dangerous were the attacks Erasmus had to suffer from Paris. The Sorbonne, the faculty of theology of the University of Paris, was considered to be one of the most important institutions of the church, and its utterances had great weight. From 1523 Erasmus' difficulties increased, and as early as 1524 the influential syndic of the Sorbonne Noël Béda began an inquiry into Erasmus' *Paraphrase on Luke*. From then on the attacks became more pointed. In 1525 the faculty condemned several translations and passages from translations of Erasmus' works by Louis de Berquin. In these versions Berquin had incorporated sections from works by Luther and Guillaume Farel. Erasmus was not aware of this but sensed that something was not right. Thus far, Erasmus had come under heavy attack, but his works had never been officially condemned. How many difficulties could be caused by such a censure was evident from that passed on Luther by the faculties of Cologne, Louvain, and Paris. A lengthy correspondence with Béda was unable to prevent the conflict from becoming more acute. In 1526 the *Colloquies* were condemned, and in 1527 followed the condemnation of passages from a whole series of other works by Erasmus. These censures were officially published in 1531, to Erasmus' fury: 'It is not enough for them to kill Erasmus. They want to rob him of his honour as well, and stamp him utterly into the ground.'[24]

These official activities were accompanied by the publication of works attacking Erasmus written by well-known theologians from the Sorbonne. In 1526 Béda brought out his *Annotationes*, directed against Lefèvre d'Etaples and Erasmus. It was a mediocre work, in which all kinds of miscellaneous statements were attacked. Of quite a different calibre was the *Propugnaculum ecclesiae* of Josse Clichtove, which appeared in the same year. Clichtove made an excellent case for the right of the church to impose binding ordinances concerning fasting and abstinence. A great part of the treatise is taken up with refuting the arguments of his opponents Luther and Erasmus, but this refutation is based on the author's own examination of the questions at issue. The attack was all the more formidable because Clichtove linked Erasmus and Luther and made it appear plausible that their criticisms of ecclesiastical ordinances rested on the same foundations. The works of Béda and Clichtove can both be described as semi-official. But there were other adversaries as well, so that one may speak of a campaign against Erasmus led from Paris.

No wonder that Erasmus turned in June 1526 to the faculty of theology itself, to the highest judicial body, the Parlement of Paris, and even to King Francis I: 'If they can lie so manifestly about us, and that in published books, but we on the contrary are prevented from refuting this slander, what then is the once famous university? A den of thieves!' In this way, he maintains, they tried to force him into the camp of the enemy.[25] Erasmus saw a plan behind all this, for the game had begun at the same time in Spain, Italy, England, Brabant, France, Hungary, and Poland.[26] Such a belief reveals the persecution mania which began to take hold of Erasmus in these years and was to assume pathological forms in the thirties, when he felt that his enemies were spying on him everywhere, and that behind every attack, in the last analysis, lurked Girolamo Aleandro.[27]

But what opinions were the special targets of these attacks? It is symptomatic that many of the complaints were directed against *De esu carnium*: Paris could not stomach anything that could be interpreted as criticism of the structure of the church in the broadest sense of the word, as a weakening of that which gave the institution of the church its stability. I shall mention only a few of the charges: Erasmus doubted the doctrine of the church concerning the sacraments and the ceremonies of the church, questioned whether confession had been instituted by Christ, held fasting and abstinence up to ridicule, saw nothing in the veneration of the saints, robbed the Virgin of her honour; advised against monastic life, condemned the monastic vows. And all this is dealt with in exhaustive summaries of passages, sometimes torn from their context, from Erasmus' writings. Time and again Erasmus replied, in new apologies, just as detailed and sometimes just as petty-minded as the attacks on him. Now and then he struck the first blow in his anger. Thus in one of the works against Béda: 'I do not defend people who under the pretence of the gospel devote themselves to the flesh; I have nothing to do with the doctrine of Luther. It is, however, beyond dispute that the teaching of Luther approaches closer to the pure spiritual philosophy of Christ than the theology of Béda ... He has only one aim in view, that human institutions must be multiplied: veneration of images, choice of foods, distinctions in monastic clothing, trust in human works, weeks of penance, scholastic hair-splitting over words. I do not condemn such things, but I do condemn their excess and superstition. He says nothing of the strength of evangelical piety, or speaks so coldly of it that you feel certain that his heart is not in it.'[28] Erasmus wrote this at the same time that he had received *The Bondage of the Will* and was writing the *Hyperaspistes* against Luther.

The attacks from Spain, had they continued, would probably have been even more dangerous. Erasmus had many kindred spirits in that country, more than he knew himself. Marcel Bataillon even speaks of an 'Erasmian invasion' in those years.[29] The Spanish translator of the *Enchiridion* reported to Erasmus that the work was read at the court of the emperor, in the cities, the churches, the monasteries, even in the inns and on the roads.[30] Its declared adversaries in Spain were the mendicant friars, who launched a genuine campaign against Erasmus in 1527. The grand inquisitor and archbishop of Seville, Alonso Manrique, and the archbishop of Toledo and primate of Spain, Alonso de Fonseca, were in his favour, as was the emperor, Charles v. The result was that the representatives of the Franciscans and the Dominicans who had compiled a long list of heresies and errors in Erasmus' works were restrained by the Inquisition. In the summer of 1527 the Conference of Valladolid took place, at which the whole affair was to be discussed by all those involved. It was intended that Erasmus should also send a defence. When he received the charges in Basel, the Conference had already been postponed indefinitely because of the risk of the plague. It was never to meet again, and thus the whole affair sputtered out like a candle.

Erasmus, however, had taken the allegations seriously and did not intend to waive his defence, although he received well-meant advice from Spain not to irritate the monks to excess.[31] In March 1528 he issued his *Apologia adversus monachos quosdam hispanos* (*Apology against Some Spanish Monks*).[32] Without doubt his tendency always to justify himself played a not insignificant role in his writing this apology. But it was not the only factor, for the nature of the accusations also compelled him to reply. In the charges brought by the Spanish monks the supposed attacks of Erasmus on the structure of the church occupied an important place, as had been the case in Paris. Much more threatening, however, were the headings to the first three chapters that contained the charges: 'Against the most sacred Trinity of God; Against the divinity, dignity, and honour of Christ; Against the divinity of the Holy Ghost.' As Erasmus remarked in his self-defence, after citing the first heading, 'Who would not shudder at such a title?'[33] And rightly so. A condemnation on this point was the gravest that could be incurred, and the mere accusation exposed one to danger. Profession of faith in the Trinity still formed the basis of society, and to reject it was in any case adequate grounds for the death sentence. Erasmus did not know that during the six weeks the Conference of Valladolid had been in session it had not got much further than the discussion of these three chapters and the fourth, which dealt with Erasmus' bold pronouncements on the Inquisition; the conference had proceeded very cautiously. But he was fully aware of the need to refute this accusation at the very least.

His treatment of the first three chapters takes up half of the total pamphlet. Before defending point by point all ninety-nine passages from his works against which objections had been raised, he listed no fewer than eighty places in which he had explicitly recognized the Trinity. This was not in itself a strong argument. He discussed in detail two crucial passages, both from his edition of the New

Testament. First, concerning his handling of the *comma Johanneum* (1 John 5:7b–8a),[34] he pointed out that he had again included the longer recension in the latest edition. He neatly observed that the manuscript in which the words were to be found was fairly recent (not more than a century old, if that, he suggested), and that this manuscript contained corrections on the basis of the Vulgate.[35] In this he was closer to the truth than he realized himself. Second, concerning his remark that in the Bible the Father is often called 'God,' the Son only in a few cases, Erasmus now stated, rightly, that he had clearly said that the name 'God' for the Son only appeared 'without qualification' or 'outright' a few times. He had never denied that there were several passages in the Bible that made it clear that the Son was God.[36] Yet such a method of discussion could not remove the objections: they lay deeper. Erasmus' remark at the start carried more weight: he had always assumed that the recognition of the Trinity was so deeply rooted that he could not imagine anyone ever being able to accuse a fellow Christian of deviating from the doctrine of the church on this point.[37]

But there was more to the charges than Erasmus acknowledged, perhaps more than he dared to admit to himself. In the discussions at the Conference of Valladolid the Augustinian monk Juan de Quintana, confessor of the emperor, revealed that he had read Erasmus' works with great attention. He declared that Erasmus' statement that in theology 'one must not assert with certainty anything except that which is expressly stated in the Holy Scriptures' was flatly heretical,[38] unless Erasmus meant the words 'expressly stated' both formally and virtually, that is, not only literally but in spirit. This remark from a well-trained theologian puts us on the track of the essential contradiction. Quintana spoke as a systematic theologian; like Luther two years earlier, he missed in Erasmus a central concept by means of which the biblical data could be expounded because they found their point of unity in it. And Erasmus? In self-defence he burst out: 'If at the beginning Peter preached Jesus to a mixed public without mentioning his divine nature; if Paul likewise only called him a man before the Athenians; if it is nowhere stated that the apostles in their preaching to the people mentioned the divine nature of Jesus; if three evangelists nowhere call Christ God; if only John does so in some passages, and

Paul also ... why then am I guilty if I point this out?'[39] Quintana could have given a faultless answer to this rhetorical question. With hindsight, we can see the remarks of the exegete opposed to those of the dogmatist. We may also observe that Erasmus' protestations of orthodoxy – reiterated to the point of becoming wearisome – sound honestly meant: a deliberate departure from the doctrine of the church was in fact beyond Erasmus' scope. But his protestations also sound rather shrill, as if he has sometimes to overrule his own understanding.

Michael Servetus was present at the Conference of Valladolid as Quintana's secretary. Still very young, probably seventeen, he kept both ears open. While he had hitherto shown no interest in theology, he now began to study the Bible eagerly. Four years later he published his *De Trinitatis erroribus*, on the errors of the Trinity. Carlos Gilly has recently shown that Servetus was a keen student of Erasmus' *Annotations* on the New Testament and of several apologies, which also formed part of the dossier at Valladolid.[40] Erasmus' writings helped to determine his ideas. On several occasions one finds Erasmus' thoughts in a radicalized form in Servetus. Erasmus thought Servetus' book dangerous,[41] and similar reflections in Servetus' *Restitutio christianismi* of 1553 were to rouse such indignation in Calvin that Servetus was to meet his death at the stake in Geneva.

Erasmus managed to maintain an unstable equilibrium at best during these years. His relationship with Oecolampadius had cooled. He was alarmed to see how the structures of the old church were gradually being broken down. In the winter of 1528-9 the guilds took the initiative to force the city magistracy to take the last decisive steps, the removal of images from the churches and the replacement of the Eucharist by the Lord's Supper. In February riots broke out, and without bloodshed a number of Catholic councillors were replaced by Protestants: Basel had gone over to the Reformation. Although the Reformation party was not pleased to see Erasmus leave, in April he followed the example of prominent adherents of the old church. He moved to Freiburg im Breisgau. His letters of these two months show how strongly he was attached to the old order. Although he had never set foot in a Protestant service, he had all kinds of bad reports to give: there was only a sermon, women and children sang a psalm in German, bread was distributed as a symbol of the body of the Lord, the people gaped but in no way deplored their sins, the preaching was coarsely anti-Catholic and obviously inflammatory, and the people came out of church in a rage as if they were possessed by an evil spirit.[42] 'For our part,' he wrote to his friend Ludwig Baer, who had already left, 'we are spending our Easter without hallelujahs, without the victory meal, albeit not without the salad of the country. Meanwhile, we feel that we are sitting beside the rivers of Babylon, so that we have no desire to sing the Lord's song in a strange land.'[43]

Erasmus went from one exile to another. Freiburg did not agree with him at all; the city and its population lacked all style. But life in Basel had become impossible for him. He had to preserve his independence in order to go on working, and that would be impossible as long as he stayed there. When the celebration of communion by the Protestant rite had been made compulsory, he encouraged his confidant Bonifacius Amerbach, who had remained behind, to be steadfast on this point.[44] At the close of the year 1529 appeared his *Epistola in pseudevangelicos*, 'a letter against the so-called evangelicals,' purportedly an apologia directed against Gerard Geldenhouwer, in fact a statement of his position in the ecclesiastical conflicts. Without concealing his great reservations about the old church, he sounded a resolute no to the reformers: 'If Paul were living now, then in my opinion he would not reject the present situation of the church; he would cry out against the sins of man.'[45] Behind this statement lay Erasmus' conviction that many of the changes that had taken place in the church over the centuries were justified. But not all!

The impossible position in which Erasmus found himself, but in which he was convinced the whole of Christendom was also placed, becomes very clear if we compare two letters. In one, he emphasizes that 'an important stimulus to these troubles was given by some people who strained the rope beyond measure: they preferred to break it rather than slacken it and keep it whole.' He sums up: the pope had far too much power; the preaching of indulgences had degenerated into shameless money-making; the veneration of saints had been corrupted to superstition; church buildings were stuffed full of images; the music in services was more fitting for a wedding or a drinking-party; the mass was served by priests who lived godless lives and served it as a shoemaker practises his trade; confession had become money-making and skirt-chasing; priests and monks were shameless tyrants.[46] The other letter, also written to a friend, states: 'Now you may perhaps put to me the question whether I never felt any incitement to join a party ... Sometimes, when I ponder to myself the base and stubborn meanness of some people, I am penetrated by a truly human feeling, the yearning to take revenge ... but very soon the spirit corrects this desire of the flesh: "What does such a godless thought mean? Do not revenge yourself on the falsehood of men by turning your hands on your mother the church, which bore you as a child of Christ through holy baptism, which fed you with the word of God, which nourishes and feeds you through so many sacraments." '[47]

It appears to be by no means fortuitous or incidental that Erasmus wrote the last letter during his final weeks in Basel, the first five months later in Freiburg.

THIRTEEN

The *Colloquies*

❦

Several references have already been made to the *Colloquies*. In the sixteenth and seventeenth centuries this was Erasmus' best-known work, and during his lifetime certainly one of the most notorious. We have seen that the Sorbonne fell eagerly upon the *Colloquies* and left little of them intact. Individuals took the same view. The Dominican Ambrosius Pelargus, who was on reasonably good terms with Erasmus, wrote to him: 'I am not against your intention, but I regret the outcome, if at least it is true, as many swear, that a good part of the youth has become much worse through your *Colloquies* ... Truly, it would have been possible to think of another and much more suitable manner of exercising young people and promoting the knowledge of languages among the young. An authoritative theologian above all should not descend to such unseemly jesting.'[1] Luther agreed with Pelargus. In 1533 when the introduction of the *Colloquies* at the school of Wittenberg was threatened, he said: 'On my deathbed I shall forbid my children to read the *Colloquies* of Erasmus. For he puts into the mouths of others his completely godless view, in conflict with the faith and the church. Let him rather laugh at me and other people.'[2] Strong emotions, great indignation!

And yet the *Colloquies* began with a very simple idea. Around the turn of the century Erasmus was living in Paris as a poor student. To support himself he gave lessons to young men from well-off families, and that occupation forced him to think about the best method of instilling the necessary knowledge of Latin into his pupils. This could not be done, he realized, by the interminable study of grammars, but through a lively treatment in dialogues between master and pupil. The method was not unknown, but Erasmus applied it in his own way. Twenty years later, in 1518, Froben, without Erasmus' knowledge, published a little book under his name containing linguistic exercises in the form of simple conversations such as he had dictated at that time. Erasmus was not very happy with the edition. It was his work, but with many faults. When he observed that the book found buyers, he himself prepared an improved edition, which appeared at Louvain. This edition too sold well. Its popularity was easy to explain. One could find in it, for example, a great number of variations of possible forms of greeting, the right way to inquire about someone's health, the Latin names for all kinds of family relationships, examples of correct and incorrect Latin – in short it was a highly practical handbook. That was important at the time. Cultivated young people needed not only a passive command of Latin but also the ability to use it actively. Erasmus assumed that children of seven or eight could begin to learn Latin, and that the teacher had to strive from the start to impart good Latin by means of memorization of much-used phrases. Erasmus knew that children learned with pleasure and ease through imitation. His method was original in that, unlike many others, he tried hard to imbue the pupil with a feeling for the distinction between Latin and dog-Latin. Erasmus himself, following Lorenzo Valla, spoke of 'kitchen maid's elegance.'[3]

The verdicts quoted earlier have little to do with this unpretentious book. As was repeatedly the case with Erasmus, he only gradually discovered the possibilities offered by a particular form. In March 1522 a totally new edition of the *Colloquies* appeared, much more detailed, in which the simple hints occupied only the first part; these were followed by much more extensive dialogues, mostly with two speakers, about the most varied subjects. A new edition was necessary within months, with a few new or expanded dialogues. Eleven more official editions followed in the years up to 1533, each one with new material, until in the end forty-eight items were included. In this form the *Colloquies* achieved their great popularity, but also came under heavy attack from very varied quarters.

The popularity was as natural as the criticism. The conversations are almost all lively scenes, not overlong, in which sixteenth-century society as a whole passes before us: the so-called noble youth, the overdressed citizen's wife who will not be outdone by her neighbour, the pilgrims whom the guides at the holy places lead by the nose, the dying man pestered by representatives of the different monastic orders, the alchemist in search of the philosophers' stone, the jack of all trades and master of none, the young woman who is married off to a decrepit greybeard with venereal disease. One could go on. Of course there are some unsuccessful dialogues, but they are few. The speakers are types but not clichés; Erasmus manages to include enough surprises. It is striking that small children are almost absent, but on the other hand there are many young people and quite a number of women who, against all convention of the time, often speak very sensibly. The clergy, especially the monks and the friars, come off badly almost without exception. Franz Bierlaire, who has written two good books about the *Colloquies*, has character-ized them as table-talk, a description with which Erasmus himself, who mentions with approval free and convivial conversations at table at which nothing and no one remains uncriticized, might agree.[4] He did not pay too much attention to them, sometimes writing three in a single day.[5]

This criticism in fact was the cause of all the attacks. In the society of the time, the church and its servants held an important place, so privileged that corruption was ever-present. All through the Middle Ages, one finds harsh criticism of all the phenomena of degenera-tion in the church. But the criticism of Erasmus and his contempo-raries was of another character. It no longer accepted the whole ecclesiastical structure as self-evident but stood outside it. It judged and condemned the existing order from a distance, not merely rebuking abuses, but voicing doubts about the essence of the institution of the church. To many of his contemporaries, Erasmus seemed in so doing to be striking at the heart of religion itself. Luther felt this no differently from Pelargus. And then there was the form. The angry Dominican theologian Ambrosius Catharinus said of Erasmus, after his death, that he 'had been the first to sow the worst seed of all in the field of the Lord and then had said: "It was a game, an exercise in eloquence, I was not speaking seriously." That is nothing but saying "I have slandered God for a joke," so that he himself is pushed into hell by the devils as a joke.'[6] The dialogue form gave Erasmus the freedom to approach a subject from more than one angle. In an apologia he observed, 'I am treated cavalierly if

I am held responsible for everything said, either seriously or in jest, in whatever role, in the *Colloquies*.'[7] That is one side; Erasmus disclaims responsibility for what his creations assert. But it is also part of his nature, that only by letting various persons illustrate different aspects of a case can he do himself full justice. There are many points of resemblance between the *Colloquies* and the *Praise of Folly*, but one is certainly important: in both works Erasmus shows great commitment, but as a spectator and not as a player.

But one should not treat the *Colloquies* too earnestly. In the first place they were intended for young people as a help in the teaching of Latin. Bierlaire has listed an impressive number of cities and territories where the *Colloquies* were prescribed for use in schools,[8] from as early as 1523 in Zwickau until the end of the century. Above all in England and the Lutheran part of Germany, the *Colloquies* had a great influence; in spite of Luther's attack on the book, it was introduced at Wittenberg in 1533. But it was also popular in Catholic territories and countries, as in Bavaria, Spain, and Portugal. By Erasmus' death a hundred editions had already been issued. Special anthologies intended for schools soon appeared, as did translations and even an expurgated edition that Catholic pupils could use without objection which turned the conversation on rash vows into a discussion on pious vows. The influence of the *Colloquies* was not confined to the sixteenth century. The Elzevier editions of the second half of the seventeenth century are well known: handsome pocket format volumes, well printed, and to a great extent intended for export from Amsterdam to England. Twenty more editions appeared in the eighteenth century, the majority of them for schools. Although the *Colloquies*, with many other books by Erasmus, appeared on many lists of forbidden books from the 1540s, several schools in Catholic countries continued to use it in teaching for a long time. Editions are even known from which the name of Erasmus was omitted, apparently to avoid possible difficulties.

Why schools attached so much value to it is expressed very well by a schoolmaster from Brugge, who found the revised edition of the *Colloquies* of 1522 equally important for old and young. Everyone should study it and learn it by heart, he advises, for everyone wishes the conversation he carries on every hour to be crystal clear and perfect. Through the *Colloquies*, he promises Erasmus, the youth of

Brugge will become the best educated in the world, a joy to men of letters and a stimulus to their elders.[9] In his eulogy he voices the honourable expectation which was associated with education and above all with classical teaching. Language is not a mere tool; its goal is to train pupils in humanity, in which language is the bridge between the young person and the ideals he absorbs from good literature. As early as 1524, in the foreword to his new edition of the *Colloquies*, Erasmus expressed this conviction succinctly: the book 'makes better Latinists and better men of many.' Not only do literature and virtue stand side by side, they are seamlessly interwoven.[10]

It is not possible to review all the colloquies. I prefer to choose a few that illustrate this connection between language and culture. 'The Abbot and the Learned Lady,' for example, presents at first sight a simple situation.[11] The colloquy begins with the abbot's amazement at the lady's room, which is full of books – and not just in French, but in Latin and Greek. It ends with the lady's threat – and Margaret Roper, the erudite eldest daughter of Thomas More probably served as her model – 'If you are not careful, the net result will be that we'll preside in the theological schools, preach in the churches, and wear your mitres!' Such a situation must lead to the depiction of two types, each playing a fixed role. The abbot is stupidity personified, a lover of hunting, court life, drinking, coarse pleasure, money, and honour. The woman is noble, polite, educated, and also realizes that it is a woman's job to manage the household and to bring up the children. All the elements for a cheap tragedy are present, and yet Erasmus manages to avoid this danger.

He does so by stating the theme at the outset. The abbot says loftily that women of high rank may well be permitted something with which to beguile their leisure. Then the following conversation takes place:

Magdalia Are court ladies the only ones allowed to improve their minds and enjoy themselves?
Antronius You confuse growing wise with enjoying yourself. It's not feminine to be brainy. A lady's business is to have a good time.
Magdalia Shouldn't everyone live well?

Antronius Yes, in my opinion.
Magdalia But who can have a good time without living well?
Antronius Rather, who can enjoy himself if he does live well?
Magdalia So you approve of those who live basely if only they have a good time?
Antronius I believe those who have a good time are living well.

This exchange raises the question that runs through the whole dialogue and is answered in opposite ways by the two partners: is living well having a good time, or is having a good time living well? The abbot is eager to demonstrate that an agreeable life is the highest good. That is why he does not tolerate any learning among his sixty-two monks, not even any books in their cells: it would make them rebellious. That is why he himself has not a single book: what would he do with it? A woman must stick to her distaff; everything else is nonsense. Books do not bring wisdom. The lady, on her part, considers it possible to have a good time only if one lives well. The whole dialogue thus becomes one great misunderstanding. The abbot understands nothing of the lady's arguments, nor does he understand how stupid his own answers are. Only once does something get through to him, when he cries: 'You strike me as a sophistress, so keenly do you dispute.' His masculine self-esteem does not permit him to see how far the roles have been reversed: the abbot is inferior to the lady in everything. As in the *Praise of Folly*, appearance and reality change places, until at last the lady reveals the truth. After she said that women will come to play first fiddle in the church, the abbot exclaims: 'God forbid!' The answer is: 'No, it will be up to you to forbid. But if you keep on as you've begun, geese may do the preaching sooner than put up with you tongue-tied pastors. The world's a stage that's topsy-turvy now as you see. Every man must play his part or – exit.' The cause of this reversal lies in education; the lady learns Latin 'to converse daily with authors so numerous, so eloquent, so learned, so wise; with counsellors so faithful.'

Erasmus does not express any view here on who the authors might be, Christian or non-Christian. There is a passage in 'The Godly Feast,' however,[12] in which he explicitly discusses the relationship between ancient culture and Christian faith, the ancient heritage of ideas and Christian feeling. Is there a difference between the word of a human being and the word of the Christian? In this conversation, a number of friends meet in a beautiful and well laid out garden just outside the city. One may think of Froben's garden and of some people from Basel and its neighbourhood. It is 1522, and the unity of the humanist circle in Basel has not yet been broken. One of the guests, after a lengthy conversation on the meaning of a statement of St Paul, excuses himself for raising a point from the profane authors. Then he cites a passage from Cicero, who presents Cato the Elder as saying, 'Nor am I sorry to have lived, since I have so lived that I do not think I was born in vain. And yet I depart from this life as from an inn, not from a home ... O glorious day, when I shall join that company of souls and leave this tumult and contagion!' He adds, 'What could a Christian have said more reverently?' Another guest adds at once: how many Christians have lived in such a way that they have the right to let these words pass their lips? A third quotes as his contribution Socrates' words, 'The human soul is placed in this body as if in a garrison, which it may not abandon except by the commander's order or remain in longer than suits him who stationed it there.' Is this not entirely in accordance with the words of Paul and Peter, who both called this body a tent? 'What else does Christ proclaim to us than that we should live and watch as though we were shortly to die, to exert ourselves in good deeds as though we were to live forever? When we hear that "O glorious day" don't we seem to hear Paul himself saying "I desire to depart and be with Christ?"' The first speaker agrees: one can detect a certain self-confidence in Cato's words that does not befit a Christian. Let us listen to what Socrates said before he drank the hemlock. He does not know if God will approve what he has done, but he has good hope that God will take his efforts as well meant. 'I think I've never read anything in pagan writers more proper to a true Christian.' 'An admirable spirit surely,' promptly adds one of the guests, 'in one who had not known Christ and the Sacred Scriptures. And so, when I read such things of such men I can hardly help exclaiming "Saint Socrates, pray for us."' Another interjects, 'As for me, there are many times when I do not hesitate to hope confidently that the souls of Virgil and Horace are sanctified.'

This passage tells us a great deal. It shows exactly the synthesis which Erasmus had found between faith and culture, between deep admiration for classical antiquity and being seized by Christ. His yardstick was the Christian faith, and by it he measured the heroes of the ancient world. This has often been presented the other way round. Christianity and antiquity are said to stand alongside each other with equal rights, or Christianity is said to be merely the reshaping of pagan content. This colloquy shows that the relationship was otherwise. The conversation as a whole deals with biblical passages and Christian faith. Erasmus inserted this section into it organically. There is a difference between Cato and Socrates on the one hand and biblical pronouncements on the other, but there is no absolute distinction. On one point Erasmus shows the reality of what he had said in general terms in the *Enchiridion*: 'No matter where you find truth, attribute it to Christ.'[13] Something of God comes through in the word of man, without the heathen thereby becoming a Christian. The emphasis is rather on the effect of God's Spirit, which is broader than is commonly realized.[14] When, at the beginning of the passage under discussion, the first speaker apologizes for being about to cite a profane author, the host says, 'On the contrary, whatever is devout and contributes to good morals should not be called profane. Sacred Scripture is of course the basic authority in everything: yet I sometimes run across ancient sayings or pagan writings – even the poets' – so purely and reverently and admirably expressed that I can't help believing their authors' hearts were moved by some divine power. And perhaps the spirit of Christ is more widespread than we understand, and the company of saints includes many not in our calendar.' The last sentence points in the same direction as 'Sancte Socrates, ora pro nobis,' an expression of the graceful seriousness characteristic of Erasmus.

Nowhere does Erasmus give such unqualified proof of his high esteem for languages as in 'The Apotheosis of Reuchlin,'[15] written very soon after he had received word of Reuchlin's death. The most important part depicts the dream of a pious Franciscan in Tübingen at the moment of Reuchlin's death. He sees Reuchlin pass with the Hebrew greeting of peace over the bridge from this world to a lovely green meadow, clothed in a brilliant white garment and followed at a distance by black and white birds, the colours of the habit of the Dominicans who had persecuted him so bitterly and from whom he was now safe. On the other side, he is received by Jerome – not dressed, as in the well-known pictures, in the robes of a cardinal and accompanied by a lion, but in crystal garments – with the words: 'Hail, most holy colleague.' Then the heavens open, the divine majesty appears, and the two colleagues are taken up into heaven. The colloquy ends with the prayer that the reporter had already composed before Reuchlin's death: 'O God thou lover of mankind, who through thy chosen servant Johann Reuchlin hast renewed to the world the gift of tongues, by which thou didst once from heaven, through thy Holy Spirit, instruct the apostles for the preaching of the gospel, grant that all men everywhere may preach in every tongue the glory of thy son Jesus.'

Finally, an example of the link between languages and Christian faith today. In several colloquies Erasmus takes up contemporary issues. He tries to get to the heart of the matter without theological jargon, using biblical arguments, thus translating theological questions and demonstrating a new way of practising theology. Naturally, this procedure often involved criticism of the official theology. A clear example is offered by the well-known 'Examination concerning Faith' from the edition of March 1524[16] in which a Lutheran is interrogated by another (or Luther by Erasmus). This is done on the basis of the Apostle's Creed. On every point the Lutheran appears to affirm the creed, so that the interrogator in the end asks in amazement why there is a war between the Lutherans and the orthodox.[17] No wonder Erasmus' publication of this piece gave such offence!

A brilliant example is also offered by 'A Fish Diet' from the edition of 1526.[18] The piece is a slice of life, a conversation between a fishmonger and a butcher. The reader sees the fishmonger before him, wiping his nose on his sleeve, untroubled by the butcher's claim that not long after eating a fish pie nine people died – accidents in business are unavoidable. He is shrewd enough to hope that the church will one day forbid the eating of fish: that can only help his sales. The butcher leads the conversation, but the fishmonger is no fool, so that good arguments are brought forward on both sides. The main theme is of course the Lenten fasting and the associated eating of fish that every year brought Erasmus, so he himself was convinced, to the brink of the grave. Naturally, the conversation widens to include the commands of the church in general. One can say that the author translates the theological discussions into generally intelligible language and chooses a starting point in everyday life. As so often, Erasmus makes a plea for mildness: why should a Christian be saddled with stricter laws than the Jews of old? He has a new argument, the new world, not long discovered. Its wealth is being plundered, but he has never heard of any attempt to introduce Christianity to those lands. What an opportunity to show that being a Christian means faith and love, not harsh rules![19] At one point the butcher asks if all papal and episcopal laws in the church are binding. The answer is that yes, they are. But it soon appears that this is too rash an assertion, for the decisions of some popes have been revoked by their successors. Then the conversation takes the following turn:

Butcher Then Peter had authority to establish new laws?
Fishmonger He had.
Butcher And Paul too with the other apostles?
Fishmonger Each of them had in his churches appointed to him by Peter or Christ.
Butcher And is the power for Peter's successors equal to that of Peter himself?
Fishmonger Why not?

A virtuous dialogue, continued by the inquiry whether there is any distinction in authority between the laws of the pope and those of the bishops. Then suddenly a surprise question from the butcher bursts the whole bubble: 'If the regulations of prelates are worth so much, what does the Lord mean in Deuteronomy by threatening so sternly against anyone's adding or taking away anything from the law?' The fishmonger cannot be caught out by this; it is not a matter of the alteration of the law, but of a wider or stricter explanation of it, depending on the circumstances of the time. The butcher persists: Does the interpretation then have more authority than the law? When the fishmonger does not understand this, he makes it clearer:

Butcher Divine law commands us to help a parent. According to the Pharisees' interpretation, whatever is placed in the offering is given to one's father, because God is the father of all men. Doesn't divine law yield to this interpretation?

Fishmonger That is surely a false interpretation.

Butcher But after the authority of interpreting has once been handed over to them, how am I to tell whose interpretation is right, especially if the interpreters differ among themselves?

The butcher is advised to listen to the word of the bishops, but is not satisfied with this. The advice to follow the doctors of theology is also unwelcome: they are often more stupid than illiterates and the learned can never agree. Finally the fishmonger passes a verdict of Solomon: 'Select the best explanations and leave the unexplained matters to others, always adopting those views approved by the majority of lords and commons.'[20] Even today we can imagine how eagerly people for whom these topics were immediately relevant must have read such a discussion. Not without reason: the expert will have no difficulty in finding echoes of the discussions of the late Middle Ages, for example the treatise of Wessel Gansfort on the authority of the church, published not long before, in this colloquy.

In 1526 Erasmus felt obliged to add an apologia to the new edition of the *Colloquies*. In it he characterized his work as follows: 'Socrates brought philosophy down from heaven to earth, I have brought it even into games, informal conversations, and drinking-parties. For the very amusements of Christians ought to have a philosophical flavour.'[21] Many generations have been grateful to him.

FOURTEEN

One Society at Stake

The last seven years of Erasmus' life, from his move to Freiburg im Breisgau in April 1529 to his death during the night of 11/12 July 1536, were a burden to him. He had suffered for many years from attacks of fever, kidney stones, and gout, but now his bodily ailments began to weigh more heavily on him. In Freiburg he felt himself completely out of his element, in spite of the honours shown to him. It was a relief when he was able to return to Basel in May 1535. Friends in Rome, England, France, Germany, and Poland were dying, and Erasmus grew lonely, a natural result of old age. More and Fisher had been executed, his enemies appointed to high positions, and everywhere Aleandro was burrowing to undermine him. Erasmus also lost some of his intellectual energy. He became aware that he could do less and that he was growing dependent on others. Certainly he was proud that his writings were still selling well,[1] yet it sounds almost pitiable when he writes that he was good for nothing but study and could only withdraw into himself, with his books for consolation.[2] He grew more suspicious than ever, and even the secret offer of the cardinal's hat in 1535 gave him little satisfaction, although he felt rather flattered: 'an ape clad in silk, as they say.'[3]

He had a deeper cause for concern, the turn events were taking in the world around him: 'If I had known before that this generation would arise, I would not have written much of what I have written, or I would have written otherwise.'[4] A common phenomenon of old age, this reaction, but one can read in his writings of these years how anxious he was. Of course Erasmus worried about his own personal situation; it would have been impossible for such an egocentric person not to. But what alarmed him even more was the falling apart of society, of the community of Christian Europe. We can scarcely imagine how a contemporary experienced the period around 1530. From the perspective of hindsight we speak of the 'Reformation' or the 'Glaubensspaltung' and think first of an ecclesiastical phenomenon and only after that of its possible social consequences. For many who lived through those years a world was passing away and the existing order was disintegrating around them. The Peasants' Wars of the years 1524 and 1525 were a traumatic experience for them: subjects in rebellion, castles burned to the ground, ecclesiastical and secular lords compelled to make pacts with people of the lowest sort, monasteries looted, nuns violated, even former priests lending their aid to the rebels. For adherents of the old church these events could not be separated from the revolt against the bishops and the pope, which broke up the whole established structure. Certainly Erasmus experienced these events in this way. For him the whole of society was at stake. From Luther's first appearance on the scene, he had feared this result, but the reality of the 1520s surpassed his gloomiest expectations. In these years he faced the question: can anything be saved of the old world, of the community of Christian Europe, of the existing culture? This fear did not begin in the Freiburg years, for one can find signs of it from the mid-twenties. And with good reason. There were the Peasants' Wars, and in the same years Erasmus began to realize that the breach between the followers of Luther and the existing church had become almost irreconcilable, while at the same time he observed the enmity between Luther and the Swiss reformers. But the climax came in the thirties.

For Erasmus it was self-evident that society had a Christian character; he could not imagine any other civilization than a Christian one. For all his high regard for ancient culture, the world of his time only had value for Erasmus if Christ was its centre. He had stated this in the foreword to the *Enchiridion*,[5] and he stood by it now. He emphatically rejected opposite tendencies, most clearly in the *Ciceronianus* (*The Ciceronian: A Dialogue on the Ideal Latin Style*) of 1528.[6] This remarkable work falls clearly into two sections. The first portrays a zealot for the language and style of Cicero, which he wishes to adopt in full, even in the sixteenth century. In comparison with his partners in the conversation, he is a caricature. He will not write a single word or form of a word that is not to be found in Cicero. He is unwilling to speak Latin and, if it is unavoidable, he has a few set phrases ready in order to avoid as far as possible the risk of impure language. One of the other two speakers thinks such an effort is nonsense: the world has totally changed since Cicero's day, and for that reason alone his Latin cannot be imitated. The second section contains a short survey of classical and post-classical Latin authors, and then a detailed and sometimes amusing discussion of the qualities of the most important humanists of the time and their predecessors.[7] This last part cost Erasmus a great deal of trouble: whoever was not named felt himself slighted; whoever was named felt his genius had not been fully recognized. The only one who did not protest was Erasmus – but he was painted as a prolific writer, who did not bear fruitful issue but abortions: 'writing is something different from belonging to the guild of writers.'[8]

In the middle of the *Ciceronianus* there is a passage in which Erasmus voices his concern at the tendency to introduce pagan content along with the idioms of the pre-Christian world. He begins with the example of the orator at Rome whose sermon he had heard on Good Friday 1509.[9] For him Christ had become a Greek or Roman hero; he said not a word of our sin, our redemption from the power of the devil, or our death with Christ. Erasmus could have wept when the triumphs of the Roman heroes were compared with the triumph of the cross. 'This Roman spoke so Romanly that I heard nothing about the death of Christ.'[10] Erasmus denounced the foolish fashion of wanting to express Christian content in classical Latin phrases. It was worse than foolishness, it was paganism, if a man would rather hear 'Socrates, son of Sophroniscus,' than 'Jesus, Son of God, and God.' He expresses himself bluntly: 'It is paganism, believe me ... sheer paganism ... The fact is we're Christians only in name. Our bodies may have been dipped in the holy water, but our minds are unbaptized.' No name is sweeter than that of Jesus, 'so gentle and kind ... that no calamity, however bitter, is not comforted and alleviated if you name Jesus from your heart.'[11]

Precisely because the Christian character of society was a

self-evident precondition for Erasmus, the question was whether its unity was still to be saved in any way. This question dominated his thoughts in the last ten years of his life. It was his conviction that the old way, of unity imposed by force, could no longer be followed in the present situation. Over the years various aspects of the problem demanded his attention: the persecution of heretics, the possibilities of a plurality of confessions within a single state, the maintenance of unity along with varied external forms of ecclesiastical life.

The first question was that of the persecution of heretics. For many it was a simple matter. The unity of the church was preserved by removing heretics from society. People who were accused of heresy were tried by ecclesiastical courts. If their guilt was established, they were handed over to the secular arm, which executed them. Erasmus doubted very much whether this was the appropriate method. Not that he demanded that society should stand aloof under all circumstances, or that he chose freedom of conviction in the abstract, even if this went far beyond the bounds of the Christian faith. He was afraid of paganism, and stated with indignation that 'such a monster,' had been burned in Basel, a man who did not believe in the Gospels, thought prayer harmful, did not pray to Christ as to God and man, and so on.[12] His indignation concerned the fact that such people dared to open their mouths in the general confusion, not the execution. But other things were happening. Highly respectable people of the same social position as himself were being accused and burned at the stake. They had not uttered any horrid blasphemy, but had thought somewhat differently from their accusers in 'dubious and controversial, even insignificant things.'[13] In 1523 the first followers of Luther were executed: two Augustinians were burned at the stake in Brussels. Works by Erasmus himself were officially condemned in 1526 and 1527, in fact by the Sorbonne. The words 'heresy' and 'heretic' no longer meant what they had in the carefree days when his friend Andrea Ammonio could report lightheartedly from London on the burning of heretics: 'I am not surprised that the price of firewood has gone up: every day there are a great number of heretics to make bonfires for us, and still their number continues to grow.'[14] That was in 1511, and Erasmus had answered in the same light-hearted style: 'I have less sympathy with those heretics you mention, if only because they have chosen the moment when winter is upon us to send up the price of fuel.'[15] But now it had become deadly serious, and not only for such simple souls as the brother of Ammonio's servant.

Under these grim circumstances, Erasmus was forced to reconsider his ideas on the persecution of heretics. The occasion for this was given by a sentence from his *Paraphrase on Matthew* of 1522. There he had discussed the parable of the tares in the wheat in Matthew 13, a passage that had played a role in the persecution of heretics for eleven hundred years. The tares may not be rooted out by the servants; they stay in the midst of the corn until the harvest. Erasmus had permitted himself the remark that God did not wish false apostles and heretics to be put to death, but rather that they should be tolerated until the day of the harvest. Noël Béda and the Spanish monks[16] reacted violently to his exegesis. In two apologias of 1527 and 1528,[17] which ran along parallel lines, Erasmus investigated the question of the attitude society ought now to adopt.

His first approach was to compare present practice with that of the age of Christ and the apostles, one of the constants in his thought. On this point he was very decided. Christ and his disciples were mildness itself, and until the year 800 the severest punishment was excommunication, exclusion from the community of the church. Augustine too, after an initial rejection, was willing to punish heretics, but never went further than punishment by the authorities; he even took up a position directly opposed to the killing of the Donatists, who were not only heretics but murderers too. A second line of thought was to demand a clear distinction between the task of the bishops and the theologians, and that of the authorities. The bishop must teach, improve, heal, and in the last resort, excommunicate. The authorities should not, as now, rely on the verdict of theologians and monks but must set up their own inquiry. A third constant was Erasmus' position on the role of the princes. In this respect he was rather reticent: 'I do not advise the princes either to strike down the heretics or not to do so. I show what belongs to the priestly office.'[18] Yet he started from the assumption that princes must not reach too quickly for the sword 'if those who have sinned can be cured in another way.'[19]

Of direct practical importance was his remark: 'If the situation turns into revolt and tumult, and both parties loudly insist that they must defend the Catholic church, the prince, as long as the matter is not fully investigated, must calm both parties. What objection is there to the prince removing those heretics who disturb public order?'[20] It cannot be said that this statement is entirely clear, but at any rate it shows that Erasmus saw the core of the problem. He did not live in a world in which individuals voiced their own opinions so that they could be tested by society. In his day group stood against group, and each was convinced of its own divine right. In this state of affairs, Erasmus recommended caution to the authorities, which in the first instance had to preserve public order. Is this a plea for tolerance? In his famous *De haereticis an sint persequendi* (*Are Heretics to be Persecuted?*), published in 1554 on the occasion of the execution of Servetus, Sébastien Castellio included comprehensive passages from both of Erasmus' works, and rightly so. The question of toleration did not remain the same for all time. Under the circumstances, Erasmus' words, although addressed more against a corrupt application of rules than against the persecution of heretics in itself, were a plea for toleration.

The passage cited on the role of the prince touches on a second complex of questions concerning the unity of Christian society. Erasmus was beginning to ask whether it might be possible to save this unity while recognizing the existing differences. This approach first appears in a letter to Johannes Fabri, shortly before the latter was to attend the Disputation of Baden in 1526, on the instructions of King Ferdinand, the brother of Charles v. There, it was expected, a decision would be taken on the ecclesiastical differences in Switzerland and thus also on the continued existence of the Swiss Confederation as a unit. From Erasmus' letter it is clear that he was not thinking of Switzerland alone but of Germany too, for he offered to give advice to the princes. In the middle of impracticable advice there suddenly appears this recommendation: 'And perhaps it would be better, in the regions where evil has gained the upper hand, to see that both parties were given a place of their own, and everyone left to his own conscience until time brings the possibility of unity.'[21] Furthermore, disturbances should be severely punished, and the cause of the evil corrected. This is a turning-point in Erasmus' thinking. In concrete terms it meant no less than the recognition of religious plurality within a single political unit, albeit only for the time being in districts which were, or threatened to become, Protestant.

Thereafter, the idea of plurality cropped up from time to time in Erasmus' letters, for example in a letter he wrote in 1529 to no less a person than Anton Fugger, the highly influential banker: he thought a certain balance between the parties was desirable.[22] He gave this advice very explicitly during the Diet of Augsburg in 1530. Erasmus was aware that this was a critical moment. Now negotiations were to take place between Lutherans and followers of the old church, negotiations that were to determine the future of Germany. Would it be possible to restore the unity of the Christian world? He saw no use in harsh measures, and learned that there were many in Augsburg who thought likewise, and that besides the hard-liners on both sides there were many present who wished to avoid a war at all costs. Melanchthon for example, wrote to Erasmus in forthright terms that the reformers wanted peace on honourable conditions, and asked him to use his influence with the emperor to avoid a war.[23] Erasmus even received invitations from various quarters to come to Augsburg, but felt no good would come of it.

More important, however, are his letters to Lorenzo Campeggi, who played a significant role in the diet as papal legate. As early as his first letter, Erasmus gave him the same advice as that which he had written to Fugger the previous year: to maintain the *status quo* was best; to everyone's amazement no war had yet broken out, and commercial relations had been kept up.[24] In a second letter he was more concrete. Luther was to be kept out of everything; Zwingli, Oecolampadius, and Capito were to be sent away; and perhaps it would be possible to do something for the Anabaptists – they were blinded, but there were some good people among them.[25] In August he wrote a very frank letter. First he sketched the situation: the Hapsburg hereditary lands were exhausted by the emperor's wars; the Protestant territories from the Hanseatic cities to Switzerland formed a strong chain of evil. The emperor must not let himself be led by the pope. 'I know and abhor the brutality of the leaders and partisans of the sects. But under the present circumstances, one must rather take into consideration the demands of the whole world for rest than the punishment they deserve for their shamelessness ... If the sects were tolerated on certain conditions, as the Bohemians are winked at, that would indeed be a grave evil, but less so than war, and what a war!'[26] An important distinction from the advice he gave to Johannes Fabri was that he was now thinking of a toleration for the Protestants in the Empire. A remarkable coincidence: this confidential letter, of all others, was intercepted and reprinted several times in Latin and in German translation.

After the Diet of Augsburg Erasmus gave this idea up. The course of the discussions, on which he was well informed, made it clear that such plans were no longer viable. Gradually other ideas ripened, which he finally expressed in 1533 in his *Liber de sarcienda ecclesiae concordia* (*On Repairing the Unity of the Church*).[27] The work is a commentary on Psalm 83 (84), like the commentaries of which he had already published a number since 1515.[28] The greater part of it contains a wide-ranging exegesis of this psalm, with some remarks addressed indirectly against the Protestants. The latter part[29] consists of observations on the unity of the church, which Erasmus believed appeared in this psalm. His starting-point was simple: 'He who separates himself from the community of the church and goes over to heresy or schism is worse than the man who lives an impure life without doing violence to the dogmas.'[30] Many abuses had crept into the church in the course of time: they must be removed without haste and as far as possible without disturbance. He still thought this was possible: 'This sickness has not yet become so serious that it is incurable.'[31] How was it to be cured? The last pages contain Erasmus' detailed advice. As far as doctrine is concerned, this was very brief. He mentioned only the problem of the freedom of the will, which was especially easy to solve: it was clear, was it not, that both faith and good works were necessary and complemented each other? Erasmus paid more attention to ceremonies, and discussed prayers for the dead, the invocation of saints, the veneration of relics, fasting, feast days, images, confession, the mass, private masses, and the veneration of the host. In most cases he advised accepting plurality of rites within a single community. The weak and the strong could bear with each other in many respects, according to the rule of Paul in Romans 14 and 15. But there were differences too. In the matter of fasting and feast days, Erasmus went quite far. He pleaded for a considerable reduction in the number of feast days and a relaxation of the fasting rules. Erasmus could imagine that in some places, things had come to the point of riotous destruction of images: the people had indeed worshipped the images. His thinking was most traditional on the mass. If superstition were combatted, he saw no evil in the rite of the mass, with the exception of some later interpolations which could be removed. His intention was to suggest an arrangement that could be valid until the council could be convened, which would have to give a definitive solution.

The reactions to this short book were very varied. It found admirers and critics in both camps. Capito in Strasbourg translated it and recommended it in his introduction, but Luther was of the opinion that 'sense of duty and the truth itself will not bear this model of harmony.'[32] On the Catholic side there was the same diversity. This is understandable, for the work unmistakably starts from a certain vision. To discover this, one need only look at the famous Augsburg Confession of 1530, in its main features the work of Melanchthon. This confession consists of two parts. The first is concerned with the doctrine taught in the Lutheran churches. The second part is a lengthy defence of all the changes that had been introduced, or that the reformers desired to introduce, in the field of ceremonial. These rites occupied an important place in the practice of ecclesiastical life, and in the popular mind they were the distinguishing mark of the church. Erasmus started from the same distinction. He regarded doctrine as the affair of theologians, as neutral territory. Where doctrine affected popular faith, it was agreed that man on his own is not capable of achieving anything, that everything man does is wholly owing to God's grace.[33] That seems simple enough. The difficulty is in giving form to the life of the church, and it was there that solutions had to be looked for. His own contribution was the consideration that the unity of the Christian world would be greatly benefited if we allowed each other a wide range of views. One may say that this was a superficial response, and such criticism is just. Some years later, it was to prove that neither Rome nor Wittenberg shared Erasmus' view of the relationship between doctrine and ceremonial. One should also recall that the irenically minded had been trying for more than ten years to escape from the problem in this way. The man to whom Erasmus dedicated this work was Julius Pflug, who in all the discussions between Catholics and Protestants from 1534 essentially defended this model of unity, together with Bucer, Capito's colleague in Strasbourg.

Culture, society, and the community of Christian Europe are, as we have seen, central themes for Erasmus. Only in the last named work, *De sarcienda ecclesiae concordia*, was Erasmus explicitly concerned with the church. This is typical of his outlook. He constantly took his point of departure from society as a whole, and its Christian character was a given. One may say that his heart was in Christianity, much less in the church. Whenever he uses the word 'church' he is thinking either of liturgy in the broadest sense of the word, of all the ways in which religion assumes an external form, or of the organizational nature of the church, of the bishops, the pope, Rome. For that reason, in his thinking as a whole the church does not occupy a prominent place. It had too much to do with externals, with compulsion. This does not alter the fact that Erasmus wished to be faithful to it.

In the *Hyperaspistes* I of 1526 there is a sentence in which he very clearly defines his attitude towards the church: 'I put up with this church until I see a better one, and it is forced to put up with me until I become better.'[34] This is a typically Erasmian statement: a touch of self-mockery, a certain detachment with regard to the church, but in spite of all reservations, loyalty. In the last part of his *Erasme et l'Italie*, Renaudet treated it as the key. In his opinion Erasmus was here expressing his longing for a third church, a renewed and rejuvenated church, a church that had to arise in Rome, with the cooperation of the Holy See. But the context of Erasmus' words makes it clear that he was, in this case, rejecting fellowship with Luther's church and explicitly professing his loyalty to the church of Rome. An almost identical expression in a contemporary letter points in the same direction.[35] It is undeniable – and this is the core of truth in Renaudet's argument – that Erasmus was not enthusiastic about the church of his own day. He dreamed of a united and uniform Christian world. He saw the church of Rome as an obstacle on the path to that ideal rather than a help. But there was no sense in leaving it and attaching himself to the church of the Reformation, which in spite of its pretensions did not deviate any less from his ideal. Such a step would only deserve consideration if a church existed that approached nearer to the ideal. So, loyalty to the church? Perhaps this is to state it too positively. It remained the Catholic church 'from which I have never deviated.'[36]

Erasmus' return to Basel was a homecoming. No one spoke to him about differences in doctrine,[37] order reigned, and the laws governing public morality were exemplary.[38] Erasmus lodged with his friend Hieronymus Froben and worked hard. His sigh two weeks before his death, 'if only Brabant were closer,'[39] may have been meant, but a return there was no more than a pipedream. The Netherlands were not really attractive, and Basel had become his spiritual home. Or is this saying too much? The Basel circle of humanists had fallen apart, and silence gradually enfolded Erasmus. At bottom he had always been a solitary person. He had his patrons, he had had fellow students, there were young people whom he educated and who served him as secretaries and clerks, but of true friends he had always had few. His reply to Zwingli in 1522, when Zwingli asked him to accept the citizenship of Zürich, is eloquent: 'I wish to be a citizen of the world, to belong to everyone, or rather, to be alien to everyone.'[40] These words have little to do with cosmopolitanism, but much with a sense of independence closely akin to solitariness.

The last months were difficult. Erasmus suffered badly from gout or rheumatism, so that he was unable to leave his room. Beatus Rhenanus gives us the following impression: 'When, for some new edition, he went through one by one letters he had formerly received from various friends, and very many of those he picked up were from people who had died, he said again and again, "He too is dead," and at length, "I do not wish to live any longer, if it pleases Christ the Lord."'[41] Finally he caught dysentery and died from it after three weeks. To the end he was conscious and mumbled words of the psalms, and in Dutch, *Lieve God*, 'Dear God.'[42]

Erasmus was buried in the cathedral of Basel, in the presence of the professors and students of the university, the magistrates, and the mayor. The funeral oration was preached by the head of the reformed church in Basel, Osvaldus Myconius.

FIFTEEN

Erasmus and His Influence

꽃

Is it possible to paint a good likeness of Erasmus? In the preceding chapters we have sketched his features – do they form a whole? These are the questions that confront the biographer. They are peculiar to the genre, but they urge themselves even more insistently in the case of Erasmus. He is highly elusive; he slips away from attempts to place him exactly. His character has a great deal to do with this. 'I always wished to be alone,' he said of himself,[1] and indeed he did stand alone. But it is not simply a matter of his personality. His writings can be interpreted in the most various ways, and that is typical of the age of transition in which he lived. The difference of opinion existed in his own lifetime and has persisted. Even though in modern scholarship confessional and apologetic motives are less prominent than they were, this has not led to complete clarity. In more recent literature one still recognizes the old pictures, albeit in modified form. In essence one can distinguish three main types of interpretation of Erasmus.

The first picture goes back to the time when Erasmus' vision of church and society had assumed its definitive form and was familiar in a wide circle, thanks in particular to the dissemination of his ideas by means of such popular works as the *Adages*, the *Praise of Folly* and the *Colloquies*. This interpretation presents Erasmus in a very negative light. He is relativist, subjectivist, and sceptical; in short, his work is pure denial. He destroys and criticizes and does so without a fixed standard; he lives by negation. This representation first appears clearly in the attacks of the Louvain theologians, Lee, and Zúñiga on Erasmus' edition of the New Testament. In later years the criticism grows more and more violent, but without changing its character. The attacks reach their climax in the campaigns in Paris and Spain in the second half of the 1520s. They are directed against writings of a very varied nature, but all characteristic of Erasmus' outlook: along with those already mentioned, the *Enchiridion*, the *Annotations on the New Testament* and the *Paraphrases*. The accusations are of all kinds: heresy in the doctrine of the Trinity, denial of the divinity of the Son, impugning the doctrine of original sin, defending justification by faith alone, disputing the divine institution of various sacraments, especially confession and infant baptism, praising marriage at the expense of celibacy, and so on. These criticisms, however disparate they may seem at first sight, start from a common assumption: that through an exegesis of the Bible that does not remain within the fold of ecclesiastical tradition, Erasmus is undermining the dogma of the church and thus opening the door to all imaginable forms of heresy, including that of the Reformation. Moreover, in this vision of Erasmus and the reproaches made against him, Luther agrees wholly with the Catholics who were the enemies of both. In Protestant circles, the image of Erasmus was to a great extent determined by Luther's *The Bondage of the Will*, in which he branded Erasmus as a Lucian, an Epicurus, a scoffer who denied the existence of any superhuman power, while against Erasmus' *diatribe*, value-free investigation, he set his own *assertio*, a positive confessional affirmation. In 1534 he published a short polemic against Erasmus, a letter to his friend Nikolaus Amsdorf,[2] in which he elaborated his criticism in such a way that even in details it paralleled that of Erasmus' opponents in the old church. In this type of interpretation Erasmus is judged according to a standard of content: what doctrine has he taught? But behind this lies the verdict that for Erasmus there is no objective truth. That is why he is regarded as a greater danger to the church than the Protestant or Catholic adversary.

This view has held its ground through the centuries. Around 1900 Heinrich Denifle depicted the Reformation as a process of secularization, and identified a subjective conception of faith, the autonomy of the individual, and relativism as its characteristic features. In his eyes, Erasmus stood alongside Luther as the champion of these tendencies. No one nowadays would speak of

Luther in these terms. On the contrary, in more recent Catholic historiography the judgment passed on Luther has been positive. This has not, however, led to a higher esteem for Erasmus, but has rather been to his detriment: he is seen as vagueness and indefiniteness personified. Joseph Lortz for example calls him *vollendete Undeutlichkeit*, 'the perfection of unclearness.'[3]

We find the same picture of Erasmus, but with the opposite appreciation, among the historians who see him as a precursor of the Enlightenment or of nineteenth-century Catholic modernism. Renaudet, for example, started from this point of view,[4] and the Dutch expert on the sixteenth century Herman A. Enno van Gelder refined the thesis considerably by speaking of the two reformations of the sixteenth century: the Reformation of Luther, he argues, ultimately preserved the values of Catholicism, whereas Erasmus was the representative of a much more far-reaching 'reformation,' one which preached the autonomy of man and was not to reach its culmination until the eighteenth century.[5]

We find a second picture in its most acute form in Hutten:[6] Erasmus as the weak, conscienceless man, cowardly, covetous, and ready to fall in with the winning side. That in his opinion is especially true of Erasmus' attitude to Luther. Although it has become clear enough that Erasmus agrees with Luther, he has never stated this publicly, and now he is drawing back out of fear. This image of Erasmus rests on the conviction that he basically stands side by side with Luther. Hutten even issued an urgent summons to Erasmus in 1520 to say so openly and to join with him in the struggle against Rome. A certain conception of the Reformation lies behind this view: for Hutten it is a liberation movement. He finds in Erasmus' works, in his criticism of all kinds of ecclesiastical abuses and in his rejection of pointless ceremonies, the commitment to freedom with respect to the curia and to Italy in general that he regards as the decisive motive for reformation. In this interpretation, Erasmus is not judged by the doctrines he taught but by his view of the structure of the church. The greatness of Erasmus thus lies in his rejection of the church as an institution defined by its hierarchy and its sacraments.

But even before Luther appeared on the scene, several opponents of Erasmus had seen his significance in similar terms, that is, in the critical character of his work. In Maarten van Dorp's protest in 1514 against the *Praise of Folly* and the proposed edition of the New Testament, the attack on the structure of ecclesiastical authority was the crucial point. Exactly the same charges are heard from the critics of the 1520s. At first sight, their criticism gives the impression of being concerned with all kinds of disparate things: Erasmus repudiates the Inquisition, he identifies errors in the Bible, he polemicizes against ecclesiastical ceremonies, he wishes to reduce the number of holy days, thinks fasting harmful, is an opponent of indulgences, sets himself against celibacy, thinks monastic life senseless, demands that the church should permit divorce, and so on. Erasmus' critics saw a central idea behind all these opinions: Erasmus is attacking the existing structure of the church in the broadest sense of the word, he is stripping it of everything that gives it stability as an institution.

This type of interpretation recurs in several versions in the history of later scholarship. For a long time it determined the customary Lutheran image of Erasmus, above all in the eighteenth and nineteenth centuries, when the depiction of the Reformation as a liberation movement was at its height. In the Netherlands in the eighteenth and nineteenth centuries we find a related view, which assumes that Erasmus was the first reformer, who by reason of his criticism of the church and his theological activity deserved this title more than Luther, and whose follower and popularizer Luther is supposed to have been. The concept of Erasmus as a forerunner of the Reformation, a reformer before the Reformation, particularly widespread in the last century, goes a little less far in the same direction.

A third view of Erasmus was that of his contemporary admirers. They saw him as the renewer of the church and of theology, who reached back across the Middle Ages, a period of decay, to the theology of the first centuries and reshaped it in the service of a reformation of the church on the model of the ideal – and idealized – church of the first centuries. In the eyes of these men, the penetrating criticism that Erasmus practised had a positive goal. The ideals of Erasmus remained alive among many into the twenties, when the extent of the schism in the church, which had begun to reveal itself, had not yet been realized. The leading adherents of Luther were almost without exception kindred spirits of Erasmus. Melanchthon always honoured him as the restorer of *sacrae litterae;*

to the end he was under his influence and kept up his contact with him. Unlike Cranach, who even painted Erasmus among the circle of the reformers, Melanchthon inclined to the view that Erasmus belonged to neither party. The reformers of Switzerland and southern Germany were to a significant extent the pupils of Erasmus. They found his attitude in the controversy over the Eucharist incomprehensible, and reproached him for it, but they continued to honour him as the man with whom the whole movement had begun. In the Catholic camp too, there were many for whom Erasmus remained the great mentor; and they included princes, prelates, and magistrates. Many saw in him the only man who could have averted the threatened tearing apart of the church.

This view of Erasmus is scarcely to be found in the earliest historiography of the Reformation period. The contradictions between Rome and the Reformation were too great for that. The interpretation of Erasmus found in the most recent literature, however, is very close to it.

The first two types of interpretation mentioned contain elements of truth to the extent that they reflect certain facets of Erasmus' aims and his personality. Both stress the critical aspects of his thought, and both turn him into a champion of an ideal of freedom that comes close to detachment. But they miss the heart of Erasmus' ideals, and thereby fail to recognize both his spirituality and his goal, while the over-illumination of certain traits produces a diffuse picture.

When I myself set out to draw a portrait of Erasmus in a sixteenth-century setting, I start with the third interpretation. One can only do justice to Erasmus if one sees him against the background of medieval theology and piety, which he knew and in which he was rooted, and at the same time realizes that he explicitly distanced himself from it and went back to the primitive church and theology as the sources of renewal. In this way I also define my vision with regard to the tendency of the last twenty years to locate Erasmus' theology so wholly within the framework of the medieval tradition that scarcely anything original is left. One should also be wary of a presentation that sketches him as an original theologian in every respect. In my view, Erasmus' importance for the culture of his day can be concretely defined, and his influence on theology determined within this context. It is sensible to identify his influence clearly; it is not very sensible to study him deeply in areas in which he made no original contribution.

It is however impossible to do this until a basic theme has been identified, a theme that underlay Erasmus' work as a whole and through which he is to be understood. This basic theme was excellently expressed by the Louvain professor Maarten van Dorp. In one of his letters to Erasmus we find a lengthy passage in which he inveighs vehemently against the new fashion of granting the tribe of grammarians, poets, and rhetoricians, the experts in *bonae litterae*, an exalted position. Does Erasmus really believe that a poet or a Greek scholar is worth more than a theologian? He concludes this passage with a brilliant tirade in which he poses the question: What sort of people will be grateful to Erasmus for his edition of Jerome? Not the jurists, the physicians, or the philosophers. 'But you made it for people interested in grammar. Let the grammarians then sit on the throne and act as censors of all the other disciplines ... But there is some risk that serious scholars may refuse to bow beneath their sceptres ... [The grammarians] think that they know all subjects, because they understand the actual words and the structure of the sentences. So we need no universities. The school at Zwolle or Deventer [two small towns in the Netherlands] will be quite enough.'[7] The whole passage drips with disdain. Van Dorp takes his stand against the arrogance of a despised sort of person: the schoolmaster on the throne!

He had, however, realized very well what was at the heart of Erasmus' way of thinking and had even identified the key to his life's work: Erasmus had discovered the word as the medium in the relationships of people with each other and in their dealings with God. The word forms a bridge between people. It brings man into connection with the world around him, with other people, and with God. The *Colloquies* were more than linguistic exercises or an amusing game; they reflected a reality of life. In a much less familiar work, *Lingua* (*The Tongue*), Erasmus points out the central place of the tongue, between the brain and the heart and in the immediate neighbourhood of the senses. The work culminates in a eulogy of the word of God himself, so immense that we human beings cannot comprehend it and need Christ, the Word of God, as our mediator.[8] Erasmus was fascinated by the possibilities that language offered and the dangers it posed. This bewitchment by words, characteristic of the humanist movement and revolutionary in its time, led to a reverence for texts, which spanned the centuries and brought contact with a vanished world, which became present again. The medium of language has an importance and leads a life of its own. As the Amerbachs put it, in words we quoted earlier, 'Study changes the reader, and we develop in the image of the authors whom we read daily.'[9] Once this fundamental theme is recognized, the importance of Erasmus can be concretely indicated in three ways.

The first is Erasmus' consistent application of the philological method used by the humanists in the study of texts from classical antiquity to biblical scholarship and the study of the Fathers of the church. In this lay his contribution to the development of a new method of biblical exegesis. He was not the first to use it, for Lorenzo Valla in Italy and Jacques Lefèvre d'Etaples in France had preceded him. But he was the first to work through the whole New Testament, and the first to apply this method consistently and to offer more than a slight revision of the Vulgate text. He went back to the Greek text, tried to reconstruct readings of biblical texts known to the Fathers, and incorporated into his annotations the exegesis of the early church. The result was that he undermined the authority of the great exegetical compendiums of the Middle Ages, the *Glossa Ordinaria* and the *Postillae* of Nicholas of Lyra. He felt that their biblical exegesis led too rapidly from the exposition of words and things to theological considerations and they tore the Fathers from their context and distorted their meaning. Erasmus' *Annotations on the New Testament* in particular were an attack on the established order. In them the reader found sober philological observations on the text of the Bible. In fact this method of work meant the desacralization of the holy book. In Erasmus' exegesis the tradition which had accumulated around the text of the Bible through the centuries was not respected and added to, but rejected in favour of a new beginning. In the editions that followed, this process was continued: on the basis of the text Erasmus exposed the practice and dogma of the church, and the rules of canon law, to criticism.

This was a breach with the past, although Erasmus personally considered his method to be a return to an older tradition, that of the Fathers, and their style of biblical exegesis. He did not understand the alarm he aroused and did not see that this criticism – at least if one accepted the premises of the critics – carried weight: whoever undermined authority at such a sensitive point as the Bible was for the Christian faith was attacking authority as such. Erasmus was subjectively a conservative *par excellence*, and thus not very aware of the objectively revolutionary character of his life's achievement.

Erasmus' work on the editions of various Fathers of the church, and on the translation of their works, publishing some himself and stimulating others, is directly related to his work on the New Testament. He was not the first in this field either, but rather built on the tradition that already existed at Basel. The programme worked out in the years following 1515 by Erasmus and others is impressive. A noble goal was served by these editions, the building up of a new theology, which attached itself to the theological tradition of the early church.

There is a second aspect, which perhaps had greater consequences. Van Dorp's letter, cited above, drew particular attention to the results that the hegemony of the grammarians would have for theology. He was very well aware of the consequences that Erasmus' new method of practising theology would have for the profession of the theologian. The method would be changed, the domination of systematic theology broken, and exegesis would be elevated to the place of honour. In other words, dialectic, the path to principles as it was called, would have to yield place to rhetoric. Theology would no longer be practised in accordance with the laws of strict logic. The whole scholastic method was in danger; it would have to leave the field to the methods of humanist learning, in which dialectic and rhetoric were united. We have seen that in his introductory matter to the New Testament Erasmus pleaded for a theology that would start from the terms and concepts appearing in the Bible, in order to arrive by this route at a science of theology that would be based directly on the word of Holy Scripture. Moreover, Erasmus not only preached this method of theological study in theory, but he carried it into practice. Several long excursuses in the *Annotations* give excellent examples of this, and *The Free Will* is the best imaginable example of the treatment of a theological problem by means of the detailed discussion of biblical passages that can be adduced for and against the freedom of the will. Whoever has the method of the great scholastic teachers before him will see the reversal of values that is argued for here.

A third and last element is the programme of renewal that Erasmus wished to realize. The study of the New Testament and the Fathers was not just a technical exercise, it was intended to lead to a new spirituality, a contemporary piety. Erasmus opposed the externalization of the church and of the means of grace, which did not permit man to achieve an immediate personal relationship with God, and set his face against scholasticism. In positive terms, Erasmus wanted the church to be transformed from a power-apparatus and a purely sacral community into a community that helped man to penetrate to the core, to a relationship with God. There is no point in repeating all this. This goal is one of the determining factors in Erasmus' work. It is self-evident that his high opinion of the word played an important role in all this: the word alone was sufficiently spiritual to be the vehicle of the spirit, both divine and human.

If we sketch Erasmus' contribution to the spiritual life of his age in this way, we thereby implicitly answer the question repeatedly asked, whether or not he was a theologian. Was he merely a language master? Erasmus himself adopted the name bestowed on him, *grammatistes*, schoolmaster, and wore it as a badge of honour.[10] In his defence against Lefèvre d'Etaples, he said that in spite of his doctor's title, acquired at the urging of friends, he never passed himself off as a theologian even among his intimates.[11] In the opinion of his age, he never revealed himself as a theologian in his writings either, for he did not practise the scholastic method. Nor was he a theologian in the sense that he could be shown to have a well-defined basic theological concept determining his whole thought. And yet I do not hesitate to call him a theologian. For he knew the scholastic theology of his own day and of the Middle Ages, and knew how to use it. He also possessed a phenomenal knowledge of the Fathers, of which he made fruitful use in his writings. The most important point is the integration of philological method into theology: precisely because he was a *grammatistes*, a gerund-grinder, he was a highly original theologian. The unification of *bonae litterae* and *sacrae litterae* that he made his life's goal brought theology out of its isolation and back into contact with the culture of the times. Finally, we find in his writings a concentration on two themes: the life and work of Christ and man's path to salvation. These two interrelated ideas were for him the central point of the Bible. Through them he bridged the gap between theology and pastoral practice. In thus making a direct connection between the Bible and personal life he showed the possibilities of a theology that was not remote from everyday life and its religious problems, but had a direct application for a wide group of interested persons. The *Paraphrases* on the books of the New Testament form a fine example of this.

The three aspects discussed above – the consistent application of the philological method to biblical scholarship, the effect of this on a new scholarly method, and the programme of reform of religion and society – belong together. They are parts of a whole, and through their combined effect Erasmus achieved his unique position and became the centre of a vigorous renewal movement. Existing forces were joined together in his work in pursuit of a single goal: to put the treasures of the past at the service of the Christian world for its renewal in the present. Indisputably, such a programme represents a breach with tradition. The idea of a decline in the history of civilization has its origin in humanism.

Various names have been given to this movement: Christian humanism, German humanism, the northern Renaissance. In my view, the name 'biblical humanism' is best, because it most accurately identifies the heart of the movement.[12] But the name should be reserved for those who were involved in all three aspects of it. If it is used to describe those who only adopted or applied the humanist method of biblical study, then virtually all the theologians of the twenties and thirties must be included among the biblical humanists. Luther is a good example. It might be argued that Luther was a biblical humanist because the gains won by biblical humanism occupy an important place in his exegesis of the Bible. His exegetical method as such, however, was different. He did not practise theology in the same way as Erasmus, and his ideas of the church and Christianity, were, as we shall see, profoundly opposed to the ideals of Erasmus. If 'biblical humanism' can include people like Luther, then the name describes such a vague and heterogeneous grouping that it loses its meaning. Certainly, the general occurrence of certain aspects of biblical humanistic tradition helps to explain the popularity and the resilience of the movement in the twenties. At that point the schism in the church gradually began to take shape. In spite of this, biblical humanism remained an important bond. It was no coincidence that most of the leading figures of this period in both Lutheranism and the Swiss–south-German Reformation came from this circle.

The influence of Erasmus in his own time was great. In 1534 the Franciscan Nicolaus Herborn wrote that Luther had won a certain part of the church to himself, Zwingli and Oecolampadius a certain part, Erasmus the greatest part. He added, with an allusion to Matthew 26:24, 'It would be better if that man had never been born.'[13] To assess Erasmus' influence exactly it is necessary to distinguish between his work in theology and the effect of his ideas on the movement for reform in church and society. In theology one may think of both his biblical exegesis and his theological method, since they both carried great weight with the more progressive theologians.

The exegetical method inaugurated by Erasmus aroused enthusiasm from the start. Significantly, Luther immediately used the first edition of Erasmus' New Testament in his lectures and publications. He used it critically, and his own method of biblical exegesis remained different, but in spite of his later attacks on it, Erasmus' New Testament remained the starting point for Luther's exegesis. Luther's procedure is a pattern of Reformation exegesis of the Bible in general, and at a slightly later stage for the exegetical practice of the Catholic camp also. A single example will suffice. The most thorough exegete among the reformers, John Calvin, continually brought Erasmus' exposition into his discussion of biblical texts. His successor Theodore Beza does even more than this: in his great editions of the New Testament he constantly engages in a dialogue with Erasmus. This influence was a lasting one. It is no coincidence that reprints of the *Glossa ordinaria* gradually lost ground in the sixteenth century to editions of the exegetical writings of the Fathers and of new contemporary commentaries. Works in the first category were used not only as an object of study, but also as the basis of exegesis. The last edition of the *Glossa ordinaria* dates from 1634. It was replaced by new exegetical collections, which took Erasmus as their starting point.

Closely associated with this is the influence exerted by the theological method that Erasmus introduced. Melanchthon is a striking example. The first systematic theological work of Protestant origin, Melanchthon's *Loci communes* (*Commonplaces*) clearly shows Erasmian influence. The work is guided, entirely according to humanist method, directly by the Bible. Moreover, in spite of great differences in content, it shares with Erasmus the emphasis on Christology and on man's path to salvation, rejecting all speculation and the notion that the essence of theology is to determine a doctrine of God. This was a decisive change of course in theology, the implications of which are still largely unknown to this day, but which was at any rate partly prepared by biblical humanism. That the Bible occupied the central place in the revelation of God's salvation in Protestantism is not only evident from the emphasis on the exegesis of the Bible but is also realized in another way in systematic theology. On this point, Erasmus' influence was great. How far this change of course was reversed again in the middle of the sixteenth century and how far Protestant theology reverted to the scholastic method has also been little investigated.

It is clear, however, that Herborn was not thinking of those influences in the first place. We are faced with the question: Can we speak of a penetration of Erasmian ideas in the wider sense, not confined to the profession of theology? In answering it we should recall first of all that no church developed from his ideas, as was the case with Luther, Zwingli, and Calvin. There, the structures formed a framework through which the founders' continued influence over the centuries was guaranteed to a greater or lesser extent. This was not the case with Erasmus. He did not unleash any popular movement. That was connected with the medium he used. In its beginning the Reformation in general developed against the will of the authorities. The forces which bore it along were larger groups, acted upon by the contemporary mass media, the sermon, the pamphlet, the vernacular book, and print. Erasmus wrote only in Latin and thus only reached an élite. Translations had a wider effect, but in translation many of his writings lost their persuasiveness. He had no professorial chair or pulpit, nor was he ambitious for one. Even personal contact was less important to him than was the book.

It is thus not fortuitous that the period in which Erasmus

dominated men's minds was a very short one. It began about 1515 and lasted until approximately 1525. From the middle of the twenties his influence in Germany began to lose ground before the much more forceful personality of Luther. The Erasmian period lasted longer in the Netherlands, in England, France, and Switzerland, because the Zwinglian movement and a rather undefined and open reform Catholicism received important impulses from him. As soon as a resolute and powerful movement began to make headway and to lay a more exclusive claim to men's minds – Lutheranism, Calvinism, or Counter-Reformation – Erasmus had no further chance.

Precisely because Erasmus created no institution of his own, we have to distinguish between the various movements to determine his influence. At the beginning of the 1520s a popular print of the 'divine mill' was in circulation. Christ poured the corn (the four evangelists and Paul) into the mill. From the mill came the flour (power, faith, hope, and love), which was loaded into a sack by Erasmus, and baked into bread (books) by Luther.[14] Thus Erasmus was allotted a mediating role in the processing of Holy Scripture into Reformation literature. In fact there were many in the first years of the Reformation movement who were convinced that Erasmus and the Reformation had everything to do with each other.

Yet it was quickly to appear that Erasmus could not exert any essential influence on Lutheranism, despite the fact that he and Luther had not a little in common. Both can be understood only if one is aware of the generally felt need for rest, certainty, the presence of God, and direct community with God typical of the world around 1500.[15] Both set themselves against the attempt to find relationship with God by the intensification of objective means: church and sacraments. Both were convinced that the church obscured the essentials through its too human institutions. There had to be a radical breach with all this, in order to rediscover the core of religion. Hence the two men approached each other in their criticism of the church. The difference between them is evident as soon as one asks what this core consisted of. For Erasmus it was the direct contact with God through Jesus, a joyful matter, and hence Jesus was the centre-point of our life. For Luther, it was the encounter with a God who demanded righteousness: a righteousness that man could not achieve. The only point of repose in life lay in Christ, in whom God shows his mercy. For Luther God and man were opposed, and in Christ God reconciled the world with himself; for Erasmus man was inclined towards God. For Luther, the highest human righteousness was sin, no more than sin; for Erasmus man in his best moments could approach God. For Luther, outside God there was only the devil; for Erasmus there was a natural goodness in man. Hence for Erasmus it was praise of God's goodness to say that the philosophers of classical antiquity had already understood something of God, while for Luther this was pure blasphemy.

There were more possibilities for Erasmus in the Swiss–south-German Reformation movement, the cradle of reformed Protestantism. But one certainly cannot identify reformed Protestantism with Erasmus. Zwingli resolutely rejected the idea of freedom of the will, in direct reaction to Erasmus' work, and carried out a complete break with the institutions of the church. On both points he deliberately set his face against Erasmus. It is important to recognize however, that he took over the fundamental idea of Erasmus' thought: the opposition of flesh and spirit, internal and external, higher and lower. As a result there was a deep internal relationship in the thinking of the two men: Zwingli's absolute rejection of images in the church went back directly to Erasmian motives, and his doctrine of the Lord's Supper was strongly influenced by that of Erasmus. His vision of man also suggests Erasmus rather than Luther. For him, being human was not the same as being a sinner, and like Erasmus he thought there was a bridge between the human and the divine. This opinion also determined his view of God's law. While Luther taught that the law only revealed the inability of man to observe it, Zwingli expressly stated that for the man who had received grace, God's law was the norm he had to observe and was able to keep, albeit with much stumbling. For Erasmus this was a self-evident point, which he had fervently defended against Luther. It is not surprising that Erasmus continued to be highly respected within reformed Protestantism, in spite of the later influence of Calvin, who in theology was closer to Luther than to Zwingli and certainly wanted nothing to do with Erasmus.

Within Catholicism Erasmus aroused the most varied reactions. In 1559 all his works were place on the *Index* (though the *Index* of five years later was less severe), and yet he exercised great influence within the church. This seeming contradiction need not surprise us. Erasmus set himself against things that were regarded as essential for the practice of piety at the end of the Middle Ages. His opposition to the externalization of religion was perceived by some as a liberation, by others as a surrender to the spirit of the age. Erasmus' fate within the old church was determined by the fact that some years after his programme had become widely known, Luther drew all the attention to himself. The result was that in Catholic circles too Erasmus was measured against Luther. The resistance to Erasmus from Paris offers a clear example. All kinds of genuinely Erasmian ideas were branded as Lutheran, although they had nothing to do with Luther and were often even repudiated by Luther himself.

In summary, one can say that Erasmian ideas remained, but that Erasmianism as such could not and did not survive the formation of fronts which began in the forties. This raises the question of whether Erasmus' thought-world and ideas were strong enough to continue to exist. In my opinion we have to answer this question in the negative. The internalization and spiritualization that were its most important characteristics offered no alternative. They manifested themselves above all in the spiritualist circles of the sixteenth century, but then in a form which was not that of Erasmus himself. Only in the England of Henry VIII did Erasmianism win a dominating position. Here, with the support of the crown, it was able to hold a middle course between the two rival forms of firm and militant conviction. As soon as one of them gained the field, Erasmianism could only exercise an influence as a moderating factor in the system. That is to say that Erasmus' ideas could serve as a corrective rather than as an alternative. As such they undoubtedly meant much in the sixteenth century. The period of the Counter-Reformation in the Catholic church was highly un-Erasmian – it wanted to create clarity, fix doctrine, and set up fixed frameworks for the church – but in the concrete measures of reform that were adopted for the improvement of the clergy and the laity there was an important Erasmian inheritance. Comparable claims may be made of reformed Protestantism. The rigorously implemented purging of the church, which left nothing of the old order in the liturgy, the fitting-out of church buildings, and ecclesiastical organization, might not be Erasmian in spirit as such, but the spiritualist feeling expressed in it had a great deal in common with Erasmus.

What has been said here of the sixteenth century can be applied without much difficulty to later periods. There is little question of any direct influence of Erasmus' ideas. There was never an Erasmian renaissance. Of course people have appealed to Erasmus when they found something in him that moved them. In these cases, it was not a question of adoption of Erasmus' ideals as a whole, perhaps with a certain adaptation to later times, but of recognition, a recognition of a form of piety. It seems to me that such a recognition is also a factor in the revival of research into Erasmus in the last two decades, which is motivated by more than a purely scholarly interest. This type of piety has two poles. On the one hand it is characterized by the desire for a personal and direct relationship with God. It is not the community which is primary, but the individual and his relation with God; mediation by holy things and institutions is unimportant in this relationship. Individualism and spiritualization are its essential features. On the other hand it is also distinguished by the value it attaches to peace, harmony, and joy, both in individual relationships to God and in the human community that emerges out of them. From this point of view Erasmian piety is marked by optimism and a certain superficiality. It is a piety of the lowlands rather than of the mountains, intimate rather than passionate.

Notes

✿

For explanation of the abbreviations and short titles used in these notes, see the bibliography, 221 below.

CHAPTER ONE

On the material treated in this chapter, see especially: Reedijk 'Huizinga and His Erasmus.'

1 *Epistolae obscurorum virorum* ed Aloys Bömer 2 vols (Heidelberg 1924; repr Aalen 1978) II 187:25
2 WA Tr 1 55:32–3

CHAPTER TWO

On the material treated in this chapter, see especially: Andreas; Benrath *Wegbereiter der Reformation*; Guggisberg; Huizinga 'Erasmus über Vaterland und Nationen'; *L'Humanisme allemand (1480–1540)*; Kristeller *Renaissance Thought*; Moeller 'Frömmigkeit in Deutschland um 1500' and *Deutschland im Zeitalter der Reformation*; Oberman *Forerunners of the Reformation*; Oberman and Brady *Itinerarium italicum*; Post; Renaudet *Préréforme et humanisme*; Rijk; Ritter; Rupprich; Spitz; Wohlfeil; Worstbrock.

1 *Adagia* IV vi 35 LB II 1083F–1084E
2 Allen Ep 2161:10–13
3 Allen Ep 1806:9–10

CHAPTER THREE

On the material treated in this chapter, see especially: Augustijn 'Het probleem van de *initia Erasmi'*; Boyle 'The Eponyms of "Desiderius Erasmus"'; Bradshaw; Crahay; DeMolen 'Erasmus as Adolescent'; Dolfen; Eijl; Haverals; Hyma; Kaufman 'The Disputed Date of Erasmus' *Liber Apologeticus'* and *Augustinian Piety and Catholic Reform*; Koch; Kohls *Die Theologie des Erasmus*; Mestwerdt; Pfeiffer *Humanitas Erasmiana* and 'Die Wandlungen der "Antibarbari"'; Post; Renaudet *Préréforme et humanisme*; Rice; Rummel 'Quoting Poetry instead of Scripture'; Schottenloher *Erasmus im Ringen um die humanistische Bildungsform*; Stupperich 'Zur Biographie des Erasmus von Rotterdam: Zwei Untersuchungen.'

1 Allen Ep 7:1–4 / CWE Ep 7:2–6
2 Allen Ep 20:97–101 / CWE Ep 20:97–100
3 Text in ASD V-1 1–86 / CWE 66 135–75
4 *De contemptu mundi* ASD V-1 44:108, 46:162, 50:277 / CWE 66 138, 140, 144
5 Allen I 590
6 Text in ASD I-1 1–138 / CWE 23 19–122
7 Allen Ep 46:32–42 / CWE Ep 46:37–49
8 *Antibarbari* ASD I-1 46:7–47:7 / cf CWE 23 25:32n.
9 *Antibarbari* ASD I-1 84:6–7 / CWE 23 61:10–12
10 *Antibarbari* ASD I-1 89:11–90:10 / CWE 23 66:24–68:6
11 *Colloquia* ASD I-3 531–2 / Thompson *Colloquies* 351–2
12 Allen Ep 50:7–14 / CWE Ep 50:9–16
13 Allen Ep 55:15–50 / CWE Ep 55:17–59
14 Epp 96–100, Allen Ep 1104:10–17 / CWE Ep 1104:12–18
15 Allen Ep 103:17–24 / CWE Ep 103:20–6
16 Allen Epp 81:8–9, 83:34–6 / CWE Epp 81:8–10, 83:39–42
17 *Antibarbari* ASD I-1 89:20–1 / CWE 23 67:2–3
18 *Colloquia* ASD I-3 531:1322 / Thompson *Colloquies* 351
19 Allen Ep 48:23–4 / CWE Ep 48:28–9
20 Allen Ep 108:20–55 / CWE Ep 108:23–61
21 Allen Ep 64:21–70 / CWE Ep 64:25–76
22 Allen Ep 64:74–81 / CWE Ep 64:80–8

CHAPTER FOUR

In addition to the literature mentioned in the preceding chapter, see especially: Brown; Halkin 'Erasme en Italie' and *Erasmus ex Erasmo*; Renaudet *Erasme et l'Italie*; Seebohm; Thomson and Porter.

1 Allen Ep 296:209 / CWE Ep 296:223
2 Allen Ep 159:4–5 / cf CWE Ep 159:7.
3 Allen Ep 159:59–64 / CWE Ep 159:65–8
4 Allen I 6:14–16 / CWE Ep 1341A:183–5

5 Ep 118
6 *Erasmus von Rotterdam* 51–3
7 Allen Ep 1211:245–616 / CWE Ep 1211:273–673
8 Ep 119
9 Allen Ep 200:8 / CWE Ep 200:9
10 Allen Ep 3032:417–33
11 *Hyperaspistes* II LB X 1527CD
12 Allen I 62:210–13
13 Allen Ep 3032:530–3
14 *Spongia* ASD IX-1 149 687–8n
15 Allen I 61:147–65
16 Allen Ep 2465:10–56
17 Allen Ep 253:4–9 / CWE Ep 253:8–11
18 *Ciceronianus* ASD I-2 637:20–639:21 / CWE 28:384–6
19 Reedijk *Poems* no 83
20 Allen Ep 215:14–15, 70–4 / CWE Ep 215:16–17, 77–80
21 Allen Ep 221:27–30 / CWE Ep 221:32–3
22 Allen Ep 252:15–31 / CWE Ep 252:16–32
23 Allen Ep 181:54–7 / CWE Ep 181:64–5
24 Allen Ep 227:20 / cf CWE Ep 227:25–6.
25 Allen Ep 237:17–70 / CWE Ep 237:21–79
26 Allen Ep 139:34–9 / cf CWE Ep 139:41–8.
27 Allen Ep 233:8–13 / CWE Ep 233:10–15
28 Allen Ep 260 introduction; Reedijk *Poems* nos 85–90
29 Allen Ep 237:71–89 / CWE Ep 237:80–98
30 Allen Ep 475:14–18 / CWE Ep 475:16–22
31 Allen Ep 1669:8–37
32 Allen Ep 298:16–22 / CWE Ep 298:20–6
33 Ep 263
34 Allen Ep 124:62–4 / CWE Ep 124:72–4
35 Allen Ep 138:38–51 / CWE Ep 138:45–65
36 Allen Ep 138:39–40 / CWE Ep 138:45
37 Allen Ep 172:10–12 / CWE Ep 172:12–15
38 Allen Ep 138:41–8 / cf CWE Ep 138:52–60.
39 Allen Ep 108:74–101 / CWE Ep 108:83–115
40 Allen Ep 181:31–4 / CWE Ep 181:36–40
41 Allen Ep 149:9–41 / CWE Ep 149:11–48
42 Allen Ep 181:36–8 / CWE Ep 181:41–3
43 Allen Ep 149:21–6 / CWE Ep 149:24–30
44 Allen Ep 181:29–36 / CWE Ep 181:35–41
45 Allen Ep 182:129–40 / cf CWE Ep 182:143–62.

46 Allen Ep 296:109–43 / CWE Ep 296:115–50
47 Allen Ep 296:101–9 / CWE Ep 296:107–111
48 See page 54.
49 Allen Ep 296:84–8 / cf CWE Ep 296:88–93.
50 Allen Ep 296:158–61 / CWE Ep 296:168–72
51 Hutten I 106:8–9
52 Hutten I 44:2–8

CHAPTER FIVE

On the material treated in this chapter, see especially: Auer; Benrath 'Die Lehre des Humanismus und des Antitrinitarismus'; Bijl; Coppens *Eustachius van Zichem en zijn strijdschrift tegen Erasmus*; Devereux; O'Donnell ed *Enchiridion*; Etienne; Van der Haeghen and Lenger *Bibliotheca Belgica* II 777–843; Hamm; Kohls *Die Theologie des Erasmus*; Oberman 'Luthers Reformatorische Ontdekkingen'; Renaudet *Préréforme et humanisme*; Schottenloher 'Erasmus, Johann Poppenruyter und die Entstehung des *Enchiridion militis christiani*'; Stupperich 'Das *Enchiridion militis christiani* des Erasmus von Rotterdam nach seiner Entstehung, seinem Sinn und Charakter'; Van Santbergen.

1 Text in LB V 1–66 / CWE 66:24–127
2 Allen Ep 1556:42–8
3 Allen Ep 164:2–3 / CWE Ep 164:3–5
4 Allen Ep 181:46–7 / CWE Ep 181:53–8
5 Allen Ep 1556:45–7
6 Oberman 'Luthers Reformatorische Ontdekkingen' 31; Benrath 'Die Lehre des Humanismus und des Antitrinitarismus' 28–30; Kohls *Die Theologie des Erasmus* I 177–90
7 Allen Ep 412:24–6 / CWE Ep 412:26–8
8 Van Santbergen 50
9 *Enchiridion* LB V 22E–F / CWE 66 57
10 *Enchiridion* LB V 27D–44E / CWE 66 65–93
11 John 6:63
12 John 4:23
13 *Enchiridion* LB V 30B–C / CWE 66 69
14 *Enchiridion* LB V 33E–F / CWE 66 75–6
15 *Enchiridion* LB V 28C–D / CWE 66 66
16 *Enchiridion* LB V 33C–D / CWE 66 75
17 *Enchiridion* LB V 35D–E / CWE 66 78
18 *Enchiridion* LB V 32E, 37B / CWE 66 74, 81
19 *Enchiridion* LB V 32E / CWE 66 74

20 *Enchiridion* LB V 37C–D / CWE 66 81–2
21 *Enchiridion* LB V 37F–38A / CWE 66 82
22 *Enchiridion* LB V 32F–33A / CWE 66 74
23 *Enchiridion* LB V 35B / CWE 66 79–80
24 *Enchiridion* LB V 36B / CWE 66 79
25 *Enchiridion* LB V 37A / 66 81
26 *Enchiridion* LB V 31C–E / CWE 66 71–2
27 *Enchiridion* LB V 32A / CWE 66 72
28 *Enchiridion* LB V 29B–30B / CWE 66 68–9
29 *Enchiridion* LB V 30F–31B / CWE 66 71
30 *Spiritualisme érasmien et théologiens louvanistes* 14–16
31 Allen Ep 1334:217–34, 375–81 / CWE Ep 1334:232–49, 386–401
32 *Enchiridion* LB V 22E–F / CWE 66 57
33 *Enchiridion* LB V 27E / CWE 66 65
34 *Enchiridion* LB V 11F–14E / CWE 66 41–3
35 *Enchiridion* LB V 12E–F / CWE 66 41
36 *Enchiridion* LB V 13A–E / CWE 66 41–2
37 *Enchiridion* LB V 13D, 14A–B / CWE 66 43
38 *Enchiridion* LB V 19B, 21B / CWE 66 51, 54
39 *Enchiridion* LB V 12C–D, 16B / CWE 66 40–1, 47
40 *Enchiridion* LB V 21B–C / CWE 66 54–5
41 *Enchiridion* LB V 5D–6C / CWE 66 30–1
42 *Enchiridion* LB V 6F / CWE 66 32
43 *Enchiridion* LB V 15F–17B / CWE 66 47–8
44 *Enchiridion* LB V 59C / CWE 66 118
45 *Enchiridion* LB V 55C / CWE 66 111
46 Allen Ep 181:51 / cf CWE Ep 181:58
47 *Préréforme et humanisme* 435
48 *Enchiridion* LB V 65B–C / cf CWE 66 126–7
49 Cf page 27 above.
50 Allen Ep 3032:467–8
51 *Enchiridion* LB V 65C–66A / cf CWE 66 127
52 *Colloquia* ASD I-3 177:1713–24 / Thompson *Colloquies* 38
53 *Enchiridion* LB V 44D / cf CWE 66 93.

CHAPTER SIX

On the material treated in this chapter, see especially: Miller ed *The Praise of Folly*; Gavin and Miller; Gavin and Walsh; Kaiser; Könneker; Kristeller 'Erasmus from an Italian Perspective'; Lefebvre; Miller, introduction to *Moriae encomium* in ASD IV-3 13–39; Radice; Screech; Geraldine Thompson; Williams.

1 *Moriae encomium*, prefatory letter ASD IV-3 67:2–16 / CWE 27 83
2 Allen Ep 337:126–32 / CWE Ep 337:136–40; *Adagia* II ii 40 LB II 460F
3 *The Praise of Folly* x
4 Allen I 19:6 / cf CWE Ep 1341A:690.
5 *Moriae encomium* ASD IV-3 67:14, 68:23 / cf CWE 27 83–4.
6 Allen Ep 337:91–109 / cf CWE Ep 337:98–115. Cf Horace *Satires* 1.1.24–5.
7 *Moriae encomium* ASD IV-3 81:177–8 / CWE 27 91
8 *Moriae encomium* ASD IV-3 71:1–134:184 / CWE 27 86–120
9 *Moriae encomium* ASD IV-3 96:470–1 / CWE 27 99
10 *Moriae encomium* ASD IV-3 114:800–4 / CWE 27 109
11 *Moriae encomium* ASD IV-3 128:59–130:75 / CWE 27 117–18
12 *Moriae encomium* ASD IV-3 104:572–5 / CWE 27 102
13 *Moriae encomium* ASD IV-3 122:964–6 / CWE 27 114
14 *Moriae encomium* ASD IV-3 120:942–126:22 / CWE 27 113–16
15 *Moriae encomium* ASD IV-3 130:96–120 / CWE 27 118
16 *Moriae encomium* ASD IV-3 104:591–106:619 / CWE 27 103–4
17 *Moriae encomium* ASD IV-3 134:185–178:885 / CWE 121–42
18 *Moriae encomium* ASD IV-3 176:856–7 / CWE 27 140–1
19 *Moriae encomium* ASD IV-3 136:196–201 / CWE 27 122
20 *Moriae encomium* ASD IV-3 144:362–3 / CWE 27 125
21 *Moriae encomium* ASD IV-3 138:242–3, 258–9 / CWE 27 122
22 *Moriae encomium* ASD IV-3 136:217–19 / CWE 27 121
23 *Moriae encomium* ASD IV-3 140:304–142:316 / CWE 27 124–5
24 *Moriae encomium* ASD IV-3 144:382–3 / CWE 27 126
25 *Moriae encomium* ASD IV-3 148:402–4 / CWE 27 127
26 *Moriae encomium* ASD IV-3 154:490–156:491 / CWE 27 129–30
27 *Moriae encomium* ASD IV-3 158:516–19 / CWE 27 130
28 *Moriae encomium* ASD IV-3 158:524–168:674 / CWE 27 131–6
29 *Moriae encomium* ASD IV-3 168:670–2 / CWE 27 135
30 *Moriae encomium* ASD IV-3 174:818–21 / CWE 27 139
31 *Moriae encomium* ASD IV-3 172:753–6, 768–71 / CWE 27 137–8
32 *Moriae encomium* ASD IV-3 178:886–194:277 / CWE 27 141–53
33 *Moriae encomium* ASD IV-3 178:893 / CWE 27 142
34 *Moriae encomium* ASD IV-3 186:79–189:147 / CWE 27 147–9
35 *Moriae encomium* ASD IV-3 186:84–5 / CWE 27 147
36 *Moriae encomium* ASD IV-3 189:141–6 / CWE 27 149
37 *Moriae encomium* ASD IV-3 189:147–190:155 / CWE 27 149–50
38 *Moriae encomium* ASD IV-3 190:156–192:230 / CWE 27 150–1
39 *Moriae encomium* ASD IV-3 192:229–30 / CWE 27 152
40 *Moriae encomium* ASD IV-3 193:257–194:267 / CWE 27 152–3
41 *Moriae encomium* ASD IV-3 164:611–21 / CWE 27 133

42 *Moriae encomium* ASD IV-3 185:48–186:55 / CWE 27 146–7
43 *Moriae encomium* ASD IV-3 180:943–8 / cf CWE 27 143.
44 *Moriae encomium* ASD IV-3 180:949–182:962 / CWE 27 143–4
45 *Moriae encomium* ASD IV-3 182:997–183:998 / cf CWE 27 145.
46 *Moriae encomium* ASD IV-3 182:985–7 / CWE 27 144
47 *Moriae encomium* ASD IV-3 182:974, 183:998–9 / CWE 27 145
48 *Moriae encomium* ASD IV-3 154:478–84 / CWE 27 129
49 *Moriae encomium* ASD IV-3 184:39–41 / CWE 27 146
50 *Moriae encomium* ASD IV-3 162:569–71 / CWE 27 132
51 Heb 11:1
52 *Moriae encomium* ASD IV-3 150:423–6 / CWE 27 127
53 Ep 337
54 Per Bjurström *Tekeningen uit het Nationalmuseum te Stockholm: Collectie van Graaf Tessin 1695–1770* (Paris/Brussels/Amsterdam 1970–1) 68

CHAPTER SEVEN

On the material treated in this chapter, see especially: Bouyer; Brachin; Chantraine *'Mystère' et 'Philosophie du Christ' selon Erasme*; Constantinescu Bagdat; Van der Haeghen and Lenger *Bibliotheca Belgica* II 974–87; Otto Herding, introduction to *Institutio principis christiani* in ASD IV-1 97–130 and to *Querela pacis* in ASD IV-2 3–33; Koerber; Margolin *Guerre et paix dans la pensée d'Erasme*; Mesnard; Phillips *The 'Adages' of Erasmus*; Renaudet *Etudes Erasmiennes*; Sowards *The Julius Exclusus of Desiderius Erasmus*; Stange; Tracy *The Politics of Erasmus*.

1 Allen Ep 566:34–5 / cf CWE Ep 566:38–9.
2 *Epistola contra pseudevangelicos* ASD IX-1 284:33–5
3 Text in LB II / ASD II-4, 5, 6 / CWE 31–6
4 See page 40.
5 Allen Ep 269:33–5 / CWE Ep 269:38–40
6 Allen Ep 591:33–57 / cf CWE Ep 591:38–63.
7 Allen Ep 590:18–19, 42–69 / cf CWE Ep 590:20–1, 44–71.
8 Allen Ep 344:14–16 / CWE Ep 344:16–17
9 *Adagia* 96–121
10 Text in ASD IV-1 133–219 / CWE 27 203–88
11 *Institutio principis christiani* ASD IV-1 133:21–134:24 / CWE 27 203
12 *Institutio principis christiani* ASD IV-1 145:267–8 / CWE 27 214
13 Text in ASD IV-2 59–100 / CWE 27 292–322
14 Allen I 19:2–3 / CWE Ep 1341A:686
15 ASD IV-2 29
16 Ep 858 / CWE 66 8–23

17 Allen Ep 283:152–64 / cwe Ep 283:181–96
18 Allen Ep 421:75–93 / cwe Ep 421:81–106
19 *Etudes Erasmiennes* xvii–xix, 122–89
20 Bouyer 93–135
21 *Adagia* iii iii 1 asd ii-5 164:81–93
22 *Adagia* iii iii 1 asd ii-5 166:120–1
23 *Adagia* iii iii 1 asd ii-5 164:67–168:161, citing Isa 53:2–3
24 *Ratio* lb v 97c–98f
25 *Ratio* lb v 98c–d / Holborn 223, 6–10
26 *Paraclesis* lb v 143c
27 *Paraclesis* lb v 144a–b / Holborn 148:17–24
28 *Ratio* lb v 84a–e
29 Allen Ep 858:139–54 / cwe Ep 858:148–65 / cwe 66 11–12
30 Allen Ep 858:144–9 / cwe Ep 858:153–60 / cwe 66 11
31 *Ratio* lb v 83f–84a
32 *Paraclesis* lb v 140a–b
33 Allen Ep 858:230–343 / cwe Ep 858:241–366 / cwe 66 13–17
34 *Institutio principis christiani* asd iv-1 150:441–62 / cf cwe 27 220.
35 *Ratio* lb v 96d
36 *Ratio* lb v 96f
37 *Institutio principis christiani* asd iv-1 165:930–167:995 / cwe 27 234–6
38 *Querela pacis* asd iv-2 91:701–92:723 / cf cwe 27 315.
39 *Querela pacis* asd iv-2 96:833–42 / cwe 27 319
40 *Querela pacis* asd iv-2 84:536–8 / cwe 27 309
41 *Querela pacis* asd iv-2 65:119–21 / cf cwe 27 296.
42 *Adagia* iv i 1 lb ii 966d–968c
43 *Adagia* iv i 1 lb ii 966e, 967d
44 *Paraclesis* lb v 141f
45 *Paraclesis* lb v 141f
46 *Ratio* lb v 91f–92b
47 *Ratio* lb v 86e–88c
48 Text in Ferguson *Opuscula* 38–124 / cwe 27 168–97
49 Ferguson *Opuscula* 115:976–116:1003 / cwe 27 191–2
50 *Ratio* lb v 77b–c
51 *Ratio* lb v 76a
52 *Paraclesis* lb v 137b
53 *Paraclesis* lb v 140e–f
54 *Institutio principis christiani* asd iv-1 182:494–6 / cwe 27 252
55 *Adagia* iii iii 1 asd ii-5 182:455–7
56 *Ratio* lb v 106c–107e
57 *Ratio* lb v 107c

CHAPTER EIGHT

On the material treated in this chapter, see especially: Béné *Erasme et Saint Augustin* and 'L'Exégèse des Psaumes chez Erasme'; Bentley 'Erasmus' *Annotationes in Novum Testamentum* and the Textual Criticism of the Gospels' and *Humanists and Holy Writ*; Bludau; Brown; Dolfen; Godin; Gorce; Hoffmann; Holeczek *Humanistische Bibelphilologie als Reformproblem bei Erasmus von Rotterdam, Thomas More und William Tyndale*; De Jonge 'Erasmus und die *Glossa Ordinaria* zum Neuen Testament,' introduction to *Apologia ad annotationes Stunicae* in ASD IX-2 3–49, and 'Novum Testamentum a nobis versum'; Lubac II-2 427–87; Payne 'Toward the Hermeneutics of Erasmus'; Pfeiffer *History of Classical Scholarship from 1300 to 1850*; Rabil *Erasmus and the New Testament* and 'Erasmus' Paraphrases of the New Testament'; Rummel *Erasmus as a Translator of the Classics*; Schwarz; Winkler.

1 Allen Ep 384:42–55 / CWE Ep 384:44–58
2 *Paraclesis* LB V 137–44; *Methodus* Holborn 150–62; *Apologia* LB VI**2r–**3r
3 See pages 38–9; see also CWE Ep 373 introduction.
4 Allen I 14:9–10 / CWE Ep 1341A:483–4
5 De Jonge 'Novum Testamentum a nobis versum'
6 Allen Ep 305:222–3 / CWE Ep 305:228–9
7 See page 69.
8 Allen Ep 304:86–146 / CWE Ep 304:95–156
9 Ep 337
10 Allen Ep 403:21–82 / CWE Ep 403:25–88
11 Allen Epp 541:82–6, 948:104–35 / CWE Epp 541:92–7, 948:114–19
12 Allen Ep 948:136–40 / CWE Ep 948:141–4
13 Text in LB V 75–138
14 Text in LB VI**3v–***4r
15 Ep 860
16 Allen Ep 1010 introduction
17 De Jonge 'Novum Testamentum a nobis versum' 404
18 *Apologia ad annotationes Stunicae* ASD IX-2 258:534–44
19 *Apologia* LB VI**3r
20 Allen Ep 860:34–6 / CWE Ep 860:38–40
21 *Apologia* LB VI**2v
22 Allen Ep 809:62–5 / CWE Ep 809:73–6
23 *Apologia de 'In principio erat sermo'* LB IX 111–12; Ep 1072
24 Allen I 14:5 / CWE Ep 1341A:478–9
25 *Erasmus* 135

26 *Ratio* LB V 124E–127D / Holborn 274:24–284:27; cf *Enchiridion* LB V 29A–30B / CWE 66 68–9.

27 See pages 46–53.

28 *Ratio* Holborn 280:30–3

29 Ep 396

30 *Ratio* LB V 133A–C

31 *History of Classical Scholarship from 1300 to 1850*

32 *Adagia* IV V 1 LB II 1053F

33 Text in LB VII / CWE 42–50

34 Allen Ep 710:30–1 / cf CWE Ep 710:36.

35 *Spongia* ASD IX-1 210:136–9

36 Text in ASD V-2, 3

37 Text in ASD V-2 104:247–67

38 *Capita argumentorum* LB VI**3v–**4r

39 *Ratio* LB V 134F / Holborn 299:4–5

40 *Ratio* LB V 136A–B / Holborn 301:14–20

41 See page 84.

42 *Enchiridion* LB V 25F / CWE 66 62

43 Allen Ep 456:129–43 / CWE Ep 456:142–58

44 *Capita argumentorum* LB VI **4r

45 Allen Ep 1948:36–7

46 Allen Ep 1664:63–5

47 *Ratio* LB V 82A–B

48 *Paraclesis* LB V 140C

49 LB VII**2v

CHAPTER NINE

On the material treated in this chapter, see especially: Augustijn 'Erasmus und die Juden'; Bedouelle; Bietenholz 'Erasme et le public allemand, 1518–1520'; Chantraine 'L'*Apologia ad Latomum*: Deux conceptions de la théologie'; Feld; Geiger; Junghans; *Strasbourg au coeur religieux du XVIe siècle*; Phillips *Erasme et les débuts de la Réforme française (1517–1536)*; Massaut *Critique et tradition à la veille de la Réforme en France*; Nauwelaerts; Overfield; Payne 'Erasmus and Lefèvre d'Etaples as Interpreters of Paul'; Scheible 'Luther und die Anfänge der Reformation am Oberrhein'; Schwarz; Telle; De Vocht; Wackernagel.

1 Allen Ep 421:128 / CWE Ep 421:140

2 Allen Epp 412:14–17, 457:42–8 / CWE Epp 412:15–18, 457:51–3

3 Allen Ep 809:127–33 / CWE Ep 809:147–53

4 Allen Ep 867:273 / CWE Ep 867:293–4
5 Allen Ep 867:270–1 / CWE Ep 867:291–2
6 Allen Ep 596:2–3 / CWE Ep 596:3
7 Allen Ep 412:17–19 / CWE Ep 412:18–20
8 Allen Ep 412:10–26 / CWE Ep 412:11–27
9 Allen Ep 305:181–210 / CWE Ep 305:185–218
10 Allen Ep 1206:69–70 / CWE Ep 1206:76
11 Allen Ep 335:316–20 / CWE Ep 335:327–31
12 *Hieronymi opera* (Basel 1516) V 1V
13 Z VII Ep 254:19–21
14 Ep 401
15 The term, adopted from time to time in America, is now also used by
   Junghans (*Der junge Luther und die Humanisten*) 189–93
16 Hutten I 134:11–15
17 Allen Epp 333:105–37, 334:178–206 / CWE Epp 333:112–47, 334:187–218
18 Allen Ep 798:22–3 / CWE Ep 798:23–5
19 *Spongia* ASD IX-1 140:463–78
20 Allen Ep 622:1–11 / CWE Ep 622:1–12
21 Allen Epp 808:23–5, 961:28–30 / CWE Epp 808:26–7, 961:34–6
22 Allen Ep 694:35–8; 48–50 / CWE Ep 694:36–9, 50–1
23 Allen Ep 300 introduction, Ep 713
24 Ep 1006
25 *Apologia ad Fabrum* LB IX 19B–C
26 *Apologia ad Fabrum* LB IX 17–66
27 Allen Ep 597:35–6 / CWE Ep 597:40–2
28 *Annotationes* LB VI 990F
29 *Apologia ad Fabrum* LB IX 32E
30 *Apologia ad Fabrum* LB IX 50F–51C, 53F–56E
31 *Apologia ad Fabrum* LB IX 60B–D
32 *Apologia ad Fabrum* LB IX 62B–D
33 *Apologia ad Fabrum* LB IX 63D
34 *Apologia ad Fabrum* LB IX 65C
35 Allen I 67:401–2
36 See page 79.
37 *Apologia contra Latomi dialogum* LB IX 90B
38 *Apologia contra Latomi dialogum* LB IX 94B
39 Allen Ep 785:37–8 / cf CWE Ep 785:39–40.
40 Ep 776
41 Allen Ep 786:25–6 / CWE Ep 786:26–8
42 Allen Ep 786:24 / CWE Ep 786:25–6

CHAPTER TEN

On the material treated in this chapter, see especially: Augustijn *Erasmus en de Reformatie* and 'Erasmus von Rotterdam im Galaterbriefkommentar Luthers von 1519'; Blockx; Ducke; A. Freitag, introduction to *De servo arbitrio* in WA 18 551–99; Holeczek 'Die Haltung des Erasmus zu Luther nach dem Scheitern seiner Vermittlungspolitik 1520/21'; Junghans; Lohse *Martin Luther*; Maurer; Moeller 'Die deutschen Humanisten und die Anfänge der Reformation'; Renaudet *Erasme, sa pensée religieuse et son action d'après sa correspondance (1518–1521)*; Schätti; Scheible 'Melanchthon zwischen Luther und Erasmus'; Scribner; Stierle; Thompson *Inquisitio de fide*.

1 Z VII 139:15–17
2 See pages 74, 78–9.
3 Allen Ep 858:189–96, 593–8 / cf CWE Ep 858:200–8, 627–32 / CWE 66 12–13, 23
4 *Epistola ad fratres Inferioris Germaniae* ASD IX-1 392:402–4
5 Allen Ep 1167:273–4 / CWE Ep 1167 305–7
6 WA Br 1 91:34–5
7 Allen Epp 993:44–51, 1033:96–102 / CWE Epp 993:52–9, 1033:107–12
8 Allen Epp 1053:33–5, 1060:19–35 / CWE Epp 1053:36–9, 1060:24–43
9 Ep 939
10 Allen Ep 933:30–1 / CWE Ep 933:36–7
11 Allen Ep 980:37–8 / cf CWE Ep 980:43–4.
12 See pages 161–71.
13 Allen Ep 1041:28–38 / CWE Ep 1041:32–45
14 *Spongia* ASD IX-1 202:908–18
15 Allen Ep 1195:9–11 / CWE Ep 1195:14–16
16 Allen Ep 1141:11–14, 29–31 / CWE Ep 1141:14–17, 35–8
17 Allen Ep 1143:11 / CWE Ep 1143:13
18 Allen Ep 1143:76–7 / CWE Ep 1143:81–2
19 Allen Ep 1153:15–92 / CWE Ep 1153:20–103
20 Ep 1153
21 *De concordia* ASD V-3 306:706–10; *Scholia* ASD IX-1 89:673–81
22 Allen Ep 1199:32–3 / CWE 1199:38
23 WA Tr 1 55:34–5
24 *Spongia* ASD IX-1 182:420–8
25 *Spongia* ASD IX-1 150:702–10
26 Allen Ep 1164:56–8 / CWE Ep 1164:66–8
27 Allen Ep 1164:73–5 / CWE Ep 1164:85–6
28 Allen Ep 1165:39–41 / CWE Ep 1165:44–5

29 Allen Epp 1186:7, 1203:23–5 / CWE Epp 1186:8–9, 1203:29–32
30 Allen Ep 1192:63–5 / cf CWE Ep 1192:70–5.
31 Allen Ep 1218:28–37 / CWE Ep 1218:31–40
32 Allen Ep 1522:11–14
33 Allen Ep 980:56–7 / cf CWE Ep 980:63–5.
34 *Spongia* ASD IX-1 190:646–60
35 Allen Ep 2613:20–1
36 Allen Ep 1690:57–60
37 *Hyperaspistes* LB X 1251B
38 Allen Ep 1329:10–16 / cf CWE Ep 1329:12–18.
39 Allen Ep 1324:87–94 / cf CWE Ep 1324:92–100.
40 Ep 1338
41 Ep 1352
42 Allen Ep 1348:30–4 / cf CWE Ep 1348:27–30.
43 WA Br 3 626:14–25
44 Allen Ep 1384:54–8
45 Allen Ep 1376:18
46 Text in ASD IX-1 91–210
47 Allen Ep 1389:68–9
48 *Spongia* ASD IX-1 162:952–3
49 *Spongia* ASD IX-1 170:109–11
50 *Spongia* ASD IX-1 192:674–5
51 Allen Ep 1385:11–12
52 Allen Ep 1397:14–15
53 Allen Ep 1418:53–5
54 Ep 1443
55 Allen Ep 1195:64–5 / cf CWE Ep 1195:74.
56 Allen Ep 1225:334 / cf CWE Ep 1225:359.
57 Allen Ep 1275:24–8
58 Allen Ep 501:48–72 / CWE Ep 501:50–76
59 See pages 48–9.
60 *Spongia* ASD IX-1 186:521
61 Allen Ep 1268:82–5 / CWE Ep 1268:90–3
62 Allen Ep 1342:932–7 / CWE Ep 1342:1029–33
63 Allen Ep 1342:926–79 / cf CWE Ep 1342:1022–78.
64 Allen Ep 1384:9–14
65 See page 169.
66 *Colloquia* ASD I-3 363–74 / Thompson *Colloquies* 179–89
67 *Correspondance de Martin Bucer* ed Jean Rott (Leiden 1979) I 3:54–6
68 See page 196.
69 *Correspondance* I 3:32–3

70 *Apologia contra Stunicam* LB IX 355E, 356D

CHAPTER ELEVEN

In addition to the literature mentioned in the previous chapter, see especially: Augustijn '*Hyperaspistes* I: La doctrine d'Erasme et de Luther sur la *Claritas Scripturae*'; Bornkamm; Boyle *Rhetoric and Reform* and 'Erasmus and the "Modern" Question: Was He Semi-Pelagian?'; Chantraine *Erasme et Luther, libre et serf arbitre*; Kerlen; Lohse 'Marginalien zum Streit zwischen Erasmus und Luther'; McSorley; Trinkaus; Zickendraht.

1 Allen Ep 1493:4–5
2 Text in LB IX 1215–48
3 Allen Ep 1500:42–61
4 Allen I 42:2 / CWE Ep 1341A:1632
5 *Hyperaspistes* LB X 1277B, 1327C–E
6 *Hyperaspistes* LB X 1277B
7 Allen Ep 1496:32–41
8 *De libero arbitrio* LB IX 1216C–D
9 *De servo arbitrio* WA 18 600:17–601:1
10 Allen Ep 1670:24–34
11 Allen Ep 1723:8
12 Text in LB X 1249–1336
13 He uses the word in the sense of 'shield-bearers' or 'champions' at Allen Ep 1334:584 / CWE Ep 1334:618.
14 Text in LB X 1335–1536
15 Allen Ep 1804:1–2
16 *Ratio* LB V 130F–132A
17 *De libero arbitrio* LB IX 1215A–1220E
18 *De libero arbitrio* LB IX 1221A–1230A
19 *De libero arbitrio* LB IX 1230A–1241D
20 *De libero arbitrio* LB IX 1241D–1248D
21 *De libero arbitrio* LB IX 1241D
22 *De libero arbitrio* LB IX 1248D
23 *De servo arbitrio* WA 18 787:11–13
24 *De servo arbitrio* WA 18 603:11–12
25 *De servo arbitrio* WA 18 786:26–32
26 *Erasme et Luther* 445–7
27 *De libero arbitrio* LB IX 1220F, 1241D
28 *De libero arbitrio* LB IX 1219B
29 *De libero arbitrio* LB IX 1248B–D
30 *De servo arbitrio* WA 18 607:14–16

31 *De servo arbitrio* WA 18 658:17–661:24

32 *De libero arbitrio* LB IX 1239A, E

33 *De servo arbitrio* WA 18 783:17–31

34 *De libero arbitrio* LB IX 1247D–1248A

35 *Hyperaspistes* LB X 1403C

36 *De libero arbitrio* LB IX 1244E–1245A

37 *De servo arbitrio* WA 18 766:8–767:18

38 *Hyperaspistes* LB X 1347A–1352E

39 Allen Ep 1804:51–4

40 *De libero arbitrio* LB IX 1244A–B

41 *De libero arbitrio* LB IX 1242B

42 *De libero arbitrio* LB IX 1217D–1218C

43 *Hyperaspistes* LB X 1423B–C

44 *De servo arbitrio* WA 18 783:31–3

45 *De servo arbitrio* WA 18 784:1–9

46 Allen Ep 1804:52–4

47 *De libero arbitrio* LB IX 1225F

48 *De servo arbitrio* WA 18 685:1–686:13

49 *De servo arbitrio* WA 18 784:9–34

50 Allen Ep 1881:1–24

51 *De libero arbitrio* LB IX 1217F

52 *De libero arbitrio* LB IX 1242F

53 *De libero arbitrio* LB IX 1246B

54 *De libero arbitrio* LB IX 1216C–D, 1246B

55 *De libero arbitrio* LB IX 1246A

56 *Martin Luther* 77–8

57 Allen Ep 3120:18–20, 47–8

CHAPTER TWELVE

On the material treated in this chapter, see especially: Augustijn *Erasmus en de Reformatie* and introduction to *De interdicto esu carnium* and *Scholia* in ASD IX-1 3–13, 53–63; Bataillon; Bierlaire *Les Colloques d'Erasme*; Farge; Gäbler; Gilly; Gilmore 'Erasmus and Alberti Pio, Prince of Carpi' and 'Italian Reactions to Erasmian Humanism'; Phillips *Erasme et les débuts de la Réforme française (1517–1536)*; Massaut *Josse Clichtove, l'humanisme et la réforme du clergé*; McConica 'Erasmus and the Grammar of Consent'; Oelrich; Payne 'Toward the Hermeneutics of Erasmus'; Renaudet *Etudes Erasmiennes.*

1 Allen Ep 1576:9–13

2 Allen Ep 1578:22–5

3 Allen Ep 1528:11

4 *Hyperaspistes* LB X 1268E
5 Allen Ep 1582:96–8
6 *De esu carnium* ASD IX-1 22:115
7 Text in ASD IX-1 19–50
8 *De esu carnium* ASD IX-1 23:130–4
9 *De esu carnium* ASD IX-1 38:590–40:611
10 Allen Ep 1315:2–4 / CWE Ep 1315:2–5
11 Allen Epp 1620:48, 1679:46–9
12 Allen Ep 2566:83–4
13 Allen Ep 1522:61–2
14 See page 50.
15 Allen Ep 1637:9–13
16 Allen Ep 1679:92
17 Allen Ep 1637:47–53
18 *Enchiridion* LB V 30E–31A / CWE 66 71
19 Allen Ep 1636:2–5
20 Allen Ep 1717:52–6
21 Allen Ep 1729:25–7
22 'Erasmus and the Grammar of Consent'
23 Allen Ep 1708:38–42
24 Allen Ep 2575:13–14
25 Allen Ep 1722:46–8, 68–70
26 Allen Ep 1753:35–7
27 Allen Ep 3127:37–46
28 *Supputatio* LB IX 718E–F
29 *Erasme et l'Espagne* 279.
30 Allen Ep 1904:17–19
31 Allen Ep 1907:24–7
32 Text in LB IX 1015–94
33 *Apologia adversus monachos* LB IX 1029F
34 See pages 93–4.
35 *Apologia adversus monachos* LB IX 1031F–1032A
36 *Apologia adversus monachos* LB IX 1040B–D
37 *Apologia adversus monachos* LB IX 1023D
38 *Modus orandi Deum* ASD V-1 146:867–9
39 *Apologia adversus monachos* LB IX 1047E–F
40 *Spanien und der Basler Buchdruck bis 1600* 277–91
41 Allen Ep 2615:335–8
42 Allen Ep 2133:65–8; *Epistola contra pseudevangelicos* ASD IX-1 292:256–65
43 Allen Ep 2136:3–6
44 Allen Ep 2631:1–52

45 *Epistola contra pseudevangelicos* ASD IX-1 308:696–8
46 Allen Ep 2205:71–123
47 Allen Ep 2136:147–59

CHAPTER THIRTEEN

On the material treated in this chapter, see especially: Baron; Bierlaire *Erasme et ses Colloques* and *Les Colloques d'Erasme*; Thompson *Colloquies*; Gutmann; Van der Haeghen and Lenger *Bibliotheca Belgica* II 467–767; Halkin et al, introduction to *Colloquia* in ASD I-3 3–23; Heep; Margolin *Erasme Declamatio de pueris statim ac liberaliter instituendis*; Schneider; Thompson *Inquisitio de fide*; Geraldine Thompson.

1 *Bellaria epistolarum Erasmi Rot. et Ambrosii Pelargi vicissim missarum* (Cologne 1539) G 2a, b
2 WA Tr 1 397: 2–5
3 *Colloquia* ASD I-3 78:60–1
4 *Spongia* ASD IX-1 172:139–51
5 *Purgatio adversus epistolam Lutheri* ASD IX-1 478:987–8
6 Allen Ep 1804:256n
7 *Apologia adversus monachos* LB IX 1069C
8 *Les Colloques* 123–47
9 Allen Ep 1286:17–30 / CWE Ep 1286:20–33
10 *Colloquia* ASD I-3 124:22–5 / Allen Ep 1476:9–10
11 *Colloquia* ASD I-3 403–8 / Thompson *Colloquies* 219–23
12 *Colloquia* ASD I-3 251:610–254:712 / Thompson *Colloquies* 65–8
13 *Enchiridion* LB V 9D–E / CWE 66 36
14 See page 84.
15 *Colloquia* ASD I-3 267–73 / Thompson *Colloquies* 81–6
16 *Colloquia* ASD I-3 363–74 / Thompson *Colloquies* 179–89
17 See pages 131–2.
18 *Colloquia* ASD I-3 495–536 / Thompson *Colloquies* 314–57
19 *Colloquia* ASD I-3 504:336–505:356 / Thompson *Colloquies* 323–4
20 *Colloquia* ASD I-3 507:441–510:532 / Thompson *Colloquies* 327–9
21 *Colloquia* ASD I-3 746:179–81 / Thompson *Colloquies* 680

CHAPTER FOURTEEN

On the material treated in this chapter, see especially: Augustijn 'Gerard Geldenhouwer und die religiöse Toleranz'; Bierlaire *La familia d'Erasme*; Blom; Castellion; Coppens *Erasmus' laatste bijdrage tot de hereniging der christenen*; Hentze; Lecler; Phillips 'Some Last Words of Erasmus'; Pollet; Reedijk 'Das Lebensende des Erasmus'; Renaudet *Erasme et L'Italie*;

Schätti; Stupperich *Der Humanismus und die Wiedervereinigung der Konfessionen.*

1 Allen Ep 2798:37–9
2 Allen Epp 2651:26–8, 2795:1–11
3 Allen Ep 3048:92
4 Allen Ep 2892:51–3
5 See pages 78–80.
6 Text in ASD I-2 598–710 / CWE 28 342–448
7 *Ciceronianus* ASD I-2 656:34–710:3 / CWE 28 408–48
8 *Ciceronianus* ASD I-2 681:4–5 / cf CWE 28 425.
9 See page 34.
10 *Ciceronianus* ASD I-2 639:9–10 / CWE 28 386
11 *Ciceronianus* ASD I-2 645:16–646:3 / CWE 28 394
12 *Epistola ad fratres Inferioris Germaniae* ASD IX-1 378:116–17
13 *Apologia adversus monachos* LB IX 1056F
14 Allen Ep 239:37–38 / CWE Ep 239:41–3
15 Allen Ep 240:38–9 / CWE Ep 240:42–4
16 See pages 000–000.
17 *Supputatio* LB IX 580C–583F; *Apologia adversus monachos* 1054B–1060A
18 *Supputatio* LB IX 582F
19 *Supputatio* LB IX 580F
20 *Supputatio* LB IX 581A–B
21 Allen Ep 1690:107–110
22 Allen Ep 2192:125–31
23 Allen Ep 2357:6–23
24 Allen Ep 2328:79–86
25 Allen Ep 2341:8–18
26 Allen Ep 2366:37–9, 54–5
27 *De concordia* ASD V-3 257–313
28 See pages 101–2.
29 *De concordia* ASD V-3 300:496–313:952
30 *De concordia* ASD V-3 301:513–15
31 *De concordia* ASD V-3 303:588
32 WA 38 276:15–16
33 *De concordia* ASD V-3 304:625–42
34 *Hyperaspistes* LB X 1258A
35 Allen Ep 1640:26–9
36 *Hyperaspistes* LB X 1257F
37 Allen Ep 3054:9–11
38 Allen Ep 3049:68–70

39 Allen Ep 3130:28–9
40 Allen Ep 1314:2 / cf CWE Ep 1314:1–3.
41 Allen I 70:508–12
42 Allen Ep 3134:21–4; Allen I 53:29–54:36

CHAPTER FIFTEEN

On the material treated in this chapter, see especially: Boyle *Erasmus on Language and Method in Theology*; Chomarat; Denifle and Weiss; Enno van Gelder; Flitner; Gäbler; Holeczek *Erasmus Deutsch* I; Joachimsen; Kaegi; Kinney; Kohls *Die theologische Lebensaufgabe des Erasmus und die oberrheinischen Reformatoren*; Lortz; Maeder; Mansfield; McConica *English Humanists and Reformation Politics under Henry VIII and Edward VI*; Olin; Raeder; Renaudet *Etudes Erasmiennes*; Scheible; Tuynman; Juan Luis Vives *In pseudodialecticos* ed Charles Fantazzi; Wiedenhofer.

1 *Hyperaspistes* LB X 1252A
2 WA Br 7 2093
3 Lortz I 133
4 See page 5.
5 *The Two Reformations in the Sixteenth Century*
6 See pages 128–9.
7 Allen Ep 347:155–63 / CWE Ep 347:167–76
8 *Lingua* ASD IV-1A 30:136–40, 172:860–8 / CWE 29 266, 405–7
9 See page 109.
10 Allen Ep 456:129–43 / CWE Ep 456:142–58
11 *Apologia ad Fabrum* LB IX 66B
12 See pages 109–10.
13 Allen Epp 2899:22–4, 2906:60–3
14 *Erasmus Deutsch* I 13
15 See pages 53–5.

Bibliography

SHORT-TITLE LIST OF TEXTS USED

Allen   *Opus epistolarum Des. Erasmi Roterodami* ed P.S. Allen,
       H.M. Allen, and H.W. Garrod, 11 vols and index, Oxford
       1906–58

ASD   *Opera omnia Desiderii Erasmi Roterodami* Amsterdam 1969–

CWE   *Collected Works of Erasmus* Toronto 1974–

Ferguson *Opus-*   *Erasmi opuscula: A Supplement to the Opera omnia* ed Wallace
    cula   K. Ferguson The Hague 1933

Holborn   *Desiderius Erasmus Roterodamus: Ausgewählte Werke* ed Hajo
       Holborn and Annemarie Holborn Munich 1933; repr 1964

Hutten   *Ulrichi Hutteni Equitis Germani opera* ed Eduardus Böcking,
       7 vols, Leipzig 1859–69; repr 1963–6

LB   *Desiderii Erasmi Roterodami opera omnia* ed Jean Leclerc,
       10 vols, Leiden 1703–6; repr 1961–2

Reedijk *Poems*   *The Poems of Desiderius Erasmus* ed Cornelis Reedijk Leiden
       1956

Thompson *Col-*   *The Colloquies of Erasmus* ed and trans Craig R. Thompson
   loquies   Chicago 1965

WA   *D. Martin Luthers Werke, Kritische Gesamtausgabe* Weimar
       1883–

WA Br   *D. Martin Luthers Werke, Kritische Gesamtausgabe: Briefwechsel*
       18 vols, Weimar 1930–85

WA Tr   *D. Martin Luthers Werke, Kritische Gesamtausgabe: Tischreden*
       6 vols, Weimar 1912–21

z   *Huldreich Zwinglis Sämtliche Werke 7–11: Zwinglis Briefwechsel*
       ed Emil Egli et al / *Corpus Reformatorum 94–8* (Leipzig
       1911–35)

LITERATURE CITED

Actes du Congrès Erasme ... *Rotterdam 27–29 octobre 1969* Amsterdam/ London 1971

Allen, P.S. *Erasmus: Lectures and Wayfaring Sketches* Oxford 1934

Andreas, Willy *Deutschland vor der Reformation: Eine Zeitenwende* 6th ed Stuttgart 1959

Auer, Alfons *Die vollkommene Frömmigkeit des Christen: Nach dem Enchiridion militis Christiani des Erasmus von Rotterdam* Düsseldorf 1954

Augustijn, Cornelis *Erasmus: Vernieuwer van kerk en theologie* Baarn 1967

– *Erasmus en de Reformatie: Een onderzoek naar de houding die Erasmus ten opzichte van de Reformatie heeft aangenomen* Amsterdam 1962

– 'Erasmus und die Juden' *Nederlands Archief voor Kerkgeschiedenis* n s 60 (1980) 22–38

– 'Erasmus von Rotterdam im Galaterbriefkommentar Luthers von 1519' *Lutherjahrbuch* 49 (1982) 115–32

– 'Gerard Geldenhouwer und die religiöse Toleranz' *Archiv für Reformationsgeschichte* 69 (1978) 132–56

– 'Het probleem van de *initia Erasmi' Bijdragen: Tijdschrift voor filosofie en theologie* 30 (1969) 380–95

– '*Hyperaspistes* I: La doctrine d'Erasme et de Luther sur la *Claritas Scripturae*' 737–48 in *Colloquia Erasmiana Turonensia* II

Avarucci, G. 'Due codici scritti da "Gerardus Helye" padre di Erasmo' *Italia medioevale e umanistica* 26 (1983) 215–55

Bainton, Roland H. *Erasmus of Christendom* New York 1969

Baron, Hans 'Erasmus-Probleme im Spiegel des Colloquium *Inquisitio de fide' Archiv für Reformationsgeschichte* 43 (1952) 254–63

Bataillon, Marcel *Erasme et l'Espagne* Paris/Bordeaux 1937 / *Erasmo y España* 2nd ed Mexico City/Buenos Aires 1966

Bedouelle, Guy *Le Quincuplex Psalterium de Lefèvre d'Etaples: Un guide de lecture* Geneva 1979

Béné, Charles *Erasme et Saint Augustin ou l'influence de Saint Augustin sur l'humanisme d'Erasme* Geneva 1969

– 'L'exégèse des Psaumes chez Erasme' 118–32 in *Histoire de l'exégèse au* XVIe siècle ed Olivier Fatio and Pierre Fraenkel Geneva 1978

Benrath, G.A. 'Die Lehre des Humanismus und des Antitrinitarismus' 1–70 in Carl Andresen *Handbuch der Dogmen-und Theologiegeschichte* III Göttingen 1984

– ed *Wegbereiter der Reformation* Bremen 1967

Bentley, Jerry H. 'Erasmus' *Annotationes in Novum Testamentum* and the Textual Criticism of the Gospels' *Archiv für Reformationsgeschichte* 67 (1976) 33–53

– *Humanists and Holy Writ: New Testament Scholarship in the Renaissance* Princeton 1983

Bierlaire, Franz *Les Colloques d'Erasme: Réforme des études, réforme des moeurs et réforme de l'Eglise au xvie siècle* Paris 1978

– *Erasme et ses Colloques: Le livre d'une vie* Geneva 1977

– *La familia d'Erasme: Contribution à l'histoire de l'humanisme* Paris 1968

Bietenholz, Peter G. 'Erasme et le public allemand, 1518–1520: *Examen de sa correspondance selon les critères de la publicité intentionelle ou involuntaire*' 81–98 in *L'Humanisme allemand (1480–1540)*

– *History and Biography in the Work of Erasmus of Rotterdam* Geneva 1966

Bijl, S.W. *Erasmus in het Nederlands tot 1617* Nieuwkoop 1978

Blockx, Karel *De veroordeling van Maarten Luther door de Theologische Faculteit te Leuven in 1519* Brussels 1958

Blom, Nicolaas van der 'Die letzten Worte des Erasmus' *Basler Zeitschrift für Geschichte und Altertumskunde* 65 (1965) 195–214

Bludau, August *Die beiden ersten Erasmus-Ausgaben des Neuen Testaments und ihre Gegner* Freiburg im Breisgau 1902

Bornkamm, Heinrich 'Erasmus und Luther' *Luther-Jahrbuch* 25 (1958) 3–22

Bouyer, Louis *Autour d'Erasme: Etudes sur le christianisme des humanistes catholiques* Paris 1955

Boyle, Marjorie O'Rourke 'The Eponyms of "Desiderius Erasmus"' *Renaissance Quarterly* 30 (1977) 12–23

– 'Erasmus and the "Modern" Question: Was He Semi-Pelagian?' *Archiv für Reformationsgeschichte* 75 (1984) 59–77

– *Erasmus on Language and Method in Theology* Toronto/Buffalo 1977

– *Rhetoric and Reform: Erasmus' Civil Dispute with Luther* Cambridge, Mass/London 1983

Brachin, Pierre 'Vox clamantis in deserto: Réflexions sur le pacifisme d'Erasme' 247–75 in *Colloquia Erasmiana Turonensia* I

Bradshaw, Brendan 'The Christian Humanism of Erasmus' *Journal of Theological Studies* n s 33 (1982) 411–47

Brown, Andrew J. 'The Date of Erasmus' Latin Translation of the New Testament' *Transactions of the Cambridge Bibliographical Society* 8 (1984) 351–80

Buck, August ed *Erasmus und Europa* Wiesbaden 1988

Castellion, Sebastien *De haereticis an sint persequendi* facsimile reproduction of the edition of 1554 ed Sape van der Woude Geneva 1954

Chantraine, Georges 'L'Apologia ad Latomum: Deux conceptions de la théologie' 51–75 in *Scrinium Erasmianum* II

– *Erasme et Luther, libre et serf arbitre. Etude historique et théologique* Paris/Namur 1981

– 'Mystère' et 'Philosophie du Christ' selon Erasme: Etude de la lettre à P. Volz et de la 'Ratio verae theologiae' (1518) Namur/Gembloux 1971

Charlier, Yvonne Erasme et l'amitié d'après sa correspondance Paris 1977

Chomarat, Jacques Grammaire et rhétorique chez Erasme 2 vols Paris 1981

Christ-von Wedel, Christine Das Nichtwissen bei Erasmus von Rotterdam: Zum philosophischen und theologischen Erkennen in der geistigen Entwicklung eines christlichen Humanisten Basel/Frankfurt am Main 1981

Colloque Erasmien de Liège: Commémoration du 450e anniversaire de la mort d'Erasme ed Jean-Pierre Massaut Paris 1987

Colloquia Erasmiana Turonensia: Douzième stage international d'études humanistes, Tours 1969 2 vols Paris 1972

Colloquium Erasmianum: Actes du Colloque International réuni à Mons du 26 au 29 octobre 1967 à l'occasion du cinquième centenaire de la naissance d'Erasme Mons 1968

Commémoration Nationale d'Erasme: Actes Bruxelles, Gand, Liège, Anvers 3–6 juin 1969 Brussels 1970

Constantinescu Bagdat, Elise La 'Querela pacis' d'Erasme (1517) Paris 1924

Coogan, Robert 'The Pharisee against the Hellenist: Edward Lee versus Erasmus' Renaissance Quarterly 39 (1986) 476–506

Coppens, Joseph Erasmus' laatste bijdragen tot de hereniging der christenen Brussels 1962

– Eustachius van Zichem en zijn strijdschrift tegen Erasmus Amsterdam/London 1974

La correspondance d'Erasme et l'épistolographie humaniste: Colloque international tenu en novembre 1983 ed Alois Gerlo and Paul Foriers Brussels 1985

Crahay, Roland 'Recherches sur le Compendium Vitae attribué à Erasme' Humanisme et Renaissance 6 (1939) 7–19, 135–53

DeMolen, Richard L. 'Erasmus as Adolescent: "Shipwrecked am I, and lost, 'mid waters chill"' Bibliothèque d'Humanisme et Renaissance 38 (1976) 7–25

– The Spirituality of Erasmus of Rotterdam Nieuwkoop 1987

Denifle, Heinrich and Weiss, Albert Maria Luther und Luthertum in der ersten Entwickelung 2 vols, 2nd ed Mainz 1904–9

Devereux, E.J. Renaissance English Translations of Erasmus: A Bibliography to 1700 Toronto/Buffalo/London 1983

Dolfen, Christian Die Stellung des Erasmus von Rotterdam zur scholastischen Methode Osnabrück 1936

Ducke, Karl-Heinz Das Verständnis von Amt und Theologie im Briefwechsel zwischen Hadrian VI. und Erasmus von Rotterdam Leipzig 1973

Eckert, Willehad Paul *Erasmus von Rotterdam: Werk und Wirkung* 2 vols Cologne 1967

Eijl, E.J.M. van 'De interpretatie van Erasmus' *De contemptu mundi'* in *Pascua Mediaevalia: Studies voor Prof. Dr. J.M. de Smet* ed R. Lievens, E. Van Mingroot, and W. Verbeke Louvain 1983

Enno van Gelder, H.A. *The Two Reformations in the 16th Century: A Study of the Religious Aspects and Consequences of Renaissance and Humanism* 2nd ed The Hague 1964

El Erasmismo en España ed M. Revuelta Sañudo and C. Morón Arroyo Santander 1986

Erasmus ed T.A. Dorey London 1970

Erasmus of Rotterdam: The Man and the Scholar ed J. Sperna Weiland and W.Th.M. Frijhoff Leiden 1988

Essays on the Works of Erasmus ed Richard L. DeMolen New Haven/London 1978

Etienne, Jacques *Spiritualisme érasmien et théologiens louvanistes: Un changement de problématique au début du XVIe siècle* Louvain/Gembloux 1956

Faludy, George *Erasmus of Rotterdam* London 1970

Farge, James K. *Orthodoxy and Reform in Early Reformation France: The Faculty of Theology in Paris 1500–1543* Leiden 1985

Feld, Helmut 'Der Humanisten-Streit um Hebräer 2, 7 (Psalm 8, 6)' *Archiv für Reformationsgeschichte* 61 (1970) 5–35

Flitner, Andreas *Erasmus im Urteil seiner Nachwelt: Das literarische Erasmus-Bild von Beatus Rhenanus biz zu Jean le Clerc* Tübingen 1952

Gäbler, Ulrich *Hyldrych Zwingli: Eine Einführung in sein Leben und sein Werk* Munich 1983

Gavin, Joseph A. and Miller, Clarence H. 'Erasmus' additions to Listrius' commentary on *The Praise of Folly' Erasmus in English* 11 (1981–2) 19–26

Gavin, Joseph A. and Walsh, Thomas M. '*The Praise of Folly* in Context: The Commentary of Girardus Listrius' *Renaissance Quarterly* 24 (1971) 193–209

Gedenkschrift zum 400. Todestage des Erasmus von Rotterdam ed Historische und Antiquarische Gesellschaft zu Basel Basel 1936

Geiger, Ludwig *Johann Reuchlin, sein Leben und seine Werke* Leipzig 1871; repr Nieuwkoop 1964

Gilly, Carlos *Spanien und der Basler Buchdruck bis 1600: Ein Querschnitt durch die spanische Geistesgeschichte aus der Sicht einer europäischen Buchdruckerstadt* Basel/Frankfurt am Main 1985

Gilmore, Myron P. 'Erasmus and Alberto Pio, Prince of Carpi' 299–318 in *Action and Conviction in Early Modern Europe: Essays in Memory of E.H. Harbison* ed Theodore K. Rabb and Jerrold E. Seigel Princeton 1969

- 'Italian Reactions to Erasmian Humanism' 61–115 in *Itinerarium Italicum: The Profile of the Italian Renaissance in the Mirror of Its European Transformations*, ed Heiko A. Oberman and Thomas A. Brady Leiden 1975
Godin, André *Erasme lecteur d'Origène* Geneva 1982
Gorce, Denys 'La patristique dans la réforme d'Erasme' 233–76 in *Reformation, Schicksal und Auftrag: Festgabe Joseph Lortz* (Baden-Baden 1958) I
Guggisberg, Hans R. *Basel in the Sixteenth Century: Aspects of the City Republic before, during, and after the Reformation* St Louis, Missouri 1982
Gutmann, Elsbeth *Die 'Colloquia Familiaria' des Erasmus von Rotterdam* Basel/Stuttgart 1968
Haeghen, Ferdinand van der and Lenger, Marie-Thérèse *Bibliotheca Belgica: Bibliographie Générale des Pays-Bas* II Brussels 1964
Halkin, Léon-E. 'Erasme en Italie' 37–53 in *Colloquia Erasmiana Turonensia* I
- *Erasmus ex Erasmo: Erasme éditeur de sa correspondance* Aubel 1983
- *Erasme parmi nous* Paris 1987
Hamm, Berndt *Frömmigkeitstheologie am Anfang des 16. Jahrhunderts: Studien zu Johannes von Paltz und seinem Umkreis* Tübingen 1982
Haverals, Marcel 'Une première rédaction du *De contemptu mundi* d'Erasme dans un manuscrit de Zwolle' *Humanistica Lovaniensia* 30 (1981) 40–54
Heep, Martha *Die 'Colloquia familiaria' des Erasmus und Lucian* Halle 1927
Hentze, Willi *Kirche und kirchliche Einheit bei Desiderius Erasmus von Rotterdam* Paderborn 1974
Hoffmann, Manfred *Erkenntnis und Verwirklichung der wahren Theologie nach Erasmus von Rotterdam* Tübingen 1972
Holeczek, Heinz *Erasmus Deutsch* I Stuttgart-Bad Cannstatt 1983
- 'Die Haltung des Erasmus zu Luther nach dem Scheitern seiner Vermittlungspolitik 1520/21' *Archiv für Reformationsgeschichte* 64 (1973) 85–112
- *Humanistische Bibelphilologie als Reformproblem bei Erasmus von Rotterdam, Thomas More und William Tyndale* Leiden 1975
Huizinga, Johan *Erasmus* Haarlem 1924 / trans F. Hopkin *Erasmus of Rotterdam* New York/London 1924; repr 1952; repr *Erasmus and the Age of Reformation* New York 1957
- 'Erasmus über Vaterland und Nationen' 34–49 in *Gedenkschrift zum 400. Todestage des Erasmus von Rotterdam*
L'Humanisme allemand (1480–1540): XVIIIe Colloque international de Tours Munich/Paris 1979
Hyma, Albert *The Youth of Erasmus* Ann Arbor 1930
Joachimsen, Paul '*Loci communes*: Eine Untersuchung zur Geistesgeschichte des Humanismus und der Reformation' *Luther-Jahrbuch* 8 (1926) 27–97

Jonge, Henk Jan de 'Erasmus und die *Glossa Ordinaria* zum Neuen Testament' *Nederlands Archief voor Kerkgeschiedenis* n s 56 (1975) 51–77

– '*Novum Testamentum a nobis versum*: The Essence of Erasmus' Edition of the New Testament' *Journal of Theological Studies* n s 35 (1984) 394–413

Junghans, Helmar *Der junge Luther und die Humanisten* Weimar 1984

Kaegi, Werner 'Erasmus im Achtzehnten Jahrhundert' 205–27 in *Gedenkschrift zum 400. Todestage des Erasmus von Rotterdam*

Kaiser, Walter *Praisers of Folly: Erasmus, Rabelais, Shakespeare* Cambridge, Mass 1963

Kaufman, Peter Iver *Augustinian Piety and Catholic Reform: Augustine, Colet, and Erasmus* Macon 1982

– 'The Disputed Date of Erasmus' *Liber Apologeticus*' *Medievalia et Humanistica* n s 10 (1981) 141–57

Kerlen, Dietrich *Assertio: Die Entwicklung von Luthers theologischem Anspruch und der Streit mit Erasmus von Rotterdam* Wiesbaden 1976

Kinney, Daniel 'More's Letter to Dorp: Remapping the Trivium' *Renaissance Quarterly* 34 (1981) 179–210

Kisch, Guido *Erasmus und die Jurisprudenz seiner Zeit: Studien zum humanistischen Rechtsdenken* Basel 1960

Koch, A.C.F. *The Year of Erasmus' Birth and Other Contributions to the Chronology of his Life* Utrecht 1969

Koerber, Eberhard von *Die Staatstheorie des Erasmus von Rotterdam* Berlin 1967

Kohls, Ernst-Wilhelm *Die Theologie des Erasmus* 2 vols Basel 1966

– *Die theologische Lebensaufgabe des Erasmus und die oberrheinischen Reformatoren* Stuttgart 1969

Könneker, Barbara *Wesen und Wandlung der Narrenidee im Zeitalter des Humanismus: Brant-Murner-Erasmus* Wiesbaden 1966

Kristeller, Paul Oskar 'Erasmus from an Italian Perspective' *Renaissance Quarterly* 23 (1970) 1–14

– *Renaissance Thought* New York 1961

Krüger, Friedhelm *Humanistische Evangelienauslegung: Desiderius Erasmus von Rotterdam als Ausleger der Evangelien in seinen Paraphrasen* Tübingen 1986

Lecler, Joseph *Histoire de la tolérance au siècle de la Réforme* 2 vols Paris 1955

Lefebvre, Joël *Les fols et la folie: Etude sur les genres du comique et la création littéraire en Allemagne pendant la Renaissance* Paris 1968

Lohse, Bernhard 'Marginalien zum Streit zwischen Erasmus und Luther' *Luther: Zeitschrift der Luther-Gesellschaft* 46 (1975) 5–24

– *Martin Luther: Eine Einführung in sein Leben und sein Werk* Munich 1981

228 Bibliography

Lortz, Joseph *Die Reformation in Deutschland* 2 vols Freiburg im Breisgau 1939, 1940

Lubac, Henri de *Exégèse médiévale: Les quatres sens de l'Ecriture* II-2 Paris 1964

McConica, James K. *English Humanists and Reformation Politics under Henry VIII and Edward VI* Oxford 1965

– 'Erasmus and the Grammar of Consent' 77–99 in *Scrinium Erasmianum* II

McSorley, Harry J. *Luthers Lehre vom unfreien Willen nach seiner Hauptschrift De Servo Arbitrio im Lichte der biblischen und kirchlichen Tradition* Munich 1967

Maeder, K. *Die Via Media in der Schweizerischen Reformation: Studien zum Problem der Kontinuität im Zeitalter der Glaubensspaltung* Zürich 1970

Mansfield, Bruce *Phoenix of His Age: Interpretations of Erasmus c 1550–1750* Toronto/Buffalo/London 1979

Margolin, Jean-Claude *Guerre et paix dans la pensée d'Erasme* Paris 1973

– *Erasme 'Declamatio de pueris statim ac liberaliter instituendis': Etude critique, traduction et commentaire* Geneva 1966

– *Recherches Erasmiennes* Geneva 1969

Markish, Simon *Erasme et les Juifs* n p 1979

Massaut, Jean-Pierre *Critique et tradition à la veille de la Réforme en France* Paris 1974

– *Josse Clichtove, l'humanisme et la réforme du clergé* 2 vols Paris 1968

Maurer, Wilhelm 'Melanchthons Anteil am Streit zwischen Luther und Erasmus' *Archiv für Reformationsgeschichte* 49 (1958) 89–115

Meissinger, Karl August *Erasmus von Rotterdam* 2nd ed Berlin 1948

Mesnard, Pierre *L'essor de la philosophie politique au XVIe siècle* 3rd ed Paris 1969

Mestwerdt, Paul *Die Anfänge des Erasmus: Humanismus und 'Devotio Moderna'* Leipzig 1917

Miller, Clarence H. ed *Desiderius Erasmus 'The Praise of Folly'* New Haven/London 1979

Moeller, Bernd 'Die deutschen Humanisten und die Anfänge der Reformation' *Zeitschrift für Kirchengeschichte* 70 (1959) 46–61

– *Deutschland im Zeitalter der Reformation* Göttingen 1977

– 'Frömmigkeit in Deutschland um 1500' *Archiv für Reformationsgeschichte* 56 (1956) 5–31

Nauwelaerts, Marcel Augustijn 'Erasme à Louvain. Ephémérides d'un séjour de 1517 à 1521' 3–24 in *Scrinium Erasmianum* I

Newald, Richard *Erasmus Roterodamus* Freiburg im Breisgau 1947; repr Darmstadt 1970

Oberman, Heiko Augustinus *Forerunners of the Reformation: The Shape of Late Medieval Thought Illustrated by Key Documents* London 1967
- 'Luthers Reformatorische Ontdekkingen' 11–34 in *Maarten Luther: Feestelijke Herdenking van zijn Vijfhonderdste Geboortedag* Amsterdam 1983
- and Brady, Thomas A. *Itinerarium Italicum: The Profile of the Italian Renaissance in the Mirror of Its European Transformations* Leiden 1975
O'Donnell, Anne M. ed *Erasmus 'Enchiridion Militis Christiani': An English Version* Oxford 1981
Oelrich, Karl Heinz *Der späte Erasmus und die Reformation* Münster 1961
Olin, John C. 'Erasmus and His Place in History' 63–76 in *Erasmus of Rotterdam: A Quincentennial Symposium* ed Richard L. DeMolen New York 1971
- *Six Essays on Erasmus and a Translation of Erasmus' Letter to Carondelet, 1523* New York 1979
Overfield, James H. 'A New Look at the Reuchlin Affair' 165–207 in *Studies in Medieval and Renaissance History* 8 ed Howard L. Adelson Lincoln 1971
Payne, John B. *Erasmus: His Theology of the Sacraments* Richmond, Va 1970
- 'Erasmus and Lefèvre d'Etaples as Interpreters of Paul' *Archiv für Reformationsgeschichte* 65 (1974) 54–83
- 'Toward the Hermeneutics of Erasmus' 13–49 in *Scrinium Erasmianum* II
Pfeiffer, Rudolf *Humanitas Erasmiana* Leipzig/Berlin 1931
- *History of Classical Scholarship from 1300 to 1850* Oxford 1976
- 'Die Wandlungen der Antibarbari' 50–68 in *Gedenkschrift zum 400. Todestage des Erasmus von Rotterdam*
Phillips, Margaret Mann *The 'Adages' of Erasmus: A Study with Translations* Cambridge 1964
- *Erasme et les débuts de la Réforme française (1517–1536)* Paris 1934; repr Geneva 1978
- *Erasmus and the Northern Renaissance* rev ed Woodbridge 1981
- 'Some Last Words of Erasmus' 87–113 in *Luther, Erasmus and the Reformation: A Catholic-Protestant Reappraisal* ed John C. Olin, James D. Smart, and Robert E. McNally New York 1969
Pollet, J.V. 'Origine et Structure du *De Sarcienda Ecclesiae Concordia* (1533) d'Erasme' 183–95 in *Scrinium Erasmianum* II
Post, Regnerus Richardus *The Modern Devotion: Confrontation with Reformation and Humanism* Leiden 1968
Rabil, Albert jr *Erasmus and the New Testament: The Mind of a Christian Humanist* San Antonio 1972
- 'Erasmus's Paraphrases of the New Testament' 145–61 in *Essays on the Works of Erasmus* ed Richard L. DeMolen New Haven/London 1978

Radice, Betty 'Holbein's Marginal Illustrations to the *Praise of Folly*' *Erasmus in English* 7 (1975) 8–17

Raeder, Siegfried 'Luther als Ausleger und Übersetzer der Heiligen Schrift' I 253–78, II 800–5 in *Leben und Werk Martin Luthers von 1526 bis 1546: Festgabe zu seinem 500. Geburtstag* ed Helmar Junghans 2 vols Berlin 1983

Reedijk, Cornelis 'Huizinga and His Erasmus: Some Observations in the Margin' 413–34 in *Hellinga Festschrift/Feestbundel/Mélanges: Forty-three Studies in Bibliography Presented to Prof Dr Wytze Hellinga* Amsterdam 1980

– 'Das Lebensende des Erasmus' *Basler Zeischrift für Geschichte und Altertumskunde* 57 (1958) 23–66

Renaudet, Augustin *Erasme et l'Italie* Geneva 1954

– *Erasme, sa pensée religieuse et son action d'après sa correspondance (1518–1521)* Paris 1926

– *Etudes Erasmiennes (1521–1529)* Paris 1939

– *Préréforme et humanisme à Paris pendant les premières guerres d'Italie (1494–1517)* 2nd ed Paris 1953

Rice, Eugene F. 'Erasmus and the Religious Tradition, 1495–1499' *Journal of the History of Ideas* 11 (1950) 387–411

Rijk, Lambertus Marie de *Middeleeuwse wijsbegeerte: Traditie en vernieuwing* Amsterdam 1977

Ritter, Gerhard 'Die geschichtliche Bedeutung des deutschen Humanismus' *Historische Zeitschrift* 127 (1923) 393–453

Rummel, Erika *Erasmus and His Catholic Critics* 2 vols Nieuwkoop 1989

– *Erasmus as a Translator of the Classics* Toronto/Buffalo/London 1985

– *Erasmus' 'Annotations' on the New Testament: From Philologist to Theologian* Toronto 1986

– 'Quoting Poetry instead of Scripture: Erasmus and Eucherius on *Contemptus Mundi*' *Bibliothèque d'Humanisme et Renaissance* 47 (1983) 503–9

Rupprich, Hans *Die deutsche Literatur vom späten Mittelalter bis zum Barock* 2 parts = Boor, Helmut de and Newald, Richard *Geschichte der deutschen Literatur von den Anfängen bis zur Gegenwart* IV-1, 2 Munich 1970, 1973

Schätti, Karl *Erasmus von Rotterdam und die römische Kurie* Basel 1954

Scheible, Heinz 'Luther und die Anfänge der Reformation am Oberrhein' 15–39 in *Luther und die Reformation am Oberrhein: Eine Austellung* Karlsruhe 1983

– 'Melanchthon zwischen Luther und Erasmus' 155–80 in *Renaissance-Reformation: Gegensätze und Gemeinsamkeiten* ed August Buck Wiesbaden 1984

Schneider, Elisabeth *Das Bild der Frau im Werk des Erasmus von Rotterdam* Basel 1955

Schoeck, Richard J. *Erasmus Grandescens: The Growth of a Humanist's Mind and Spirituality* Nieuwkoop 1988

Schottenloher, Otto *Erasmus im Ringen um die humanistische Bildungsform: Ein Beitrag zum Verständnis seiner geistigen Entwicklung* Münster 1933
- 'Erasmus, Johann Poppenruyter und die Entstehung des *Enchiridion militis christiani'* *Archiv für Reformationsgeschichte* 45 (1954) 109–116

Schwarz, Werner *Principles and Problems of Biblical Translation: Some Reformation Controversies and Their Background* Cambridge 1955

Screech, Michael Andrew *Ecstasy and the Praise of Folly* London 1980

Scribner, R.W. 'The Erasmians and the Beginning of the Reformation in Erfurt' *The Journal of Religious History* 9 (1976–7) 3–31

Scrinium Erasmianum ed Joseph Coppens 2 vols Leiden 1969

Seebohm, Frederic *The Oxford Reformers of 1498: Being a History of the Fellow-Work of John Colet, Erasmus, and Thomas More* London 1867

Seidel-Menchi, Silvana *Erasmo in Italia 1520–1580* Turin 1987

Smith, Preserved *Erasmus: A Study of His Life, Ideals and Place in History* New York/London 1923; repr New York 1962

Sowards, J. Kelley *Desiderius Erasmus* Boston 1975
- *The Julius Exclusus of Desiderius Erasmus* Bloomington/London 1968

Spitz, Lewis W. *The Religious Renaissance of the German Humanists* Cambridge, Mass 1963

Stange, Carl *Erasmus und Julius II.: Eine Legende* Berlin 1937

Stierle, Beate *Capito als Humanist* Gütersloh 1974

Strasbourg au coeur religieux du XVIe siècle: Actes du Colloque international de Strasbourg (25–29 mai 1975) ed Georges Livet, Francis Rapp, and Jean Rott Strasbourg 1977

Stupperich, Robert 'Das *Enchiridion militis christiani* des Erasmus von Rotterdam nach seiner Entstehung, seinem Sinn und Charakter' *Archiv für Reformationsgeschichte* 69 (1978) 5–23
- *Erasmus von Rotterdam und seine Welt* Berlin/New York 1977
- *Der Humanismus und die Wiedervereinigung der Konfessionen* Leipzig 1936
- 'Zur Biographie des Erasmus von Rotterdam: Zwei Untersuchungen' *Archiv für Reformationsgeschichte* 65 (1974) 18–36

Telle, Emile V. *Erasme de Rotterdam et le septième sacrement: Etude d'évangélisme matrimonial au XVIe siècle et contribution à la biographie intellectuelle d'Erasme* Geneva 1954

Thompson, Craig R. *'Inquisitio de fide,' a Colloquy by Desiderius Erasmus Roterodamus 1524* 2nd ed Hamden 1975

Thompson, Geraldine *Under Pretext of Praise: Satiric Mode in Erasmus' Fiction* Toronto/Buffalo 1973

Thomson, D.F.S. and Porter, H.C. *Erasmus and Cambridge: The Cambridge Letters of Erasmus* Toronto 1963

Tracy, James D. *Erasmus. The Growth of a Mind* Geneva 1972

– *The Politics of Erasmus: A Pacifist Intellectual and His Political Milieu* Toronto/Buffalo/London 1978

– 'Two Erasmuses, Two Luthers: Erasmus' Strategy in Defence of *De Libero Arbitrio*' *Archiv für Reformationsgeschichte* 78 (1987) 37–60.

Trinkaus, Charles 'Erasmus, Augustine, and the Nominalists' *Archiv für Reformationsgeschichte* 67 (1976) 5–32

Tuynman, P. 'Erasmus: functionele rhetorica bij een christen-ciceroniaan' *Lampas* 9 (1976) 163–95

Van Santbergen, René *Un Procès de religion à Louvain: Paul de Rovere (1542–1546)* Brussels 1953

Vives, Juan Luis *In pseudodialecticos: A Critical Edition* ed Charles Fantazzi Leiden 1979

Vocht, Henry de *History of the Foundation and the Rise of the Collegium Trilingue Lovaniense 1517–1550* 4 vols Louvain 1951–5

Wackernagel, Rudolf *Humanismus und Reformation in Basel* Basel 1924

Wiedenhofer, Siegfried *Formalstrukturen humanistischer und reformatorischer Theologie bei Philipp Melanchthon* 2 vols Bern/Frankfurt am Main/Munich 1976

Williams, Kathleen ed *Twentieth Century Interpretations of the 'Praise of Folly': A Collection of Critical Essays* Englewood Cliffs, NJ 1969

Winkler, Gerhard B. *Erasmus von Rotterdam und die Einleitungsschriften zum Neuen Testament: Formale Strukturen und theologischer Sinn* Münster 1974

Wohlfeil, Rainer *Einführung in die Geschichte der deutschen Reformation* Munich 1982

Worstbrock, Franz Josef *Deutsche Antikerezeption 1450–1550* Part 1: *Verzeichnis der deutschen Übersetzungen antiker Autoren* Boppard am Rhein 1976

Zickendraht, Karl *Der Streit zwischen Erasmus und Luther über die Willensfreiheit* Leipzig 1909

Index

Erasmus Studies

※

A series of studies concerned with Erasmus and related subjects